Tax Guide 504

CONTESTING IRS PENALTIES

by

Holmes F. Crouch
Tax Specialist

Published by

20484 Glen Brae Drive
Saratoga, CA 95070

ISBN 0-944817-66-1

LCCN 2002102086

Printed in U.S.A.

Series 500
Audits & Appeals

Tax Guide 504

CONTESTING IRS PENALTIES

[2nd Edition]

For other titles in print, see page 224.

The author: **Holmes F. Crouch**
For more about the author, see page 221.

PREFACE

If you are a knowledge-seeking **taxpayer** looking for information, this book can be helpful to you. It is designed to be read — from cover to cover — in about eight hours. Or, it can be "skim-read" in about 30 minutes.

Either way, you are treated to **tax knowledge** . . . ***beyond the ordinary***. The "beyond" is that which cannot be found in IRS publications, FedWorld on-line services, tax software programs, Internet chatrooms, or e-mail bulletins.

Taxpayers have different levels of interest in a selected subject. For this reason, this book starts with introductory fundamentals and progresses onward. You can verify the progression by chapter and section in the table of contents. In the text, "applicable law" is quoted in pertinent part. Key phrases and key tax forms are emphasized. Real-life examples are given . . . in down-to-earth style.

This book has 12 chapters. This number provides depth without cross-subject rambling. Each chapter starts with a head summary of meaningful information.

To aid in your skim-reading, informative diagrams and tables are placed strategically throughout the text. By leafing through page by page, reading the summaries and section headings, and glancing at the diagrams and tables, you can get a good handle on the matters covered.

Effort has been made to update and incorporate all of the latest tax law changes that are *significant* to the title subject. However, "beyond the ordinary" does not encompass every conceivable variant of fact and law that might give rise to protracted dispute and litigation. Consequently, if a particular statement or paragraph is crucial to your own specific case, you are urged to seek professional counseling. Otherwise, the information presented is general and is designed for a broad range of reader interests.

The Author

INTRODUCTION

The IRS — Internal Revenue Service — collects approximately 1.5 *trillion dollars* annually ($1,500,000,000,000) from U.S. citizens and U.S. residents. Of this amount, nearly 20% derives from penalties and interest, classed as: ***additions to tax***. The 20% of 1.5 trillion dollars turns out to be nearly 30 billion dollars ($30,000,000,000). Consequently, penalties comprise BIG BUSINESS for the IRS.

For Congress, tax penalties are the magic carpet to enhancing revenue . . . without raising taxes. The number of penalties and their severity keep always increasing. Generally, the penalty rates range from a low of 5% to a high of 75%, depending on the nature of the offense. The rates apply to the amount of tax due as determined by the taxpayer, PLUS any additional tax due, as determined by the IRS. The ultimate form of penalty is the IRS's power to levy and seize your money, marketable assets, and real estate.

Congress has given the IRS wide discretion in its imposition of penalties on taxpayers. The purpose for doing so is to:

(1) encourage voluntary compliance with applicable tax law;

(2) act as a deterrent to undesired taxpayer behavior; and

(3) promote effective and efficient administration by the IRS.

Unfortunately, in the real world of IRS administration, penalties often are imposed as a "bargaining whip," as a "punishment pyramid," and as a "power thrill" by some IRS employees at all levels. Although the ***IRS Restructuring and Reform Act of 1998*** is supposed to change the IRS's behavior towards penalties, don't **you** count on it! Penalties add substantial revenue to the U.S. Treasury and stigmatize those who are obligated to pay the penalties.

Over the course of one's lifetime, all individuals face the possibility of one or more tax penalties being assessed against them. The possibility extends over a period of from 35 to 50 years (from age 21 or lower, to age 71 or higher). It is our position, therefore, that any penalty of $100 or more per year should be vigorously contested. The contestation should be based on reasonable grounds, adequate records, and on one's good faith understanding of what the applicable law was intended to accomplish.

All total, there are about 100 different tax penalties that can be imposed (or recommended) by the IRS. Criminal penalties (fines and prison time) can only be imposed by a U.S. District Court. All penalties (civil and criminal) apply across the board to individuals, small businesses, large corporations, exempt organizations, specialized industries, family trusts, foreign entities, departing aliens . . . and so on.

Quite obviously, we cannot address — nor do we intend to address — every conceivable penalty that might apply. However, we will address 15 of the more common penalties faced by individual taxpayers and small businesses. Such penalties include those applicable to nonfiling of returns, late filings, frivolous filings, fraudulent filings, late payments, understatements, overvaluation, disregard of rules, false statements, willful neglect, foreign transfers, omission of information, tax evasion, transactions in cash, interference with the IRS . . . and other tax wrongdoings.

Our goal here is to present selected penalty laws, then give examples of how and why the penalties apply. More importantly, we want to explain what **you** can do to remove or lessen each penalty. Towards this end, where pertinent, we cite court cases, IRS regulations, and practical pointers for standing your ground in your effort to have a penalty removed. If the IRS does not remove a penalty when you think you have reasonable grounds for its doing so, there are established procedures to follow. To succeed in such procedures, however, you must be persistent.

Sure, you can swallow a $50 or $100 penalty now and then over the years. And many taxpayers choose to do so. Little do they realize that even minuscule penalties stay on your data-base summary records that the IRS keeps. It is not beyond the IRS's tactics in court proceedings to hammer at you under oath about a $50 tax penalty that you've forgotten about, some 10 or 20 years ago. Our point is that if you have any reasonable basis whatsoever, attempt to expunge every penalty from your record that you can.

CONTENTS

1

FAILURE TO FILE OR PAY

Two Common IRS Penalties Are: (A) Failure To File A Return When Required, And (B) Failure To Pay The Full Amount When Due. For EACH Of (A) Or (B), Three Separate Penalties May Apply (Totaling 6). A 7th Penalty — Called: MAXIMUM TAX POSSIBLE — Applies When The IRS Prepares A "Substitute Return" For You. As Per Section 6651, If REASONABLE CAUSE Can Be Shown, The Penalties Can Be Removed . . . Or Lessened. This Requires Attachment To Your Return Or Payment: Form 4571, EXPLANATION (Etc.). Removing The 7th Penalty Requires That A "True, Correct, And Complete" Return Be Filed.

It is common knowledge that a tax return is required to be filed each year that one's gross income exceeds designated threshold amounts. The thresholds differ depending on one's filing status (single, married, etc.), employment status, age status, and exemption status. In the broadest general sense, the thresholds range from about $10,000 to around $15,000 per year. This is the $15,000 vicinity of the "poverty line" in the U.S. The net result is that approximately 130,000,000 (130 million) tax returns are required to be filed each year with the IRS.

The filing requirement is based on your *gross* income. It is NOT based on net income (gross minus deductions) nor on taxable income (net minus exemptions). It could be that, with deductions, exemptions, and credits, no tax would be due. For example, one might have a gross income of $150,000 and pay no tax . . .

legitimately. Contrarily, one might have an income of $15,000 and pay some small amount of tax. Can't you see the inequity that would arise, if filing were based strictly on the amount of tax to pay? Without filing, the $150,000 case could have substantially overstated its deductions, exemptions, and credits.

If one fails to file, or files and fails to pay, or pays and fails to file, penalties apply. The term "failure to file" includes nonfilings, late filings, and misfilings (wrong form, wrong tax year). The term "failure to pay" includes nonpayments, late payments, and mispayments (wrong name, wrong Tax ID). For these failings, various penalties apply. Among such penalties are:

(1) Basic failure-to-file penalty;
(2) Fraudulent failure-to-file penalty;
(3) Basic failure-to-pay penalty; and
(4) Increased failure-to-pay penalty.

In this chapter, we want to introduce to you the administrative processes involved in asserting these penalties. At the same time, we want to give you some examples of how and why such "failings" occur. Our assumption is that the failings are inadvertent and proscrastinative. They may also be the result of inattentiveness and ordinary carelessness. Accordingly, we want to familiarize you with Tax Code Section 6651 (the basic law on failure-to-file penalties), and on what constitutes "reasonable cause" for removing said penalties. Where there is willful intent, the removal of penalties is more difficult.

What Constitutes a "Return"

Before any failure-to-file or failure-to-pay penalty can be imposed, a tax return must be filed. This implies that you can avoid the penalty by not filing a return. No way! When required, any person liable for tax . . . *shall make a return or statement according to the forms and regulations prescribed by the* [IRS] . . . *and include therein the information required.* [IRC Sec. 6011(a).]

In the Supreme Court case of *E. Badaracco, Sr.* (SCt, 84-1 USTC ¶ 9150, 104 SCt 756), the court held that in order to constitute a return, four conditions must be met. These court-mandated conditions are—

1. There must be sufficient data to calculate the tax liability;
2. The document must purport to be a return;
3. There must be an honest and reasonable attempt to satisfy the requirements of tax law; and
4. The taxpayer must execute the return under penalty of perjury.

These requirements apply to all types of income tax returns, gift tax returns, death tax returns, and excise tax returns.

In all cases, the IRS-prescribed forms carry the statement:

> *Under penalties of perjury, I declare that I have examined this return and accompanying schedules and statements, and to the best of my knowledge and belief, they are true, correct, and complete.*
>
> (Your signature)

This clause is known as the jurat clause. It should be read carefully before signing, and it must be signed.

Other than timely filing and timely paying, the acceptable filing of a return takes place in one of three procedures, namely:

A. The voluntary filing of a delinquent return.
B. Involuntary filing after notice and demand by the IRS to do so . . . or face more penalties.
C. The preparation of a "substitute return" by the IRS.

The penalty rates are the same, regardless of how or when the (delinquent) return is filed. The penalties accrue from the date that the return was originally due (including extensions of time).

Tampered Returns Invalid

Many taxpayers file their (purported) returns on time, but they "tamper" with the official forms. Most tampering is done in such a way that the forms are incomplete and, therefore, deemed *invalid*. The tampering is done partly as a matter of gamesmanship, and partly as a means of "tricking the system." Some do it as a matter of conscientious objection to the tax laws, and others do it as a religious protest against the use of taxpayer money for unpopular causes and excessive government spending programs.

Whatever the reason for tampering with a return, the IRS regards the return as invalid. It is immediately classed *unacceptable* as the required filing. When so, the purported return is usually sent back to the taxpayer with a notice and demand that a proper return be prepared. Those tampered returns which are not sent back are retained by the IRS as documentary evidence of "willful intent." Three or more tampered returns, three or more years in a row, becomes proof positive that you have no voluntary intent to comply with the tax laws.

For instructional purposes, we have extracted the nutshell essence of nine specific Tax Court cases involving invalid returns. The cited cases give you an idea of what some taxpayers will do to trick the tax system. The cited extractions are:

(1) A return with no information on it other than an arbitrary amount labeled: "tax due." —*D.M. Peebles*, TC Memo 1956-160

(2) A return which did not show the sources of income, deductions, or credits, nor any computation of tax.
—*D.E. Swope*, TC Memo 1990-82

(3) A "tentative" return showing an "estimated" tax due, without backup information as to income, deductions, or credits.
—*J.J. Kramer*, TC Memo 1996-513

(4) On the income lines of Form 1040, various constitutional arguments were entered: nothing else.
— *Wittowell*, TC Memo 1981-631

(5) A return on which asterisks were inserted on some lines, while most other lines were left blank; the asterisks were footnoted arguments. —*R.L. Turk*, TC Memo 1991-198

(6) A return on which the wages line was filled in as "nontaxable receipts." —*R.H. Perkins*, TC Memo 1985-125

(7) A signed blank form with attachments advancing protestor arguments, without mentioning specific (applicable) tax code sections. — *R.L. Herd*, TC Memo 1994-580

(8) A return with each relevant line containing the word "object" with an asterisk "Fifth Amendment." — *J.R. Williams, Jr.*, TC Memo 1994-560

(9) A timely filed return which was neither signed nor sworn to. — *M.L. Swedelson*, TC Memo 1991-10

Many tampered returns involve strikeouts or insertions in the penalties-of-perjury statement (called: the *jurat* clause). Everything else can be complete on a return, but, if the jurat clause is tampered with, the return is invalid. However, various courts have held that if a taxpayer **adds under his signature** (without altering the jurat clause) such words as paid, submitted, or filed "under protest," the added words are not tampering. Every taxpayer has the right to protest against the IRS under the First Amendment.

Penalty Section 6651

Section 6651 of the Internal Revenue Code (IRC) is titled: ***Failure to File Tax Return or to Pay Tax.*** It comprises approximately 1,350 statutory words. This number is too much to memorize or to quote here verbatim. The 1,350 words are arranged into the following subsections, namely:

(a) Additions to the Tax

(b) Penalty Imposed on Net Amount Due

(c) Limitations and Special Rule

(d) Increase in Penalty for Failure to Pay Tax in Certain Cases

(e) Exception for Estimated Tax

(f) Increase in Penalty for Fraudulent Failure to File

(g) Treatment of Returns Prepared by [IRS]

(h) Limitation on Penalty on Individual's Failure to Pay for Months During Period of Installment Agreement.

Of particular interest, there is a Congressional footnote to Subsection 6651(a). In the IRS Restructuring Act of '98, that agency is now forbidden from labeling and data-basing a delinquent filer who tampered with his return as: ***Illegal Tax Protestor.*** Such a designation was the IRS's own stigmatizing creation: never authorized by any law. Once a person was so labeled by the IRS, the "illegal protestor" designation stayed on a taxpayer's record forever. It became a form of penalty chasing by the IRS to pyramid all penalties possible on a protestive taxpayer. Under the '98 Act, the IRS must expunge such designations from its records. The IRS is now authorized to use the designation: ***Nonfiler.*** This new designation, however, . . . *shall be removed . . . once the taxpayer has filed income tax returns for two consecutive taxable years and paid all taxes shown on such returns* [Sec. 3707, P.L. 105-206].

While not self-evident in the subsections listed above, Section 6651 actually consists of **seven** separate penalties. There are four in subsection (a) alone. We regard subsection (g): Returns Prepared by the IRS, also as a penalty. The IRS will never prepare for you a return which is "true, correct, and complete." It prepares the shabbiest of returns possible in order to extract maximum tax and maximum penalties.

The most modest of all failure-to-file penalties is the 60-day penalty. It is the last of four separately paragraphed items in Section 6651(a). It reads in pertinent part—

> *In the case of a failure to file a return . . . within 60 days of the date prescribed . . . , the addition to tax under paragraph (1) shall not be less than the* ***lesser of*** *$100 or 100 percent of the amount required to be shown as tax on such return.*

This is like a 60-day grace period for filing. The worst you pay is $100 . . . provided that at least some amount of tax is shown on the return. This is part of the new emphasis on encouraging voluntary compliance when filing a little late.

Three Basic Penalties

Section 6651(a): ***Addition to the Tax***, prescribes three penalty paragraphs. Each is a separate penalty unto its own. Paragraph (1) addresses failure to file; paragraph (2) addresses failure to pay; and paragraph (3) addresses failure to pay, after being given notice of a deficiency in the tax self-assessed. All three paragraphs are prefaced with the words — "In the case of failure." Pertinent portions of these paragraphs are cited herewith.

> Section 6651(a)(1) — *In case of failure to file any return required . . . there shall be added to the amount required to be shown as tax* [due] *on such return* ***5 percent*** [per] *month or fraction thereof during which such failure continues, not exceeding 25 percent in the aggregate.*

> Section 6651(a)(2) — *In case of failure to pay the amount shown as tax* [due] *on any return . . . there shall be added to the amount shown as tax* [due] *on such return* ***0.5 percent*** [per] *month or fraction thereof during which failure continues, not exceeding 25 percent in the aggregate.*

> Section 6651(a)(3) — *In case of failure to pay any amount in respect of any tax required to be shown on a return . . . which was not so shown . . . within 21 days from the date of notice and demand therefor . . . there shall be* ***added to*** *the amount of tax stated in such notice and demand 0.5 percent* [per] *month or fraction thereof during which such failure continues, not exceeding 25 percent in the aggregate.*

Paragraph (3) applies only when you are notified by the IRS that the amount of tax shown due on your return is understated. That is, the IRS has examined your return in some manner, and found a "deficiency" therein. In the worst case scenario, all of the failure to file and pay penalties could add up to 75% of the tax due.

As so stated in Section 6651(b): ***Penalty Imposed on Net Amount Due***, it is the UNPAID portion of the tax to which the penalties apply. This means that if your taxes are overpaid via withholdings and/or estimated prepayments, no penalties would apply. That is, provided you file within three years of the due date.

Three Enhanced Penalties

In addition to the three basic penalties in subsection (a) of Section 6651, there are three "enhanced" penalties: two in subsection (d) and one in subsection (f). All three are substitutions for those penalties designated in paragraphs (1), (2), and (3) of subsection (a). The percentage amounts in subsection (a) are increased by subsections (d) and (f).

Subsection 6651(d): ***Increase in Penalty for Failure to Pay Tax in Certain Cases***, states that—

> *In the case of each month (or fraction thereof) beginning . . . 10 days after the date on which notice and demand for immediate payment is given under section 6331(a), . . . paragraphs (2) and (3) of subsection (a) shall be applied by substituting "1 percent" for "0.5 percent" each place it appears.*

The reference to Section 6331(a) is: ***Levy and Distraint; Authority of IRS***. As per such section, the IRS can enforce collection of any unpaid tax . . . *by levy upon all property and rights to property belonging to* [the notified] *person.* As per subsection 6331(d), a "Notice of Intent to Levy" is sent to delinquent taxpayers who negligently refuse to pay. A 10-day demand is issued after other more subtle reminders have been sent, and to which no meaningful response from the taxpayer has been received. The IRS means business, when it sends you a 10-day demand. Its intent is to levy upon your liquid assets (wages, bank accounts, investments, etc.) and collect the unpaid tax, with or without your consent.

Subsection 6651(f): ***Increase in Penalty for Fraudulent Failure to File***, states that—

> *If any failure to file any return is fraudulent, paragraph (1) of subsection (a) shall be applied (i) by substituting "**15 percent**" for "5 percent" each place it appears, and (ii) by substituting "**75 percent**" for "25 percent."*

The diagnosis of "fraudulent failure to file" derives from the willful intent not to file, as surmised by the IRS. The IRS presumes such intent through such telltale signals as: (A) repeated tampering with a return, (B) placing assets out of levy reach, (C) disguising sources of income, and (D) adversarily insisting that no tax is due. Purportedly, the IRS has the burden of proving fraudulent failure to file. For recalcitrant nonfilers, the IRS asserts the penalty without any proof-positive evidence whatsoever. It is not until the penalty is challenged in court by the taxpayer that the IRS has to carry its burden of proof. The IRS notoriously refuses to honor its burden, until some judge, face-to-face, mandates that it do so.

The "Maximum Tax" Penalty

The 7th and last penalty authorized by Section 6651 is its subsection (g): ***Treatment of Returns Prepared by IRS***. This subsection states—

> *In the case of any return made by the IRS under section 6020(b) . . . such return shall be treated as the return filed by the taxpayer for purposes of determining the amount of the addition under paragraphs (2) and (3) of subsection (a).*

The idea here is that if a person fails to make a return when required to do so, the IRS can make one for him. When it does so, it need only use the gross income information that it gets electronically from brokers and payers. It uses "single" filing status; no dependents, no deductions; no credits. The result is the maximum possible tax conceivable. Furthermore, Section 6020(b)(2) says that—

> *Any return so made* [by the IRS] *shall be prima facie and sufficient for all legal purposes.*

For example, suppose you have no reportable regular sources of income. You have a parcel of land for which you paid $120,000. You sold the land for $100,000 thereby taking a capital *loss* of $20,000. Legally, you owe no tax. However, the real estate closing person has to report the $100,000 gross proceeds to the IRS (or he'll be penalized). The IRS uses the $100,000 as your willfully unreported income. It computes your tax as $25,000. To this amount it adds the fraudulent failure-to-file penalty (75%) and the enhanced failure-to-pay penalty (25%). It then demands $50,000 plus interest from you. By the IRS filing an egregiously erroneous return on your behalf, it is setting the stage for the levy and seizure of your assets. And, it's all constitutionally legal!

In this example, and others like it, you always have the option of filing a "true, correct, and complete" return, proving that no tax is due. The moral here is: never — NEVER — let the IRS prepare a return for you. In the worst of situations, you can file a tentative return timely, then amend and correct it, up to three years later.

Showing of Reasonable Cause

For summary purposes at this point, we present Figure 1.1. We are trying to stress in this figure that, by allowing the IRS to prepare your return, you are subjecting yourself to the worst penalty of all. You will be assessed the maximum conceivable tax and penalty, so as to "get your attention." DO NOT ignore an IRS-prepared return.

Fortunately, all seven penalties in Section 6651 contain the statutory phrase—

> *unless it is shown that such failure is due to reasonable cause and not due to willful neglect . . .*

In other words, the penalties are imposed unless you can show reasonable cause that they should not be imposed.

What constitutes "reasonable cause"?

The IRS provides guidance on this, via its Regulation 301.6651-1(c): ***Showing of reasonable cause.*** This is a 1,000-word regulation. Its essence is that—

> *A taxpayer who wishes to avoid the addition to the tax for failure to file a tax return or pay tax must make* ***an affirmative showing*** *of all facts alleged as a reasonable cause for his failure . . . in the form of a written statement containing a*

declaration that it is made under penalties of perjury. [Emphasis added.]

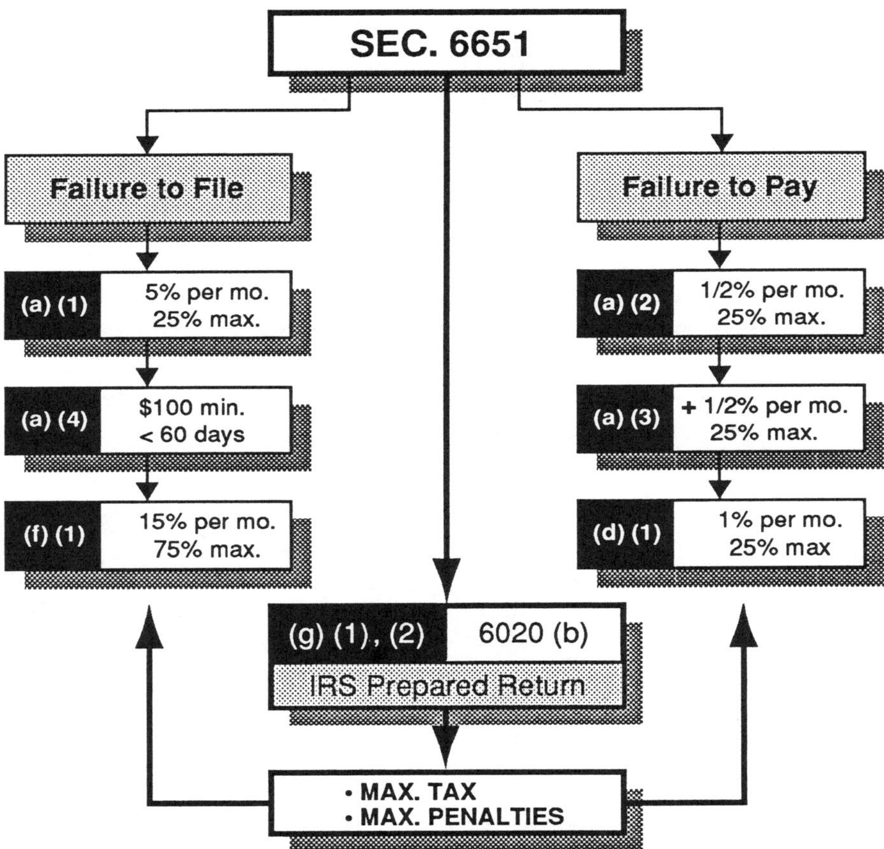

Fig. 1.1 - Summary Highlights of the Section 6651 Penalties

The regulation goes on to set forth certain good faith criteria which the IRS will consider.

There are two criteria for establishing reasonable cause: A — for failure to file, and B — for failure to pay. Both rely on your exercising **ordinary business care and prudence**. Criterion A requires that, despite such care and prudence, you were unable to file within the prescribed time. Criterion B requires that, despite such care and prudence in providing for payment, you were unable to pay, or, if paying, you would suffer undue hardship. In evaluating your extent of "ordinary business care and prudence," the IRS will examine your prior history of compliance, your financial condition, your accessibility to records, the length of time between the cited event and the prescribed date(s), and whether the circumstances were beyond your control. Expecting compassion from the IRS just won't work. It is solely a revenue **collection** agency.

Death, serious illness, unavoidable absences, mailed on time but delivered late, sending to the wrong IRS processing center, reliance on professional tax advice, inability to obtain key records, honest mistakes, and other similar facts and circumstances are duly considered. Claiming ignorance of the tax law, forgetfulness, or just being "too busy" with other matters will be disregarded by the IRS. If you really have a valid reason for filing late or for paying late, press forward and say so. Comprehend and apply the principles set forth in Figure 1.2.

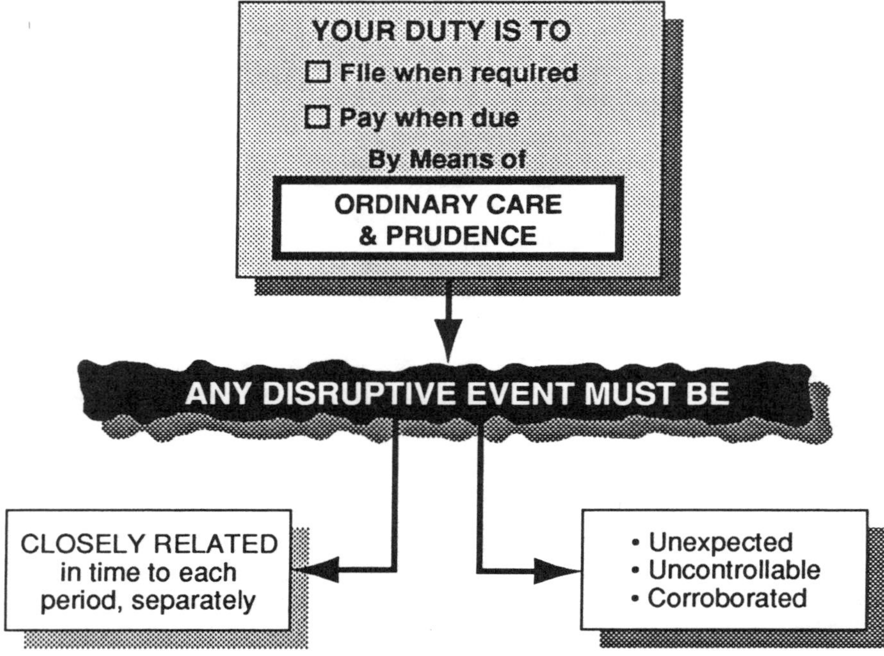

Fig. 1.2 - Basic Principles for Removing Section 6651 Penalties

Failure of Burden

The burden of establishing reasonable cause is squarely on you, the taxfiler/taxpayer. This is what is meant by the term: *an affirmative showing*, in the IRS regulation above. The IRS and various courts have long held that the absence of willful neglect, in and of itself, is insufficient for establishing reasonable cause. Nor is it sufficient to merely state that one has such cause. To avoid the penalty or have it removed, you must present positive evidence with corroborative statements, as appropriate. There are well over 3,000 documented court cases where reasonable cause was asserted by the taxpayer, but where no substantive evidence was presented. Unfortunately, when in doubt, the courts always favor the IRS . . . and its imposition of penalties.

Most failures for carrying one's burden of proof arise from variations of "collectivity of causes" rationale. That is, instead of driving the reasonable cause point home on one specific set of facts and circumstances, an assortment of causes is put forward. The fact that several causes are put forward simultaneously is viewed by the IRS and the courts as nonspecific. The penalties are upheld because the causes do not represent "ordinary business care and prudence."

Typical of the collective causes *rejected* by the IRS and the courts are:

- Varying degrees of ill health over the years;
- Bankruptcy, and loss of money and records;
- Old age with investments in nonliquid assets;
- Traumatic expulsion from a partnership;
- Heavy workload and lack of sleep;
- Stress over marital problems and spousal records;
- Income allegedly belonging to someone else;
- Reliance on tax advice from religious sects;

- Accountant held up returns because not paid for services;
- Tax laws too complicated; subject to different interpretations;

. . . and on and on.

The adamant position of the IRS and Tax Court is that a showing of reasonable cause must include evidence that—

One — You *scheduled* the preparation of your return in a timely manner, including extension of time to file.

Two — Despite your best efforts to file on time, you were prevented from doing so by unexpected and unforeseen events. Describe the events in semi-detail.

Three — You *set aside* enough funds reasonably to pay the tax when due, including extension of time to pay.

Four — Your set-aside funds were not used for high living, exotic vacations, or fancy cars; the funds were used for urgent medical, legal, and educational needs, including job search expenses.

The long and short is that you have a duty to schedule in advance the preparation of your return, and a concurrent duty to set aside enough funds to pay the tax when due. Ordinary business care and prudence must shine forth.

Use Form 4571 or Equivalent

Ever heard of Form 4571?

Probably not. Its official title is: ***Explanation for Filing Return Late or Paying Tax Late*** It is a very short form as most tax return forms go. Its vertical length is about $3^1/2$ inches. There is a small-print instruction at the center right of the form which says—

Continue below if necessary.

The preprinted format of Form 4571 is presented in Figure 1.3.

FORM 4571	EXPLANATION FOR FILING RETURN LATE OR PAYING TAX LATE	
Name & Address (as shown on return)	Your Tax ID	
	Spouse's ID (if joint return)	
	Form Number	Tax Period
I did not file or pay on time because: (Continue below, if necessary)		
Under penalties of perjury, I declare that the above statement, to the best of my knowledge and belief, is true, complete, and correct.	Your signature ▶	Date
	Spouse's signature (if joint return) ▶	Date
(Explanation continued)		

Fig. 1.3 - General Format of IRS Form 4571

Aside from your name, address, Tax ID, and signature, you must enter in the spaces indicated the tax return form number and the tax period to which the return relates. You must use a **separate** Form 4571 for *each* tax return and *each* tax period which is delinquent. You cannot aggregate several delinquent returns on one Form 4571. This is because each return period is a separate event of its own, with separate reasons for filing late or paying late. If appropriate, you can repeat the causal event and circumstances up to three return periods. If you repeat your reasonable cause grounds more than three times, it will appear that you have entangled yourself into a chronic pattern of late filings and late payments.

The sole objective of Form 4571 is to complete the preprinted lead-in statement—

I did not file the above tax form or pay the required tax on time because: . . . [in your own words].

Your own words should be succinct, factual, and nonrambling. The causal event should relate as closely as possible to the regular due date of the return. Preferably, the event should have occurred within six months before, or within six months after, the regular due date. Whatever the event may be, it should have the characteristics of being sudden, unforeseen, and uncontrollable.

As Figure 1.3 clearly indicates, the validity of your Form 4571 depends on your not tampering with the preprinted jurat clause: *Under penalties of perjury, I declare that* . . . .

When properly signed by you, Form 4571 should be attached to the **face** of the tax return to which it relates. It should be attached about midway down, so that the tax return heading and preliminary information are not obscured. If necessary, fold Form 4571 in such a way that when unfolded, any attachments to it (documents, medical bills, photographs, drawings, etc.) fold out into full view to IRS processing personnel. How the IRS handles Form 4571 and its attachments from this point on is beyond your control. Because IRS personnel are often careless — they may damage or detach and throw away your Form 4571 — by all means keep a reproducible copy for your records. As additional insurance, send your delinquent return and/or payment by Certified Mail.

An Example That Worked!

For good cause shown, the IRS **will remove** a failure-to-file-or-pay penalty. We have a true case on point. The tax return (Form 1040) was for 1992 . . . due April 15, 1993. The return was filed on August 25, 1997 — some 4 years 4 months and 10 days late. With Form 4571 and *photographs* attached to the return, a total of $26,445 in tax, penalties, and interest was removed.

The taxpayer was a self-employed, unmarried woman, working as a mortgage broker. As a passenger, driving home with a friend on November 11, 1992, the two were in a near-fatal auto accident. Though hospitalized for only five days, she was unable to work for several years thereafter. In August 1996, the IRS sent her a notice requesting payment of $32,155 in tax, penalties, and interest for 1992.

About a year after receiving the IRS notice, the taxpayer filed her 1992 return. It showed that she only owed $3,453 in tax. Attached to the face of the return was Form 4571. It read—

> I was in a car accident on 11-12-92 and suffered severe lacerations to head (10 internal stitches; 25 external stitches), concussion, and chronic pain in neck and upper back. Was hospitalized but have been unable to work. Had to spend all available money on medical treatment and self-support. See photographs attached.

The photographs alone were traumatic and convincing. They showed a woman with blackened eyes; stitches and swelling to the right face and forehead; facial expression of true pain and suffering; with stiff neck and shoulders.

On November 24, 1997 (about 90 days after filing her 1992 return), the IRS responded to her Form 4571 as follows:

> *As you requested, we changed your account for 1992 to correct it* [as follows}:

Account balance before change	*$32,155*
Decrease in tax	*15,209 CR*
Late filing penalty removed	*3,877 CR*
Estimated tax penalty removed	*644 CR*
Decrease in interest charged	*6,904 CR*
Additional penalty since notice	*209*
Amount you now owe	*$ 5,710*

The "notice" to which the $209 refers was a ***Request for Tax Payment*** that was sent to the taxpayer in August 1996. Her Form 4571 did not provide information as to her medical status in 1996. Consequently, the additional penalty for $209 was not removed.

Prepare to Appeal

Not every explanation for failure to file or failure to pay is accepted by the IRS. Much depends on the credibility of your statements, and on whether there are indicators of lack of due diligence on your part. If your Form 4571 or other explanatory attachments have been ignored or rejected, and you still feel strongly about your position, prepare to appeal.

Sometimes — not always — you are offered the option to appeal. If so, a little flyer is enclosed: ***Your Rights as a Taxpayer***. The flyer is not particularly helpful, though it does give an 800 phone number, a fax number, and an Internet address that you can contact for further information. The Appeals Office within the IRS is an independent operation of its own. This means that an IRS person other than he or she who initially reviewed your explanation will take another look at it.

Be advised, however, that your right of appeal is limited to initiating the process within 30 days after the date of your rejection notice. Thus, you have to decide rather promptly whether to, or not to, appeal. If the penalty is less than $100, you may decide to swallow it. Otherwise, appeal it. The experience you gain will stand you well, as you face the IRS throughout the next 35 to 50 years of your filing tax returns.

Regulation 601.106(a): ***Appeals functions; General***, states that the purpose of the Appeals process is—

> *To resolve tax controversies without litigation to the extent possible. Appeals is to approach these controversies in a fair and impartial manner to both the taxpayer and the government.*

Paragraph (1)(iii) of the above regulation requires that the Appeals process be initiated at the request of the taxpayer. This means that you directly contact the Appeals Office for the IRS District where you live. Get information on how to proceed — THEN PROCEED. Initiate the process by a written request, properly addressed.

At this point, we just want you to *mull over* the possibility of engaging the IRS Appeals process. We'll give you more of the details in Chapter 12: Appealing Within IRS. In the meantime, there are a lot more penalties you should know about. Rarely does the IRS limit its assertions to one penalty only; more often, multiple penalties are imposed.

2

UNDERPAYMENT OF ES TAX

An Underpayment Penalty Applies When The Amount of Tax Due At End Of Year Is $1,000 Or More. If Your Income Not Subject To Withholdings Is Significant, ESTIMATED PREPAYMENTS Are Required. The Prepayments Start 9 Months BEFORE The Year Ends, And Must Target 90% Or More Of The Final Tax. Otherwise Quasi-Quarterly Penalties Apply To The Amounts Underpaid. Request For WAIVER Of The Penalties Is Made On Form 2210 With Documentation On Any Casualty, Disaster, Retirement, Disability, Or Other "Unusual Circumstances." The ES Underpayment Penalty Is An Endless Nuisance.

The letters "ES" refer to: *Estimated* tax. More specifically, they refer to the **prepayment** of one's estimated tax. The "ES" appears on Form 1040-ES and other ES forms for estates and trusts, and nonresident aliens. The ES tax is not a tax on the year completed. It is a tax on the current year which is not yet completed. It is a prepayment of tax *before* the regular April 15 due date, for the year completed.

Did you know that there is a prepayment-of-estimated-tax law?

It is not a front-end law: "Thou shalt prepay next year's tax." Instead, it is a back-end law. Its title is: ***Failure by Individual to Pay Estimated Income Tax*** [Section 6654]. Whenever you see the word "failure" in the title to a tax law, you know — or should know — that it is a penalty law. It establishes what you are supposed to prepay, and if you fail to do so, a penalty applies. While the underpayment penalty itself is not devastating — order of 6% to 9% — it is an irritating nuisance, nevertheless.

Accordingly, in this chapter we want to familiarize you with the ES penalty law, and how to comply with it. We particularly want to explain what you can do to avoid or minimize any associated penalty. There is also a corporate ES penalty law (Sec. 6655), but we will not address corporation underpayments.

Fortunately, for individuals (and estates and trusts), there is an ES tax threshold below which no penalty applies. If your ES tax (after withholdings and credits) is **less than $1,000**, no penalty applies. This is approximately equivalent to $3,600 of income which is not subject to regular withholdings. This is quite a low threshold in the food chain of revenue for Big Government.

Introduction to Section 6654

The ES tax prepayment concept began in 1954. It was introduced as a way to whip self-employed persons (including farmers and fishermen) into some parity with employees whose salaries and wages were subject to withholdings. A "tax whip" always involves the imposition, or threat of imposition, of a penalty of some kind. Have you ever received an IRS computer notice where the threat of a penalty was not in the forefront? A tax whip is intended to browbeat you into an emotional frenzy for instant compliance. It is designed to prevent the rationalizing of your probable total income for the oncoming tax year.

In those early days, the ES underpayment was 6% of 70% of one's estimated tax, less applicable prepayments. In other words, the effective penalty was 4.2% (70% x 6%). It applied when one's then self-employment net income exceeded $400. That's only a $16.80 penalty ($400 x 4.2%). So, what did the IRS and Congress do? They progressively upped the penalty to make it as aggravating and as irritating as possible to more and more persons.

Thus, today, we have a 1,635-word penalty law designated as IRC Section 6654. It consists of 13 separate subsections . . . as presented in Figure 2.1. Take a moment and glance down the 13 subsectional titles listed.

The shortest subsection is (m): ***Regulations***. It reads:

Section 6654	FAILURE BY INDIVIDUAL TO PAY ESTIMATED INCOME TAX	
Subsec.	**Title (edited)**	**Word Count**
(a)	Addition to the Tax	65
(b)	Amount & Period of Underpayment	105
(c)	Required Installments & Due Dates	30
(d)	Amount of Required Installments	585
(e)	Exceptions	190
(f)	Computed After Application of Credits	55
(g)	Application of Withholdings on Wages	90
(h)	Where Return Filed Before Before Jan 31	50
(i)	Rules for Farmers & Fishermen	155
(j)	Rules for Nonresident Aliens	90
(k)	Fiscal Years & Short Years	55
(l)	Estates & Trusts	150
(m)	Regulations	15
13 Subsecs.	Approximate Total Words ▶	1,635

Fig. 2.1 - Subsections and Word Count of Estimated Tax Law for Individuals

> *The* [IRS] *shall prescribe such regulations as may be necessary to carry out the purposes of this section.*

Obligingly, the IRS has prescribed approximately 12,000 words (11,650 by our count) of regulatory text.

Continuing with our introduction to Section 6654, its subsection (a) gives a gist overview. Said subsection: ***Addition to the Tax***, reads—

> *Except as otherwise provided in this section, in the case of any underpayment of tax by an individual, there shall be added to the* [regular income] *tax . . . an amount determined by applying—*
>
> *(1) the **underpayment rate** established under section 6621,*
>
> *(2) to the amount of underpayment,*

> *(3) **for** the period of the underpayment.* [Emphasis added.]

The long and short of Section 6654(a) is that there are *three* variables that you have to chase around each year. These variables are: (1) penalty rate, (2) amount of underpayment, and (3) period of underpayment.

Penalty Rate: Short-Term Interest

Note above that Section 6654(a)(1) does not use the term "penalty rate" directly. Instead, the term "underpayment rate" is used. Functionally, the two terms are the same. The underpayment rate is a penalty predicated upon federal short-term interest rates. "Short-term" because the penalty applies only to that period of time of one year or less: April 15 to April 15. After the close of the taxable year on December 31, the ES penalty continues until the computed tax is paid on or before April 15th.

The reference in Section 6654(a)(1) to Section 6621 is: ***Determination of Rate of Interest***. Section 6621(a)(2): ***Underpayment Rate***, says—

> *The underpayment rate established under this section shall be the **sum** of—*
>
> *(A) the Federal short-term rate determined during the 3rd month following the taxable year, plus*
> *(B) 3 percentage points.*

This means that in March of every year, the penalty rate changes. It is not a fixed penalty rate like that when failing to file or failing to pay . . . after December 31 of each year.

Most penalties are imposed *after* an individual's tax accounting year is complete. This is NOT so with the ES tax penalty. It is imposed *before* the taxable year is complete. We portray this distinction for you in Figure 2.2. Because the add-on rate amount is imposed before the final tax for the accounting year is known, it is called "interest" rather than a penalty. Do you believe this? It is as

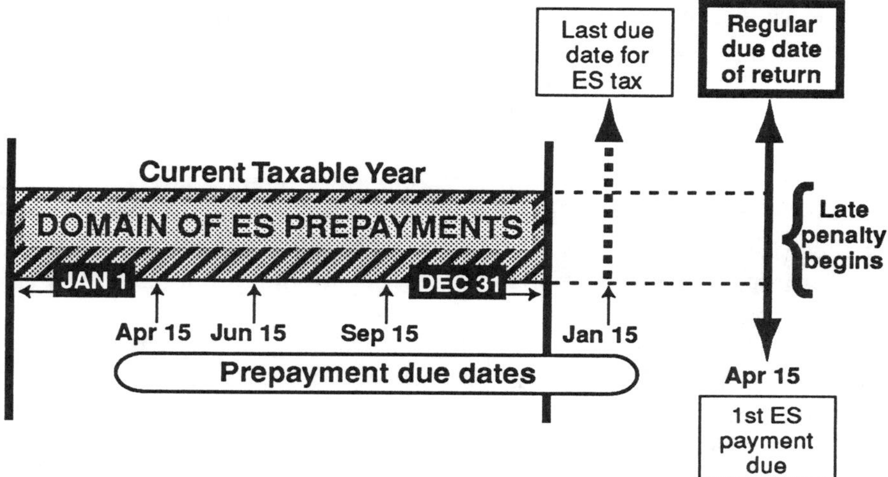

Fig. 2.2 - Crucial Dates Relating to ES Underpayment Penalty

though the IRS were charging you interest on your own money, before it is customarily due the IRS on April 15.

At the end of Chapter 1 (on page 1-17), we listed several penalties that were removed by the IRS as a consequence of reasonable cause. One of the items mentioned was—

Estimated tax penalty removed *664CR*

This wording was abbreviated. The actual IRS wording used on its "change of account" notice was—

The estimated tax penalty that was previously charged has been reduced *664CR*

This is verification of the fact that the IRS itself regards the matter as a *penalty*; not an underpayment interest rate. Over the years, the penalty rate has ranged from a low of 6% to a high of 9%.

The aggregate amount of the ES penalty is computed after the close of the taxable year. Thus, if you fail to make ES prepayments when required to do so (either through withholdings or prepayment vouchers), and you also pay late (after timely filing your return), there are *two* penalties. There is an ES underpayment penalty and, separately, a late payment penalty. See Figure 2.2 again.

Amount of Underpayment

In a manner similar to the late payment penalty (in Chapter 1), the ES penalty applies to amount unpaid when due: not to the total ES tax. The ES penalty applies to underwithholdings as well as to underprepayments. The reference for its application is the "required annual payment."

Suppose, for example, that your required annual payment is $5,000. Through withholdings and prepayments you paid $3,500 for the taxable year. Your amount of underpayment is $1,500 [5,000 – 3,500]. Because we are addressing underpayment not late payment, the ES penalty applies to **90%** of the $1,500 or $1,350. Why 90%; where does the 90% come from?

Answer: the 90% comes from subsection 6654(d)(1)(B): ***Amount of Required Annual Payment.*** This portion of the ES law reads in part—

> *The term "required annual payment" means the **lesser** of—*
>
> *(i) 90 percent of the tax shown on the return for the taxable year (or, if no return is filed, 90 percent of the tax for such year), or . . .*

Additionally, we point out that the 90% applies after offsets against the tax for allowable credits (which are not actual payments).

Computationally, the 90% shows up as follows:

Step 1 —	Your income tax	________
Step 2 —	Other taxes	________
Step 3 —	Total tax (add steps 1 & 2)	________
Step 4 —	Allowable credits	<________>
Step 5 —	Current year tax (subtract step 4 from step 3)	________
Step 6 —	Multiply step 5 by 90% (0.90)	========

Step 6 is your required annual payment . . . **for ES penalty purposes only**. This is NOT your current year total tax. Step 5 is that tax. Step 5 is computed after the current taxable year is complete (i.e., after December 31).

Step 6 is called: *the 90% rule*. That is, to avoid the ES penalty, your withholdings (if any) plus your prepayments (if any), must exceed 90% of your current year's tax. The challenge is to estimate what the 90% amount will be, in March or April, rather than at the end of the year. Projecting nine months in advance is when most estimating errors are made.

Safe Harbor Rule

If the nature of your occupation, investments, business activities, and other sources of income are too variable, there is what is called: *the safe harbor rule*. It is a 2-part rule, depending on your adjusted gross income (AGI) for the preceding year.

In March or April of any given calendar year, you should know — or have a pretty good idea — of your preceding year's tax. Instead of trying to estimate nine months in advance what your current year's tax will be, you can use your preceding year's tax as your reference base. Safe Harbor Rule A says that if your preceding year's AGI is $150,000 **or less**, you can base your ES prepayments on 100% of said tax. If your AGI **exceeds** $150,000, Rule B permits you to use 110% of such preceding year's tax.

Intentionally, we have oversimplified Rule B. The IRS and Congress, in their annual ritual of "tweaking the taxpayer," say that Rule B changes for different tax years. For years 1998, 1999, and 2000, the applicable percentages were 105%, 108.6%, and 110%, respectively. For year 2001, it was 112%. For year 2002 and thereafter, it is 110%. Therefore, if you want to be on the safe, safe harbor side for Rule B, use 112% instead of 110%. You just never know when the IRS and Congress will change their minds.

Incidentally, if you are married but filing separate returns, the AGI breakpoint between Rule A and Rule B is $75,000 . . . instead of $150,000.

In Figure 2.3, we summarize the estimating rules above. Our recommendation is that if, in March or April you expect your gross

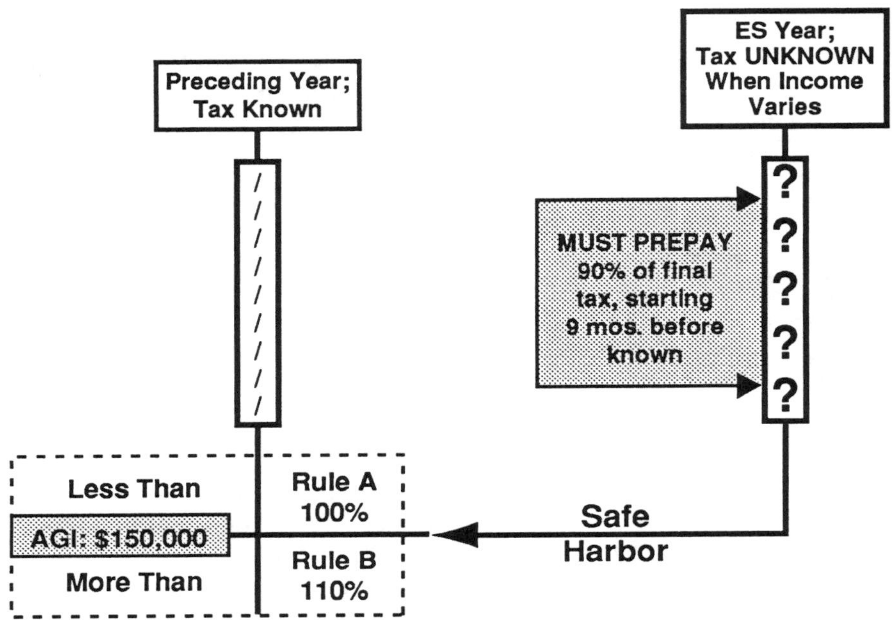

Fig. 2.3 - "Safe Harbor" Rule for Avoiding ES Underpayment Penalty

income to diminish significantly, use 90% of the preceding year's tax as your reference base. If you expect your gross income to increase significantly, use 112% as your reference base. If, as a result of these two "rules of thumb," you have overpaid your tax, you will get a refund.

Quasi-Quarterly Installments

If you are required to make ES tax prepayments, you cannot do so as you see fit. You have to follow prescribed procedures. You have to pay in four installments [Sec. 6654(c)]. Each installment has a due date of its own. There is one penalty for each installment period. As a result, there is the potential of **four** ES penalties each year! For example, there could be a 6% penalty on the 1st installment; a 4.5% on the 2nd; 3% on the 3rd; and 1.5% on the 4th.

More specifically, Section 6654(c) says—

There shall be 4 required installments for each taxable year. In the case of the following installments, the due date is:

1st .... April 15
2nd .... June 15
3rd .... September 15
4th .... January 15 of the following taxable year

Note particularly the time interval between installments. [Jan. 15–Apr. 15 (3 mo); Apr. 15–Jun. 15 (2 mo); Jun. 15–Sep. 15 (3 mo); Sep. 15–Jan. 15 (4 mo).] Quite obviously, these are not equal quarterly installments; they are *quasi-quarterly*.

Also note the due date of the 4th installment: January 15. This is NOT the 1st prepayment for the following taxable year. The 1st prepayment is April 15. There is a special reason for this installment distortion. The reason is Section 6654(h): ***Special Rule where Return Filed on or before January 31***. It reads:

If, on or before January 31 of the following taxable year, the taxpayer files a return for that taxable year and ***pays in full*** *the amount computed on the return as payable,* ***then no addition to tax shall be imposed*** *under subsection (a) with respect to any underpayment of the 4th required installment for the taxable year.* [Emphasis added.]

In other words, you may file your tax return for the just completed taxable year by January 31, and pay in full. If you do so, there is no 4th installment required . . . and no ES penalty (for that 4th installment). The net effect is that a completed return with payment by January 31 constitutes your fourth installment.

Use 1040-ES Vouchers

You are required to prepay estimated tax when your underprepaid tax through withholdings reaches $1,000 for the taxable year [Sec. 6654(e)(1)]. At this stage, you have the choice of increasing your withholdings or instituting a schedule of ES prepayments. Generally speaking, if more than 50% of your gross income is not subject to withholdings, ES prepayments are your better choice. Either prepay using Form(s) 1040-ES or pay the penalty.

If you have any doubt about how to proceed, request from the IRS its 1040-ES "Package": ***Estimated Tax for Individuals***. This is a 7-page package. It consists of four pages of 2-columnar instructions (about 4,400 words), tax rate schedules, an "Estimated Tax Worksheet" (17 computational lines), four prepayment vouchers, a payment record stub, and a list of IRS mailing addresses. The availability of this package is clear evidence that you cannot write a check to the IRS whenever it is convenient, and drop it in the mail. No, you must write four checks (or money orders) and drop each separately in the mail on or before each prescribed due date.

The lead-off instructions to the 1040-ES package say—

> *The estimated tax worksheet will help you figure the correct amount to pay. The payment vouchers in this package are for crediting your payments to your account correctly.*

After doing the ***Estimated Tax Worksheet*** (which you keep for your records), the next instruction reads—

> ***When a Penalty is Applied.*** *In some cases, you may owe a penalty when you file your return. The penalty is imposed* ***on each underpayment*** *for the number of days it remains unpaid. A penalty may be applied if you did not pay enough estimated tax for the year, or you did not make the payments on time or in the required amount.*

Another instruction tells you how to complete and use the vouchers. Each voucher is a 3" x 7" slip of paper, with entry spaces for your name, address, and social security number (including that of spouse, if any). In the upper right corner, there is a 1 1/2" x 1 1/2" box labeled: ***Amount of payment $_______________***. All four vouchers are sequentially numbered (**1**, **2**, **3**, and **4**); each displays its own due date.

On each voucher, a headnote instruction says—

*File **only** if you are making a payment of estimated tax.*

Blank vouchers or vouchers claiming overpayment credits will not be honored. The IRS wants your money: either a check or money order. Do not send cash. Payments by credit card or by debit card are authorized by Section 6311(d)(3).

What happens if you miss an ES voucher or two? Can you make up for the nonpaid or underpaid vouchers and avoid the penalty for the missed installment period?

Answer: Yes . . . and No. Yes, you can make up for the nonpaid or underpaid vouchers. No, the makeup does not avoid the penalty for the period made up. Any makeup payment in a subsequent period to cover a previous underpayment merely stops the accrual of further penalty on the underpayment.

Zero Tolerance for Underpayment

The position of the IRS — and that of Congress — is that you have a duty to arrange your financial affairs so as to make your ES voucher payments when due. This is an income tax principle of long standing. It goes back to 1913 when the Sixteenth Amendment to the U.S. Constitution was enacted. The premise then as it is today is that you owe federal income tax *concurrently* as you derive the income. Technically, therefore, the moment you receive any tax accountable money, you should set aside a portion of your receipts for your ES prepayments.

It is for the IRS's administrative convenience only that you are allowed — and required — to make your full year's estimated payments in four installments. Whether you derive income uniformly or nonuniformly makes no difference. If you derive income nonuniformly, you have the option of proportionalizing your installments (called: *annualizing*) pursuant to Section 6654(d)(2)(B). A special worksheet for this purpose is available. It is Schedule AI (Form 2210): ***Annualized Income Installment Method***. Otherwise, except for unusual circumstances, there is "zero tolerance" for failing to make ES payments when officially required and due.

The first constitutional arguments against the ES tax were settled in 1958. In that year, there were two separate U.S. Courts of Appeal (CA) cases. The two cases were—

W.H. Erwin, CA-9 (San Francisco), 58-1 USTC ¶ 9318, 253 F2d 26

and

L.L. Beacham, CA-5 (New Orleans), 58-1 USTC ¶ 9488, 255 F2d 103

In both cases it was separately held that the ES prepayment provisions were not arbitrary, nor was enactment beyond the powers granted to Congress by Article I of the Constitution. Furthermore, ES prepayments did not violate the due process clause of the Fifth Amendment, nor the definition of income tax under the Sixteenth Amendment.

A more telling case is that of *D.R. Hopkins, Jr.* BC-DC Colorado, 91-2 USTC ¶ 50,525. Here the plaintiff sought to have the ES underpayment penalties removed for three years in a row (1987, 1988, and 1989). In 1989, Hopkins filed for bankruptcy based on the termination (on 30 days' notice) of his cartage contract related to air freight business. This cartage contract was his sole source of income. Its cancellation on such short notice deprived him of funds to pay back taxes, including the ES penalties.

The case evidence showed that during the three years at issue, the plaintiff made payments to other creditors . . . but not to the IRS. Payments were made to car and truck dealers, to his mortgage company, to credit card companies, and for one "last ditch" gambling trip.

Based on this evidence, the Court ruled that—

> *The cause of the Plaintiff's inability to pay his estimated taxes lies not with the cancellation of the cartage contract. Rather, it lies in his neglect to set aside sufficient funds,* ***as those funds were being earned****, to pay the estimated taxes when due. The Plaintiff has failed to show that the* [IRS] *abused its discretion in refusing to waive the penalties.*

The point being made above is: When required, there is just no way to avoid ES prepayments via quasi-quarterly installments. So, take heed. The IRS, Congress, and the courts are not sympathetic to pleas involving "lack of funds," "money used for prior business debts," or "belief that, because of investment losses, no ES tax was due." The ES issue is not a voluntary matter. It is mandatory that you set aside adequate amounts from your income stream to pay over to the IRS when due. It is your duty to do so — all other matters notwithstanding.

Exceptions to the Penalty

The IRS has authority to waive (forgo) the ES penalty in certain cases. This authority is prescribed in Section 6654(e): ***Exceptions***. There are three groupings of these exceptions, namely:

(1) Where tax is small amount,
(2) Where no tax liability for preceding year, or
(3) Waiver in certain cases.

All three exceptions start with the statutory clause—

No addition to tax shall be imposed under subsection (a) . . . [if]

Subsection (a), recall, is titled: ***Addition to the Tax***. The term "addition to tax" is Congress's way of concealing from you the harshness of the word "penalty." "Addition to tax" and "penalty" have identical meanings.

Exceptions (1) and (2) are unlikely to be of significance for those required to make ES prepayments. Exception (1) applies where the tax on the return (after withholdings and credits) is *less than* $1,000. Exception (2) applies where there was no tax liability whatsoever, in the preceding taxable year of 12 months. Exception (2) applies, however, only if you were a U.S. citizen or U.S. resident "throughout the preceding taxable year."

Exception (3): ***Waiver in certain cases***, is where most ES penalty removal effort lies. In Case (A): ***In general***, no penalty applies IF—

> *The* [IRS] *determines that by reason of* ***casualty, disaster,*** *or other* ***unusual circumstances*** *the imposition of such addition to tax would be against equity and good conscience.* [Emphasis added.]

This "unusual circumstances" waiver pertains to events that are unexpected, unfortunate, and unforeseen. Included are the consequences that arise from fires, storms, floods, earthquakes, armed robbery, murder, rape, death, vehicular accidents, and other situations requiring your priority of attention and resources.

In Case (B): ***Newly Retired or Disabled Individuals***, no penalty applies IF—

> *The* [IRS] *determines that the taxpayer retired after having attained age 62, or became disabled in the taxable year for which estimated payments were required* ***or*** *in the taxable year* ***preceding*** *such taxable year, and such underpayment was due to reasonable cause and not to willful neglect.* [Emphasis added.]

The "newly retired or disabled" waiver is intended primarily for those who have had withholdings most of their taxpaying life, who now face ES prepayments for the first time. This waiver is practically automatic when documented evidence of being newly retired or permanently disabled is presented to the IRS.

Request Waiver on Form 2210

To request a waiver of your ES penalty, you must check the "Request waiver" box on Form 2210 and attach said form to your tax return. Form 2210 is titled: ***Underpayment of Estimated Tax by Individuals, Estates, and Trusts***. A special headnote to this form says—

> *In most cases, you* ***do not*** *need to file Form 2210. The IRS will figure any penalty you owe and send you a bill. File Form 2210* ***only if*** *one or more boxes in Part I apply to you.*

In other words, the IRS makes it easy for you to accept the penalty. If you want the penalty waived, you have to file the form, compute the penalty, indicate what portion you want waived, and attach a statement giving the reasons for wanting all or part of the penalty waived.

Part I of Form 2210 is titled: ***Reasons for Filing***. It consists of four checkboxes which we abbreviate as follows:

1a ☐ Request waiver. See "Waiver of Penalty" in instructions.

b ☐ Using annualized income installment method.

c ☐ Treating withholdings as paid on date withheld.

d ☐ Different filing status between previous and current year.

Boxes b, c, and d are optional (lower) ways to compute the penalty. They do not involve waiver or eliminating the penalty in any manner.

The complete official wording at box 1a reads:

☒ *You request a* ***waiver****. In certain circumstances, the IRS will waive all or part of the penalty. See* ***Waiver of Penalty*** *in the instructions.*

The separate instructions consist of 4 1/2 pages of 3-columnar text (about 7,000 words). You are instructed to complete Part II of Form 2210: ***Required Annual Payment*** (some 12 steps). Then you are instructed to compute the penalty in either Part III: ***Short Method*** (7 steps) or Part IV: ***Regular Method*** (39 steps) as applicable. At the computed penalty amount — on line marked: PENALTY — you show in parentheses (for subtracting) the amount you want waived. For emphasis, we suggest adding the words: **Waiver Amount Requested . . . $__________** in hand-entered bold print. To get the penalty removed, you really have to work at it. We illustrate the procedure in Figure 2.4.

The waiver instructions go on further to say—

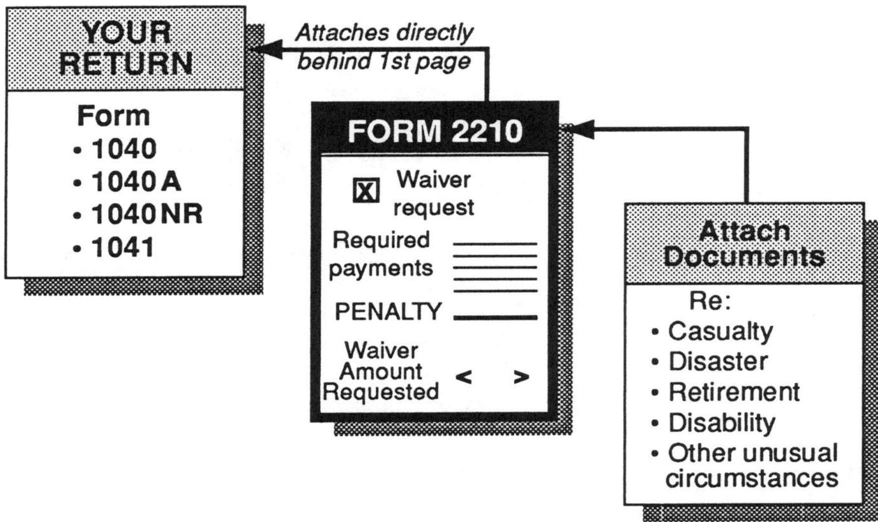

Fig. 2.4 - How Waiver Form 2210 Attaches to Your Tax Return

- *If you are requesting a penalty waiver due to a casualty, disaster, or other unusual circumstance,* ***attach documentation*** *such as copies of police and insurance company reports.*

- *If you are requesting a penalty waiver due to retirement or disability,* ***attach documentation*** *that shows your retirement date (and your age on that date) or the date you became disabled.*

- *The IRS will review the information you provide and decide whether to grant your request for a waiver.*

There is no question about it. Making ES prepayments quasi-quarterly is an irritating nuisance. If the underpayment of tax is $2,000 or less, let the IRS bill you. The penalty bill would be on the order of $100. But if your end-of-year underpayment is $10,000; $30,000; or $50,000, for example, the penalty becomes significant ($500 to $2,500 . . . or so). It is better to ES prepay.

3

FAILURE TO DEPOSIT TAX

Any Business Which Has Employees Is Subject To Mandatory Withholdings Plus Employer Contributions (Plus The Collection of Certain Excise Taxes). This Money MUST NOT Be Commingled With Gross Receipts From The Business. It Must Be Deposited In An IRS-Authorized Financial Institution. Failure-To-Deposit Penalties Apply, Ranging From 2% to 15% Of The UNDERDEPOSITED Amount. Relief From The Penalties Requires An Affirmative Showing Of REASONABLE CAUSE Due To Circumstances Beyond The Owner's Control. Two Informal Requests For Relief Can Be Sought, After Which You Must Go To Court.

Small-business owners (and large ones, too) are "deputized" by the IRS as withholding agents and collectors of certain excise taxes. The withholdings (from employees) and collections (from customers) have to be deposited in federally authorized depository institutions. The taxes can NOT be forwarded directly to the IRS. Payments made to the IRS are subject to penalties, as are deposits which are untimely made or made for insufficient amounts. It is significant to note that while several penalties apply, there is no compensation, reward, or thanks for being so deputized.

The term "failure to deposit" differs materially from that of "failure to pay" in Chapter 1. Failure to *pay* refers strictly to income tax returns. Failure to deposit refers strictly to *depository* tax returns. For small businesses, there are six such returns, namely:

Form 720 — Quarterly Federal Excise Tax Return

Form 940 — Employer's Annual Federal Unemployment Tax Return

Form 941 — Employer's Quarterly Federal Tax Return

Form 943 — Employer's Annual Tax Return for Agricultural Employees

Form 945 — Annual Return of Withheld Federal Income Tax

Form 1042 — Annual Withholding Tax Return for U.S. Source Income of Foreign Persons

For depository purposes, two different sets of rules apply. (For either set of rules, the penalties are the same.) If a business owner's total withholdings and collections exceed $50,000 for the taxable year, a complicated EFTPS (Electronic Federal Tax Payment System) must be used. That is, deposits are made electronically to the U.S. Treasury's general account directly from one's business account. Only large businesses are subject to the EFTPS rules.

If the depository amount (for a taxable year) is $50,000 or less, the less formal FTDC (Federal Tax Deposit Coupon) system may be used. Therefore, for purposes of this chapter, $50,000 *or less* is the aggregate annual depository threshold. This is the domain of small business interests for which the FTDC depository rules are intended. We want to acquaint you with these rules and the key form you must use: **Form 8109**. We particularly want to warn you about the cascading of penalties when small business owners get behind in their depository duties.

Why Deposits Necessary

A common problem among small businesses is the commingling of the gross receipts from the business with *other people's money* (OPM). For purposes of this chapter, OPM consists of: (a) withholdings from employees, (b) employer payroll contributions, (c) nonpayroll withholdings, and (d) collections of sales, use, and excise taxes. It is this OPM money that is subject to depository rules as to time and form. The deposits generally are required semiweekly (twice a week), monthly, or quarterly, depending on the type and amount of OPM.

For most small businesses, having sufficient operating cash on hand is a major problem. By commingling the OPM with gross receipts from the business, the illusion is created that one has more operating cash than there is in reality. As a deputized IRS collector, the OPM cash you have is NOT your money to use as you see fit. It belongs to the U.S. Treasury. It, too, needs operating cash. The difference is that the IRS has the power to impose irritating penalties for failure to make OPM deposits when required.

In one sense, the depository rules can be thought of as an inducement to small businesses to be more self-disciplined. Ideally, a well disciplined business would have two separate types of bank accounts of its own: one for the business, and one for the OPM. We depict this ideal arrangement for you in Figure 3.1. It is from the OPM account that money is available for the required deposits.

Unfortunately, very few small businesses can develop the monetary discipline required in Figure 3.1. In the commingling owner's mind, he is "borrowing" the OPM — temporarily, of course. When the time comes to make the required deposits, he will do so . . . somehow. The "somehow" is the borrowing of other money to deposit the OPM money, or intentionally making the deposits later or in insufficient amounts. Before long, it becomes an endless game of trying to catch up, but never being able to do so.

Some business operators regard their depository penalties as part of the cost of doing business. Little do they realize that such penalties are NOT allowable business expenses. This is so stated succinctly in IRC Section 162(f): ***Trade or Business Expenses; Fines and Penalties***. This tax law says—

> ***No deduction shall be allowed*** *under subsection (a)* [ordinary and necessary expenses for carrying on a business] ***for any fine or similar penalty*** *paid to a government* [federal, state, local, foreign] *for the violation of any law.* [Emphasis added.]

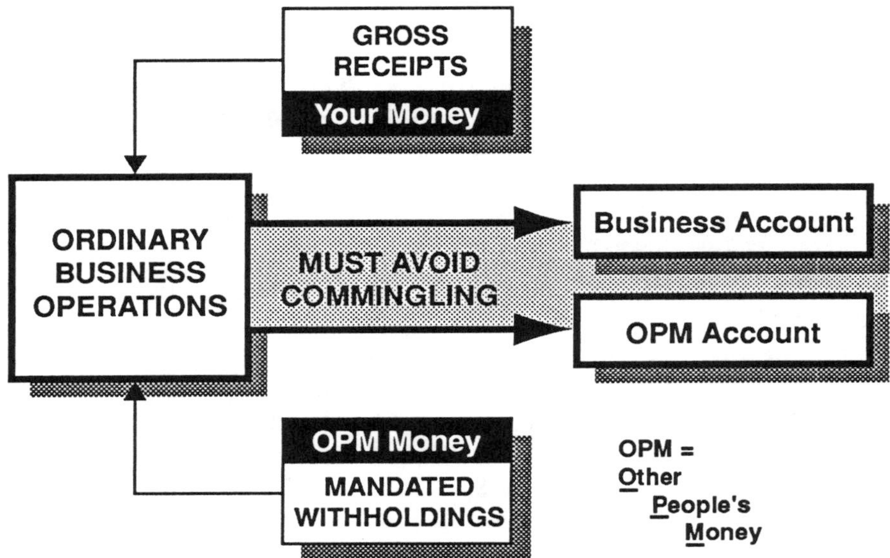

Fig. 3.1 - The Need for Two Separate Bank Accounts in Business

Thus, as a deputized collector of OPM for the IRS, any depository penalties you pay are not a deductible business expense. They are pure punishment for your lack of willingness to work free for the IRS month after month . . . year after year. Fundamentally, though, the issue is one of self-discipline — or lack thereof — in separating the OPM from your ordinary business gross receipts. See Figure 3.1 again. There is a lot of wisdom in this figure; we hope you will heed it.

Authorized Depositories

In general, you must deposit all OPM collections with a federally authorized financial institution. The deposits may be made by mailing or delivering a check, money order, or cash. Each deposit, however, must be accompanied by an **FTD** coupon ("FTD" is **F**ederal **T**ax **D**eposit). This "coupon" identifies your formal tax account to which the IRS posts credits, when funds are transferred electronically from the depository institution to the U.S. Treasury.

The basic depository law under which you are obligated is Section 6302: ***Mode or Time of Collection***. This law consists of approximately 2,200 statutory words. These words are supplemented by approximately 16,800 words of regulatory text. Depositing is big business for the IRS and U.S. Treasury. Although authorized depositories must accept cash if you offer it to them, they much prefer check or money order. The check or money order must be made payable to the depository institution itself: NOT to the IRS nor to the U.S. Treasury. It is the depository institution that forwards your OPM deposits to the U.S. Treasury.

Subsection (c) of Section 6302 is our point of focus. This subsection is titled: ***Use of Government Depositories***. It consists of about 100 words. It reads in principal part as—

> *The Secretary* [of the Treasury] *may authorize Federal Reserve banks, and incorporated banks, trust companies, domestic building and loan associations, or credit unions which are depositories or financial agents of the United States, to receive any tax imposed under the internal revenue laws, in such manner, at such times, and under such conditions as* [the IRS] *may prescribe; . . .* [including] *the manner, times, and conditions under which the receipt of such tax . . . is to be treated as the payment of such tax to the* [U.S. Treasury].

The point of Section 6302(c) is that, if you are required to make deposits of OPM money and you are not already affiliated with an authorized depository, you should become affiliated promptly. Surely, somewhere in the general vicinity of where you do business, there is such a depository. The IRS instructions on this point read—

> *Be sure that the financial institution where you make* [the] *deposits is an authorized depository. Deposits made to an unauthorized institution may subject* [you] *to the failure to deposit penalty.*

The importance of affiliating with an authorized depository is that, when the deposits are received (by the depository), they are automatically treated as received by the U.S. Treasury. If your depository due date falls on a Saturday, Sunday, or legal holiday, the next succeeding banking day is treated as the due date. It is for this reason that we encourage you to open a separate OPM (tax) account with an authorized depository in your geographic area. By doing so, there would be no loss in "float time" as would occur when transferring money between different financial institutions. Float time can cost you a 2% penalty (if 1 to 5 days) or a 5% penalty (if 6 to 15 days).

Use FTD Coupons

You must make your OPM deposits by using Form 8109: ***Federal Tax Deposit Coupon***. Once your business is assigned a Tax ID number (**EIN**: **E**mployer **I**dentification **N**umber) by the IRS, it will send you a "book of coupons." Each coupon can be used for one of about 12 different depository tax returns. As the coupons are used, the IRS will keep track of the number of deposits made. It will automatically send you additional coupon books when you need them. To be on the safe side, you should make inquiry to the IRS yourself about the coupons (Forms 8109).

The general arrangement of an FTD coupon is presented in Figure 3.2. Particularly note the bold digit-sectioned box across the top of the form. Actually, there are two boxes: a 2-digit box and an 11-digit box. The 2-digit box is for entering the *month* of the tax year for which the deposit is made. The amount of the deposit is digitized in dollars and cents. Directly below the digit-sectioned ***Amount of Deposit*** box is your EIN, name, address, and telephone number. Once you are "in the system," your EIN, etc. are preprinted by the IRS on your replacement coupon forms.

A small-print instruction above the amount of deposit says—

> *Do NOT type, please print.*

This means: hand print. The accompanying instructions go on to say—

> *Entries must be made in pencil. Please* ***use a soft lead*** *so that the entries can be read more accurately by optical scanning*

equipment. Hand print the money amount without using the dollar sign, commas, a decimal point, or leading zeros. The commas and decimal point are already shown in the entry area.

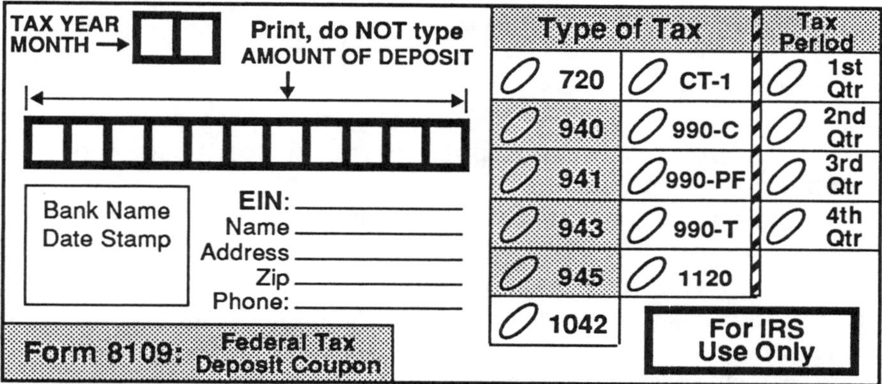
TAX YEAR MONTH →

Print, do NOT type
AMOUNT OF DEPOSIT

Bank Name
Date Stamp

EIN:
Name
Address
Zip
Phone:

Form 8109: Federal Tax Deposit Coupon

Type of Tax
720
CT-1
940
990-C
941
990-PF
943
990-T
945
1120
1042

Tax Period
1st Qtr
2nd Qtr
3rd Qtr
4th Qtr

For IRS Use Only

Fig. 3.2 - General Format of an FTD Coupon for Depositing Business Taxes

To the right of the amount of deposit, there is a block of tax return form numbers, and the quarterly tax periods to which they apply. The indicated entries are made by *hand darkening* the applicable diagonal ovals. Instructions for the hand darkening say—

1. *Make sure your name and EIN are correct.*
2. *Prepare only one coupon for each type of tax deposit.*
3. *Darken only one box for the* ***type of tax*** *you are depositing.*
4. *Darken only one box for the* ***tax period*** *for which you are making a deposit.*
5. *Use separate FTD coupons for each return period.*

We use the "IRS USE ONLY" box to ensure proper crediting to your account. ***Do not*** *darken this box when making a deposit.*

After making your deposit, the authorized institution will date stamp your coupon Form 8109. Unfortunately, you will not receive any official receipt from the depository institution. Your canceled check is your receipt. It is up to you to keep your own records of deposits. One way is to request the depository to photocopy the completed coupon, and hand you the photocopy. The original of the date stamped coupon is kept by the depository institution for *its* records. It is only after the IRS receives the coupon information electronically that your account is reconciled. At such time, settlement of your tax deposit liability is either satisfied in full, is underpaid, or is overpaid.

Application of Deposits

As an OPM-required depositor, your deposits are made on a monthly or semiweekly basis, depending on your aggregate total deposits for the preceding year. Deposits are made on a monthly basis if all employment taxes (social security, medicare, income, and unemployment: Forms 940, 941, 943, and 945) are $50,000 *or less*. Otherwise, they are made semiweekly. A monthly depositor (the focus of this chapter) must deposit the OPM accumulations within a calendar month, by the 15th day of the following month. The IRS is supposed to inform employers by November of each year which schedule to follow (monthly or semiweekly) for the upcoming year.

As the deposits are received by the IRS (from the depository institution), it credits them to the oldest past-due deposits within the same return period. Any overpayments from a previous return period are similarly applied. The consequence of this application procedure is that if you miss a deposit early in a return period, but make succeeding deposits on time, you will face multiple failure-to-deposit penalties. As the deposits are applied to old liabilities, they cause a shortfall in current liabilities. This is called: penalty *cascading*. The cascading process can quickly get out of hand.

Suppose, for example, that you are required to make a deposit of $1,000 on May 15, a deposit of $1,500 on June 15, and a deposit of $1,200 on July 15. Being cash short, you are unable to make the $1,000 deposit on May 15. You try to make up part of the May 15 shortfall by making a $1,700 deposit on June 15. Of the $1,700, the IRS credits $1,000 to the May 15 deposit and $700 to the June 15 deposit. This produces a shortfall of $800 for June 15 ($1,500 required – $700). Still trying to make up the May 15 shortfall, you make a $1,500 deposit ($1,200 required plus $300) on July 15. Of this $1,500, the IRS credits $800 to the June 15 deposit and $700 to the July 15 deposit. This produces a shortfall of $500 for July 15 ($1,200 required – $700). Altogether now, you have **three** underdeposit penalties. It's a never-ending catchup game.

The IRS will bill you separately for each of the three penalties (plus interest). You will be instructed to pay each penalty directly to the IRS. You cannot and MUST NOT use Form 8109 to credit your penalty payments. If you inadvertently do so, you'll experience a holy mess: deposit screwups, penalties on penalties, interest on underdeposits, etc.

Commencing in year 2000, taxpayers will be allowed to designate which deposit period is to be credited with a deposit.

Penalty Law Section 6656

Section 6656 of the Internal Revenue Code is titled: ***Failure to Make Deposit of Taxes***. Its subsection (a) is titled: ***Underpayment of Deposits***. The term "underpayment of deposits" means *underdeposits* relative to the deposit due date and relative to the deposit due amount. A graduated penalty applies depending on the number of days the required amount remains underdeposited.

Subsection 6656(a) reads in principal part as—

> *In the case of any failure by any person to deposit (as required . . .) on the date prescribed therefor any amount of tax imposed by* [the applicable tax return] *in such government depository as is authorized under section 6302(c)* [previously cited] *to receive such deposit, . . . there shall be imposed upon such person a penalty equal to the applicable percentage of the amount of underpayment.*

The "applicable percentage" is set forth in a graduated scale in subsection 6656(b)(1). For each amount of underpayment, the penalty rates are:

(i) 2% for deposits made 1 to 5 days late.
(ii) 5% for deposits made 6 to 15 days late.
(iii) 10% for deposits made 16 or more days late.

(iv) 15% for amounts still undeposited more than 10 days after notice and demand by the IRS for immediate payment.

The 10% penalty also applies when deposits are made to an unauthorized financial institution, or sent directly to the IRS, or attached to the return being filed. If the amount of deposit claimed as a credit on the return is overstated, the penalty jumps to 25% of the amount of deposit overclaimed [Reg. ¶ 301.6656-2].

For a small business, there could be as many as six different depository tax returns. We listed these six returns in the introduction to this chapter. They are **Form 720**: excise tax; **Form 940**: unemployment tax; **Form 941**: employer's quarterly tax; **Form 943**: agricultural employees tax; **Form 945**: withheld income tax; and **Form 1042**: withholdings from foreign persons. With this number of applicable returns, each requiring a deposit the 15th of each month, it is easy to see how a small business owner can get rattled and confused. There is just no letup in the monthly depository scheme. The FTD coupons constitute a priority lien on all available cash in a business.

Exceptions & Safe Harbors

Trying to soften (by a tad) the penalty pounding of small businesses, Congress, in its IRS Restructuring Act of '98 identified certain areas for mitigation by the IRS. One of these areas is an exception for first-time depositors. The specific tax law on point is subsection (c) of Section 6656: ***Exception for First-Time Depositors of Employment Taxes***. This exception reads in part—

> *The* [IRS] *may waive the penalty imposed by subsection (a) on a person's inadvertent failure to deposit any employment tax if—*
>
> (1) such person has a net worth of less than $2,000,000;
> (2) such failure occurs during the first quarter of the deposit requirements, or any change in such requirements; and
> (3) *the return of such tax was filed on or before the due date.*

The term "any employment tax" refers to the required filing of Forms 940, 941, 943, and 945.

Subsection (d) of Section 6656 is titled: ***Authority to Abate Penalty Where Deposit Sent to*** [IRS]. This subsection limits the eligibility for abatement to *the first time a deposit is required* IF the deposit *is inadvertently sent* to the IRS. We have reason to believe that abatement due to inadvertency would apply to other than first time deposits. Our reason is based on the fact that between July 22, 1998 (the IRS Restructuring Act) and December 31, 2001, substantial changes — called "transitional changes" — in the depository rules occurred. There is always bona fide conflict and confusion between old rules and new rules.

The softened version of underdeposit penalty impositions includes limited safe harbor rules [Reg. ¶ 31.6302-1(f)(1)]. An employer is treated as having made the required deposit if **any shortfall**: (1) does not exceed the greater of $100 or 2% of the amount required to be deposited, and (2) is deposited by the prescribed makeup date. For a monthly depositor, the shortfall makeup date is the due date for the quarterly return. The only employment tax quarterly return is Form 941: ***Employer's Quarterly Federal Tax Return***. (Forms 940, 943, and 945 are annual returns.) The Form 941 quarterly due dates are April 30, July 31, October 31, and January 31.

A de minimis safe harbor is also available. If, as a Form 941 filer, your depository taxes for the quarter are **less than $2,500**, you are not required to deposit with an authorized financial institution. Instead, you can make that quarterly payment directly to the IRS. Attach your check to Form 941, then be sure that it is filed on time [Reg. ¶ 31.6302-1(f)(4)].

These exceptions and safe harbors are truly de minimis in operational effect. The more troublesome aspect has been the $50,000 threshold beyond which all-electronic deposits were mandated. Forcing a small business to go all-electronic just to save paperwork for the IRS attests to the indifference of the IRS to small business reality. Under pressure from Congress, the IRS announced on March 22, 1999 that, commencing January 1, 2000, the all-electronic mandate would be increased from $50,000 to

$200,00. This is the kind of general relief that small businesses have long sought.

Reasonable Cause Relief

When we cited the penalty Section 6656(a) above, we intentionally omitted one particular clause. We did so because we wanted to get other depository matters out of the way, before focusing on a longstanding fallback relief provision. For good cause shown, relief from the underdeposit penalties is not limited to first-time depositors, nor to $100 shortfall depositors, nor to $1,000 quarterly employment tax filers. The relief is available to all deputized OPM (Other People's Money) collectors: large and small.

The previously omitted clause in Section 6656(a) is—

> *. . . unless it is shown that such failure is due to reasonable cause and not due to willful neglect. . . .*

This is the same clause that appears in many other penalty sections of the tax code. No one fact nor one circumstance is determinative of reasonable cause. Most good faith efforts to comply with the deposit requirements will be considered.

IRS Regulation ¶ 301.6656-1(b): ***Assertion of reasonable cause***, is most pertinent here. So much so that we cite this particular regulation in full. Accordingly, it reads:

> *To show that the underpayment* [underdeposit] *was due to reasonable cause and not due to willful neglect, a taxpayer must make an affirmative showing of all facts alleged as a reasonable cause in a written statement containing* ***a declaration*** *that it is made* ***under penalties of perjury****. The statement must be filed with the* [IRS] *district director for the district or the director of the service center where the return with respect to the tax is required to be filed. If the district director or the director of the service center determines that the underpayment was due to reasonable cause and not due to willful neglect, the penalty will not be imposed.* [Emphasis added.]

There is one very important item to note in the regulation just cited. It is the emphasized phrase: *a declaration . . . under penalties of perjury* (the jurat clause). You may explain your reasonable cause situation in any format of your choice. When you are all through explaining and documenting, your signature must appear below the jurat clause. If you don't remember its exact wording, look at the signature block on *any* tax return form. It will be there. Without the jurat to your reasonable cause explanation, your request for penalty relief will be denied. It may also be denied for other reasons.

Requests to Pursue

When a failure-to-deposit penalty is imposed, you will be notified and billed for such penalty by the IRS. The notice will be accompanied by a payment voucher which allows you to pay and receive proper credit. Instructions may also accompany the notice which apprise you of your rights to seek waiver of the penalty for reasonable cause. At this point, you have two courses of request action that you can take. We summarize and depict these two courses for you in Figure 3.3.

The first course is to prepare, in your own format, a "Request for Waiver of Deposit Penalty." State your facts and circumstances, include the jurat clause, and sign. Hand print on the voucher: "Waiver Requested. See Attached." Attach your waiver request to the voucher form, and place in the return envelope which the IRS sent to you. The envelope is bar coded to arrive at the proper processing desk at the IRS.

If your waiver request is denied, obtain from the IRS its Form 843: ***Claim for Refund and Request for Abatement***. Be sure also to obtain the official instructions to Form 843. Basically, the instructions tell you to prepare a separate Form 843 for each tax period, and indicate the type of tax and penalty involved. Make several photocopies of the blank official form; we know you'll need them. The penalty designation part appears as—

Type of tax, penalty, or addition to tax:
☐ *Employment* ☐ Estate ☐ *Gift* ☐ *Excise*

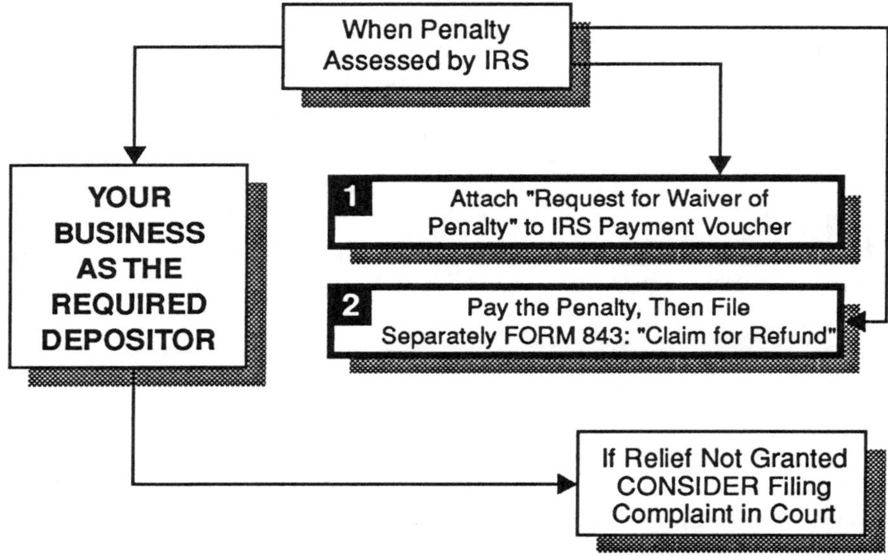

Fig. 3.3 - Two Preferable Requests to the IRS for Penalty Relief

☐ *Penalty—IRC section* ▸ ______________

Type of return filed:
☐ *940* ☐ *941* ☐ *943* ☐ *945* ☐ *Other (specify)*

For employment tax penalty purposes (Forms 940, 941, 943, and 945), **Form 843** is a CLAIM FOR REFUND. It is not a request for abatement, as its title implies. The "abatement" request applies only to those interest charges that are caused by the IRS's errors, delays, and erroneous written advice. Therefore, being a Claim for Refund, you have to *pay* the penalty before you can request its refund. This saves further accrual of interest which, in and of itself, is a psychological benefit. Thus, your second course of informal action is to pay the penalty, then immediately prepare Form 843 for a refund.

In this second course, do not attach Form 843 to the payment voucher which the IRS sends to you. Pay the amount due by voucher. Then, file your refund claim separately with the IRS center serving your area. There is adequate space on the front and back of

Form 843 to type in your explanation of why you think your claim for refund of the penalty should be allowed. The jurat clause is already preprinted on Form 843.

Within about 90 to 180 days, you should get an official response to your claim for refund. If denied, and you still want to persist, your next course is to pursue the matter through the courts. The examples which follow will give you some idea of your likelihood of success.

Where Penalties Upheld

A good percentage of reasonable cause court petitions for relief from the failure-to-deposit penalty rely on: (a) illness or death of owner, (b) lack of funds, or (c) wrongdoing of employees. None of these arguments carries much judicial weight. Such arguments are not a substitute for ordinary care and prudence when operating a business. Judicial minds are not sympathetic to the work, toil, and pain of a struggling business. A few brief examples will illustrate our point.

The penalties were upheld in the following cases where the *illness or death* of the owner was alleged:

- *Roberts Metal Fabrication, Inc.*, 93-1 USTC ¶ 50,013.

  — The poor health and frequent absences of the president and sole shareholder did not excuse his failure to establish internal controls and delegate to others his depository responsibilities.

- *Sykes & Sons, Inc.*, 95-2 USTC ¶ 50,620.

  — The illness of the person in charge of the company's business operations, and the inexperience of the family members who took over after his death, did not excuse the lack of preparation for transition to new management.

- *Bostar Foods, Inc.*, 97-1 USTC ¶ 50,285.

  — The emotional and physical stress on the corporation's president due to business financial troubles and personal family problems provided no grounds for relief, where no internal controls to monitor his tax obligations were in place.

The penalties were also upheld in the following cases where the *lack of funds* was alleged:

- *Upton Printing Co.*, 95-2 USTC ¶ 50,377
  - — Financial difficulties, causing the company to use the funds earmarked for employment tax deposits to pay creditors in an effort to continue its operation, was not reasonable cause.
- *Woodstein-Lauderdale, Inc.*, 94-2 USTC ¶ 50,461.
  - — The taxpayer's claim of insufficient funds, and his misunderstanding of the priority of federal tax deposits over other creditor claims, were not persuasive, especially since his accountant had cautioned him that penalties would apply.
- *Ray Stevens Paving Co.*, 93-2 USTC ¶ 50,539.
  - — The claim of financial hardship was disregarded where, although losing money, the corporation made million-dollar disbursements to trade creditors and their principal officers, while neglecting tax obligations.

The penalties were further upheld in the following cases where the *wrongdoing of employees* was alleged.

- *Valen Mfg. Co.*, 96-2 USTC ¶ 50,407.
  - — The total reliance on a hired bookkeeper to make the required tax deposits was unreasonable where, once the bookkeeper's errors were discovered, the required deposits (including penalties) were made.
- *Conklin Brothers, Inc.*, 93-1 USTC ¶ 50,116.
  - — Although the company controller concealed his failure to make employment tax deposits by altering checks and reports, this was ruled as undue reliance on an employee for such a major responsibility.

- *Frederick Savage, Inc.*, 95-1 USTC ¶ 50,189

  — When the more experienced of two owners left the company, the remaining owner could not assert his reliance on the failure of the former owner to instruct him on the intricacies of the depository requirements.

Elements to Establish

In the above and many similar cases, the failure-to-deposit penalty has been upheld. In the past 10 years or so, there have been 42 court cases involving Section 6656. Of this number, 36 or 85% of the penalties stood. Only six or 15% of the penalties assessed by the IRS were court removed. This raises the question: In order to escape the penalties, what are the elements of reasonable cause that have to be established?

The basic approach is to establish that the failure did not result from "willful neglect." This term is defined by case law as a "conscious, intentional disregard of, or reckless indifference to" the depository rules. The IRS, however, regards three or more depository failures as willful neglect. Particularly so if the responsible person paid other creditors before the IRS, or if the services of a tax professional were not engaged. It is standard policy for the IRS to presume willful neglect, whether it has any basis for such presumption or not. The IRS does not have to consider its own unreasonableness as an element of reasonable cause for a taxpayer.

Oddly, in failure-to-deposit cases, the IRS often does not abide by its own Regulation ¶ 301.6651-1(c)(1): ***Showing of reasonable cause***. Selected excerpts from this regulation read—

> *A failure to pay will be considered due to reasonable cause to the extent that the taxpayer has made a satisfactory showing that he exercised ordinary business care and prudence . . . if he made reasonable efforts to conserve sufficient assets in marketable form to satisfy his tax liability . . .* [yet] *nevertheless was either unable to pay the tax or would suffer an undue hardship* [such as selling assets at a substantial loss] *if he paid on the due date.*

In the following cases, the IRS **lost its assertions** that penalties were due:

- *Dana Corp.*, DC Ohio, 91-1 USTC ¶ 50,295. The corporation made estimated tax deposits six times a month. Because of conflicting rules and dates, the IRS assigned the deposits to the wrong periods.

- *American Biomaterials Corp.*, CA-3, 92-1 USTC ¶ 50,194; 954 F2d 919. The three top officers, Chairman of the Board, Chief Executive Officer, and Chief Financial Officer, embezzled all available cash and liquidity in the corporation. This incapacitated the business and rendered it unable to comply with the deposit rules. Embezzlement by the top officers was beyond the control of the employee accountant who was filing returns without the deposits.

- *Arthur's Industrial Maintenance, Inc.*, DC Va, 93-1 USTC ¶ 50,092. The company was owed substantial amounts of money by its clients. The amounts were more than sufficient to make the required deposits. Nevertheless, attempts to collect the money owed were met with bankruptcies and insolvencies.

We try to summarize in Figure 3.4 the above elements that establish reasonable cause. If you pursue your own case into court, you should be aware that it can take from three to five years to achieve resolution.

A Very Instructive Case

We have chosen to present the court case of the *Slater Corporation*, BC-DC Fla, 96-1 USTC ¶ 50,043 in more detail than those above. We do so for several reasons. First, there were 16 failure-to-deposit penalties covering four consecutive years (1991–1994). **None** of the penalties was upheld by the court! Secondly, the *Slater* case illustrates how brutal, nasty, and inhumane the IRS can be. And, thirdly, the case illustrates how — on rare occasions

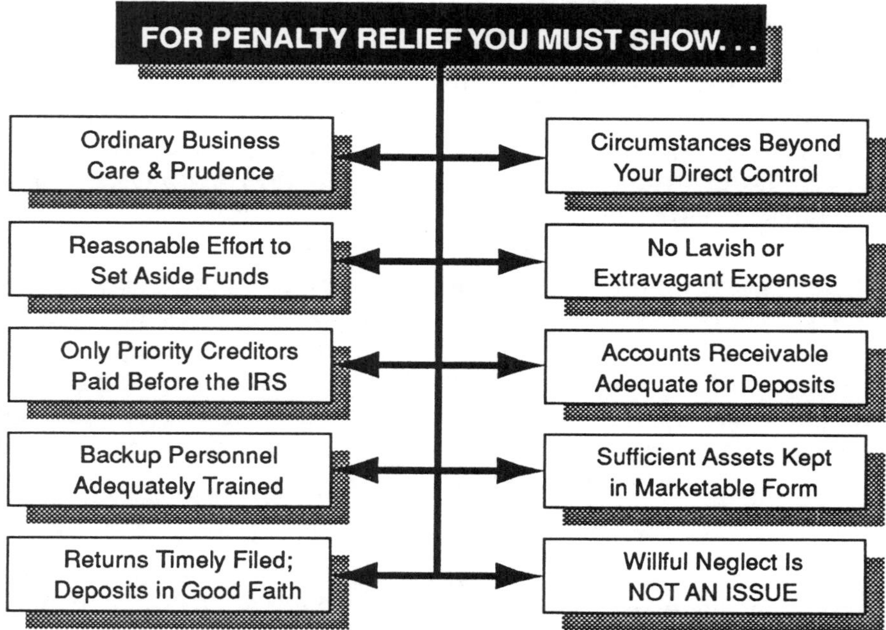

Fig. 3.4 - Key Elements to Show When Establishing Reasonable Cause

— a court can devote serious thought and analysis to the taxpayer-presented facts and circumstances. In the great majority of tax cases, the courts favor the IRS . . . because it is easier to do so.

The Slater Corporation was a general contractor overseeing numerous subcontractors engaged in the reconstruction of homes and businesses destroyed by Hurricane Andrew in 1992 (in South Florida). The work was on government-sponsored projects for which delays in payment for work performed are notorious. Even when the government payments were made many months after a project was completed, a 10% retainage was held back (in the event of complaints from property owners). Before any government payments were made, however, the Slater Corporation had to pay off all subcontractors and suppliers, and had to post performance bonds to this end. To make the prepayments to subcontractors, suppliers, and bondsmen, the Slaters advanced $300,000 of their own personal assets to the corporation. In addition, the Slaters obtained a home equity loan of $75,000 to put into the business.

Though all the facts above were known to the IRS, it still alleged willful neglect. It accused the Slaters of paying off other creditors than the IRS. It asserted that the business was not managed with ordinary care and prudence, because the Slaters did not employ a full time accountant. Although all employment tax deposits were made in full, including penalties and interest, all were "back credited," thereby always being late.

When the Slaters objected to the IRS's back crediting their deposits, they were threatened with seizure and sale of their business. This would have forced the forfeiture of their highly-leveraged performance bonds. So they petitioned for protection from the IRS through the Bankruptcy Court under Chapter 11: reorganization. At this point, the penalties totaled $48,990 and the interest on the penalties totaled $19,932 (grand total: $68,922). All required deposits were paid in full.

The Court concluded as follows:

> The Slaters' failure to timely pay the employment tax liabilities was not due to willful neglect. The evidence reveals that the Slaters and their principals contributed substantial funds to pay the tax liabilities, and that had the funds been applied towards the Slaters' current tax liabilities, certain of the penalties would not have accrued. Here, the IRS maximized and pyramided the penalties in each quarter by demanding and applying current funds to old periods, which already had incurred the maximum penalties.
>
> In sum, the Slaters are entitled to **relief from** the subject penalties in that the failure to timely deposit and pay the taxes for each period at issue was due to reasonable cause and not due to willful neglect.
>
> It is so ORDERED AND ADJUDGED.

4

NEGLIGENCE & DISREGARD

The "Penalty Of Choice" Among IRS Auditing Personnel Is The 20% Negligence And Disregard Penalty. It Is Automatically Added On To The UNDERPAYMENT Of Tax Imposed When A Return Has Been Formally Examined. Ostensibly, It Is Assessed For Failure To Keep Proper Books And Records, Noncompliance With Rules And Regulations, Or Taking A Position Which Has No Realistic Possibility Of Being Sustained On Its Merits. When Assessed, The BURDEN IS ON YOU To Establish Via "Reasonable Cause" That Relief From The Penalty Is Proper. Even Then, Some Auditors Are Unpersuaded. But You Must Try.

One of the most — if not THE most — flagrant penalties asserted by the IRS is the 20% negligence penalty. Any time a tax return is examined, and there is a discrepancy in what you compute the tax to be, and what the IRS computes it to be, the negligence penalty is asserted . . . automatically. It is virtually guaranteed to be asserted. So commonplace is the negligence penalty that it is dubbed: "the penalty of choice for lazy IRS personnel."

When an assigned IRS person computes the tax his or her way, a 20% amount is automatically added on to the underpayment amount. In most cases, the add-on is designated: Section 6662(b) penalty for negligence or disregard of rules and regulations. The IRS imposer never cites the tax law, rule, or regulation that you have allegedly disregarded. You don't believe us? If the penalty has been imposed on you, try asking the IRS: "Specifically, what rule or regulation have I disregarded?" You will not get an answer. You will be told — if you are told anything at all — that the burden of proof is on you to establish that the penalty should not apply. On your own, you have to find out that there is a reasonable cause exception to the penalty, namely: Section 6664(c).

The negligence-and-disregard penalty is one of *five* separate 20% penalties called: ***Accuracy-Related***. In this chapter, we'll address the first of the five penalties only. We'll address the others in subsequent chapters.

The idea behind an accuracy-related penalty is that you are punished for not using ordinary business care and prudence when preparing your return. What constitutes such care is best described through examples where the penalty has been upheld, and examples where the penalty has been removed. No penalty can be removed unless you take it upon yourself to affirmatively establish reasonable cause.

Our position is that your first line of reasonable-cause showing is to the IRS person, supervisor, or office from which the penalty emanated. Since the penalty was probably cavalierly applied, it can be cavalierly removed by the imposer thereof. But you must cite some applicable rule or regulation, and some specific good faith facts, to back up your removal request. If necessary, appeal the matter within the IRS. Under the IRS Restructuring and Reform Act of 1998, the IRS's Appellate Division is given wide latitude of discretion in its penalty appeal cases.

Overview of Section 6662

IR Code Section 6662 is titled: ***Imposition of Accuracy-Related Penalty***. It is comprised of about 1,500 words and is arranged into eight subsections. It is relatively a new law, having been enacted in 1989 as P.L. 101-239 (Omnibus Budget Reconciliation Act). It repealed and replaced seven prior accuracy-related penalty laws. Under the seven old laws, the IRS developed the egregious habit of *stacking penalties* for its enjoyment of giving taxpayers a hard time. This was the seed for Congress to seek to change focus from the IRS's arbitrary "stacking," to the judicious assignment of penalties.

The preamble to the accuracy penalties section of P.L. 101-239 states that—

> *The bill consolidates into one part of the Internal Revenue Code all of the generally applicable penalties relating to the accuracy of tax returns. The penalties that are consolidated are the negligence penalty, the substantial understatement penalty, and the valuation penalties. These consolidated penalties are also coordinated with the fraud penalty. The bill repeals the* [1989] *versions of these penalties. The bill reorganizes the accuracy penalties into a new structure that* ***operates to eliminate any stacking*** *of the penalties.* [Emphasis added.]

The preamble is what Congress said. Let us see what the new law itself says. See if you can pick up any content that implies the elimination of stacking.

Subsection 6662(a): ***Imposition of Penalty***, reads in full—

> *If this section applies to* ***any*** *portion of an underpayment of tax required to be shown on a return, there shall be added to the tax an amount equal to 20 percent of the portion of the underpayment to which this section applies.*

Do you see anything in these words about "no stacking"? Not really. Though, conceivably, there is some implication of such in the wording "portion of underpayment to which section applies."

Surely, you know what the term "stacking" is, when applied by the IRS with respect to penalties. Under old law, there were seven different penalties relating to the accuracy of a tax return. Some were less than 20%; some were more than 20% (as high as 50%). If all were 20%, for example, and all seven penalties were imposed simultaneously, the aggregate stack would be 140% (7 x 20%) of the portion of tax underpaid. This means that you would have to contest seven different penalties: each *separately* from the others! While you could probably have one or two (maybe three) of the penalties removed, the others would remain. It is a grinding-you-down process, to cause you to give up on the lesser amount penalties. This has always been a great revenue-producing game for the IRS.

Under new law, Regulation ¶ 1.6662-2(c) says—

> ***No stacking of accuracy-related penalty components.*** *The maximum accuracy-related penalty imposed on a portion of an underpayment may not exceed 20 percent of such portion (40 percent of the portion attributable to gross valuation misstatement), notwithstanding that such portion is attributable to more than one of the types of misconduct described in subsection (b) of this section.*

Note that there is a 40 percent penalty provision. Even Congress, it seems, cannot completely rid itself of the penalty-stacking habit.

The 5 Accuracy Components

Subsection (b) of Section 6662 is titled: ***Portion of Underpayment to Which Section Applies.*** This is the subsection in which the components of accuracy are prescribed. The popular assumption is that penalty-asserting IRS agents actually read the law that they are empowered to enforce. They **do not**! But **you** are expected to read and assimilate it. Accordingly, subsection 6662(b) reads in full as—

> *This section shall apply to the portion of any underpayment which is* ***attributable to 1 or more*** *of the following:*
>
> *(1) Negligence or disregard of rules or regulations.*
>
> *(2) Any substantial understatement of income tax.*
>
> *(3) Any substantial valuation misstatement* [of credits, deductions, etc.]
>
> *(4) Any substantial overstatement of pension liabilities.*
>
> *(5) Any substantial estate or gift tax valuation misstatement.*

*This section shall **not** apply to any portion of an underpayment on which a penalty is imposed under section 6663* [the 75% fraud penalty]. [Emphasis added.]

The administrative effect is that the 20% accuracy penalty is "destacked" from the 75% fraud penalty. When the fraud penalty is asserted, it shuts out the accuracy penalty. Still, there is an illusion here. When we get into the distinguishing details between the accuracy and fraud penalties (in Chapter 7), the above listed components are further subcomponetized. This gives added revenue effect. Congress and the IRS have no intention of reducing the overall number of penalty opportunities, nor the revenue derived from them. All that Congress did was to "consolidate and coordinate" (via Sections 6662 and 6663) the multiplicity of penalty components.

Here's an important point to note. The accuracy penalty applies only if a tax return is filed. That is, **provided** the return (income, estate, gift) is filed on time. If your return is filed late, **both** the accuracy penalty and the failure-to-file penalty (in Chapter 1) can be imposed. However, the late filing of a return is not a factor to be considered in determining whether the accuracy penalty should be imposed [Reg. ¶ 1.6662-2(a)].

How "Negligence" is Defined

The term "negligence" (and its pseudonym: disregard of rules and regulations) is defined in four places. It is defined in (a) the enacting legislation of Section 6662; (b) the tax law itself; (c) IRS regulations; and (d) case law, where the matter has been contested in court. For tax purposes, the term goes beyond that of the everyday concept of negligence. For penalty purposes, it must directly relate to some specific law or regulation.

The enacting legislative definition is—

Negligence includes any careless, reckless, or intentional disregard of rules or regulations, as well as any failure to make a reasonable attempt to comply with the provisions of the Code. In addition, . . . if the underpayment is due to a failure to include on an income tax return an amount shown on an information return . . . [such] *is strong evidence of negligence.*

The specific tax law, subsection 6662(c): ***Negligence***, reads—

The term "negligence" includes ***any failure*** *to make a reasonable attempt to comply with the provisions of* [the IR Code], *and the term "disregard" includes any careless, reckless, or intentional disregard.*

The applicable regulation with respect to defining the term is Regulation ¶ 1.6662-3(b): ***Definitions and rules.*** This regulation comprises about 480 words. It is more specific than the broad generalities above. Selected excerpts from this regulation read—

The term "negligence" includes any failure to . . .

- *(i) exercise ordinary and reasonable care in the preparation of a tax return;*
- *(ii) keep adequate books and records;*
- *(iii) substantiate items properly;*
- *(iv) include an amount of income shown on an information return; or*
- *(v) ascertain the correctness of a deduction, credit, or exclusion on a return which would seem to be . . . "too good to be true" to a reasonable and prudent person.*

This regulation also includes any *inconsistent treatment* of an item between a partner and his partnership, and between an S corporation shareholder and his S corporation. Partnership and S corporation returns are **not** income tax returns; they are "income information" returns. This is because the income, deductions, and credits pass through to the entity members, in proportion to each member's ownership interests. However, if a member advises the IRS of his inconsistent treatment, and explains his basis for the inconsistency, the negligence penalty may not be imposed. Particularly so, if Form 8082: ***Notice of Inconsistent Treatment or Administrative Adjustment Request*** is properly prepared and filed.

Disregard of Rules, Etc.

Regulation ¶ 1.6662-3(b) consists of two separate paragraphs. Paragraph (1) is titled: *Negligence*, whereas paragraph (2) is titled: ***Disregard of rules or regulations.*** We covered paragraph (1) above. Here, we want to cite paragraph (2) in full. Accordingly:

> *The term "disregard" includes* ***any*** *careless, reckless, or intentional disregard of rules and regulations. The term "rules or regulations" includes the provisions of the Internal Revenue Code, temporary or final Treasury regulations issued under the Code, and revenue rulings or notices (other than notices of proposed rule-making) issued by the Internal Revenue Service and published in the Internal Revenue Bulletin. A disregard of rules or regulations is "careless" if the taxpayer does not exercise reasonable diligence to determine the correctness of a return position that is contrary to the rule or regulation. A disregard is "reckless" if the taxpayer makes little or no effort to determine whether a rule or regulation exists, under circumstances which demonstrate a substantial deviation from the standard of conduct that a reasonable person would observe. A disregard is "intentional" if the taxpayer knows of the rule or regulation that is disregarded. Nevertheless, a taxpayer who takes a position contrary to a revenue ruling or notice has not disregarded the ruling or notice if the contrary position has a realistic possibility of being sustained on its merits.*

This regulatory description of the components of the term "disregard" is a pretty tall order. Altogether, there are roughly about 20,000 different rules and regulations emanating from about 1,800 tax laws. Ask yourself this question: How many persons in the IRS, from top officials, attorneys, on down, know the intricacies of *all* the rules and regulations? Very, very few . . . if any at all. Yet, **you** as the taxpayer are expected to know or inquire about them. Some IRS person can come along and assert — without any pertinent research whatsoever — the penalty for negligence and disregard. This forces upon you the burden of proving the IRS wrong. It is because of the difficulty of this burden that at least 90% of all accuracy penalties cite negligence or disregard of the rules as the basis for the 20% penalty. Talk about an unlevel playing field, this is it!

In Figure 4.1, we summarize the above definitional terms constituting negligence and disregard. Study the terms objectively. Then ask yourself: "Is this really a level playing field for taxpayers versus the IRS?" If you haven't already answered this question, the examples which follow may give you a broader perspective.

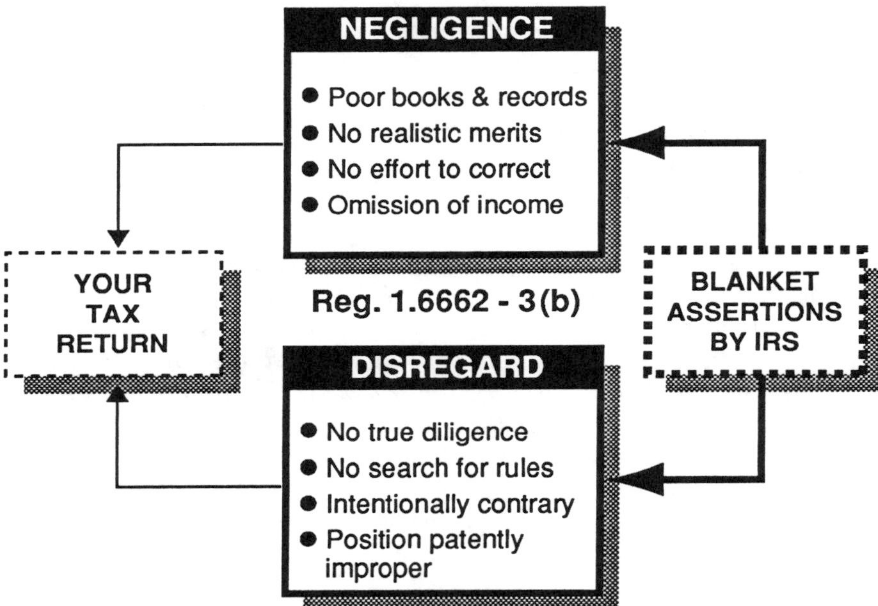

Fig. 4.1 - The Regulatory "Indicators" of Negligence and Disregard

Where Penalties Upheld

Of the 100 or so penalties in the Tax Code, the preponderant litigative issue is the negligence (and disregard) penalty. Within the past 25 years, well over 8,000 such case have been addressed in court. Of this number, our guess is that between 75% and 80% of the penalties have been upheld. It is not that this percentage of taxpayers is truly negligent; it's that "unlevel playing field." It is instructive, therefore, that we cite some specific examples where the courts have ruled in favor of the IRS. In truth, courts are seldom persuaded by good faith challenges to the validity of the IRS's assertions. Consequently, we'll simply categorize the cases, then give a nutshell digest of the position taken by the courts.

Preparation of returns by professionals. In *J. Montoro*, TC Memo 1997-281 (and about 250 similar cases), the taxpayers could not rely on the fact that an attorney, accountant, tax advisor, or tax return preparer had prepared their returns. Nor could they rely on the belief that the preparers would file the returns, where the taxpayers failed to ensure that all necessary information was provided.

Failure to seek professional advice. In *R.J. Huang*, TC Memo 1997-257 (and about 120 similar cases), the taxpayers, upon starting a new business, did not consult a tax preparer, accountant, or lawyer regarding various itemized, business, and rental deductions. As it turned out, the deductions were more personal than business, and no contrary substantiation was presented.

Private churches and religious schemes. In *S.M. Ohnmeiss*, TC Memo 1991-594 (and about 180 similar cases), the taxpayers allegedly made contributions to a private church or religious following which was not identified on their returns. Furthermore, in exchange for a vow of poverty, all personal living expenses were paid out of the contributed funds. No records were kept and no documentation was presented to substantiate the exempt status of the religious organization.

Meritless Constitutional Defenses. In *P.W. Healey*, TC Memo 1996-286 (and about 220 similar cases), the taxpayers argued against the penalties based on constitutional arguments, such as "double jeopardy," "civil forfeiture," "taking property without compensation," etc. The purpose of the penalties was to compensate government for the costs of investigation, detection, and recovery of lost money, or to compensate government for taxpayers' noncompliance.

Reasonable cause evidence not presented. In *D.R. Prince*, TC Memo 1997-324 (and about 1,500 similar cases), the taxpayers did not offer any direct evidence contesting the negligence or disregard penalties.

Family Trust Arrangements. In *W.L. Balis*, TC Memo 1992-34 (and about 100 similar cases), the taxpayers did not establish the validity of their trusts which were characterized as "family estate," "pure," "educational," "business," "common law," or other tax avoidance arrangements. The taxpayers transferred all of their real and personal property, and lifetime services to the trust, in exchange for beneficial interests therein.

Failure to keep adequate records. In *E. Beauchamp*, TC Memo 1997-393 (and about 400 similar cases), the taxpayers did not present adequate substantiation of their deduction claims, despite repeated requests from the IRS that they do so.

Tax shelters and shams. In *D.N. Merino*, TC Memo 1997-385 (and about 750 similar cases), the taxpayers knew that they were buying into a program that consisted chiefly of tax benefits and leveraged writeoffs. Warnings in the prospectuses regarding the tax risks warranted further investigation by a prudent investor, which they failed to pursue.

Where Penalties Removed

Relief from the negligence-and-disregard penalty can be sustained when you show good faith and reasonable cause in what you did. To achieve such relief, you must lay the groundwork. Foremost is that you have filed a return on time, as required. Filing late without reasonable cause of its own is an indicator of possible negligence. Secondly, you must have some credible documentation that is pertinent to the underpayment issue being raised by the IRS. Having no documentation at all is another indicator of negligence. And, thirdly, whatever arguments you advance in support of your reasonable cause must not be frivolous, groundless, or based on far-out concepts of constitutionality.

The Internal Revenue Code is the "law of the land." Congress initiated every tax law therein, and the President confirmed them. Whatever the reason for your underpayment of tax, as asserted by the IRS, you must base your penalty relief endeavors on some credible reasonable cause explanation. Relief can be — and often is — granted, as the examples which follow illustrate.

- ☐ The fact that the taxpayer hired an accountant to straighten out his books and to establish a system of proper recordkeeping indicated an effort to comply with the rules and regulations, rather than to negligently or intentionally disregard them.

  — *W.C. King*, TC Memo 1982-282

- ☐ Negligence penalties were not imposed on unsophisticated investors who reasonably relied on erroneous investment advice from a certified financial planner when investing in and claiming losses from an oil and gas tax shelter partnership. Due care does not necessarily require investors of the taxpayers' inexperience and lack of financial sophistication to independently investigate their investments.

  — *D.A. Wright*, TC Memo 1994-288

- ☐ Taxpayers were not subject to the negligence penalty for their erroneous characterization of their commodities trading as a trade or business. Given the considerable time they committed to their commodities investments, prudent persons under similar circumstances might reasonably take the position that their activities constituted a trade or business.

  — *R.W. Steffler*, TC Memo 1995-271

- ☐ When a divorce decree did not specifically designate any portion of the money payments to be received by the taxpayer as alimony payments, the court determined that it was not unreasonable for her to believe that she did not receive alimony and that her interest in her ex-husband's retirement benefits was a tax-free distribution of property. Penalties for negligence were not upheld because there was an honest misunderstanding of the law.

  — *A.L. Denbow*, TC Memo 1989-92

☐ A petroleum engineer who was employed by foreign petroleum companies in foreign countries was not subject to the negligence penalty because he made a reasonable attempt to comply with the tax laws. The engineer concluded that he was not required to file a return because he improperly claimed the foreign earned exclusion, erroneously resulting in no tax liability. The tax law in this area is complex; the engineer was not negligent for not knowing in advance how the rules ultimately would be applied in his situation.

— *D.P. Lansdown*, 96-1 USTC ¶ 50,025

Underpayment Defined

The 20% negligence-and-disregard penalty applies to an *underpayment* of tax. It does **not** apply to the full amount of tax, whether said amount is computed by you or by the IRS. However, the IRS-computed amount is the reference base for determining the underpayment. Consequently, if you intend to contest the negligence penalty, you should make sure that the IRS computation is correct. The IRS makes a lot of computational errors and misinterpretations of tax law. Establishing whether the IRS is correct or not is beyond the scope of this book.

If the IRS's computation of tax is correct, Section 6664(a): ***Underpayment***, defines the term as—

> *The amount by which any tax imposed by* [the IRS] ***exceeds the excess of***
>
> *(1) the sum of—*
> *(A) the amount shown as the tax by the taxpayer on his return, plus*
> *(B) amounts not so shown previously assessed (or collected without assessment),*
>
> *over*
>
> *(2) the amount of rebates made.* [Emphasis added.]

What does the phrase "exceeds the excess of" mean? Pretty confusing, isn't it? We'll try to clarify this phrase by recourse to IRS Regulation ¶ 1.6664-2(a): ***Underpayment defined.***

This regulation reads, in part—

The definition of underpayment also may be expressed as—

Underpayment *= W – (X + Y – Z),*

where W = the amount of tax imposed; X = the amount shown by the taxpayer on his return; Y = amounts not so shown previously assessed (or collected without assessment); and Z = the amount of rebates made.

The term "rebates" means any form of tax reduction from abatements, credits, refunds, or other repayments made to the taxpayer by the IRS. It is for administrative convenience that the IRS often makes beneficial adjustments to a tax return **before** the "tax imposed" is officially computed. When the rebates are made, they subtract from the sum of X (taxpayer computed amount) plus Y (other amounts paid by taxpayer). The net effect is that the rebates, if any, are added back into the underpayment computations.

A diagrammatic representation of the underpayment formula above is presented in Figure 4.2. The idea is to provide you with a full accounting of all amounts affecting the underpayment base. It is Step 4 in Figure 4.2 that comes nearest to explaining the statutory phrase: "exceeds the excess of." Step 5 is simply applying the 20% penalty rate.

Example How Penalty Imposed

By far, most negligence penalties are imposed when a return has been examined by an IRS auditor. The penalty is included as part of the wrap-up routine. Every auditor asserts the negligence penalty, whether justified or not.

The routine is to cite Section 6662(a) or, in the alternative, Section 6662(c). The proper citation should be Section 6662(b)(1), (b)(2), (b)(3), (b)(4), or (b)(5), as appropriate. By skipping over subsection (b), IRS auditors avoid having to separate the total understatement into its proper components. This exemplifies the poor supervision of penalty assessments by IRS management.

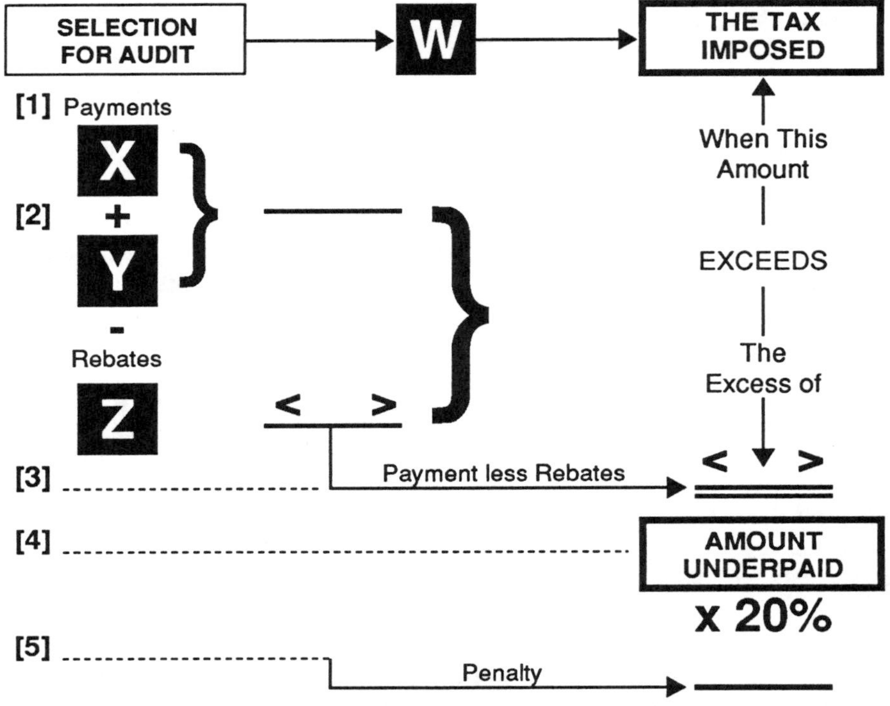

Fig. 4.2 - The Accounting Process for Establishing Underpayment of Tax

The usual procedure after an audit is to submit to the auditee a ***Report of Tax Examination Changes***. The report summarizes the adjustments increase, the corrected tax, and the total deficiency or underpayment. The 20% negligence penalty is then applied to the total deficiency, citing either IRS Sec. 6662(a) or (c). Subsection (a), recall, is Imposition; subsection (c) is Negligence. Subsection (b), which is **rarely cited** is: *Portion of Underpayment to Which Section Applies.*

Here's a real-life example. The taxpayer was a marketing consultant who did a lot of business traveling. For cost-cutting reasons, his employer did not reimburse him for all of his travel and related business expenses. Even though he had adequate substantiation of his expenses, he was office audited. Other items besides travel were also audited. When he was all through, some six months later, he received a Report of Individual Income Tax

Examination Change. The report consisted of six full-length, computer-printout pages.

For instructional purposes here, we have condensed and edited the report in Figure 4.3. The true substance and dollar figures are as shown. Note that a blanket 20% penalty is applied to the entire deficiency (understatement of tax). Note also that interest is computed separately for the deficiency *and* for the penalty. This is so that if the penalty should be abated later, recomputing the interest on the deficiency is not required.

DEPARTMENT OF TREASURY INTERNAL REVENUE SERVICE		
REPORT OF INDIVIDUAL INCOME TAX EXAMINATION CHANGES		
Name & Address of Taxpayer(s)	Date of Report:	
	Form: ________	Year: ________
	Soc. Sec. No.	**IRS District No.**
		Examiner's Name
Representative (if any):	**Filing Status**	**File No.** ________

	ADJUSTMENTS TO INCOME AND/OR DEDUCTIONS	$ Amount
A.	Adjustment INCREASE	15,096
B.	Plus Taxable Income on Return	68,585
C.	CORRECTED Taxable Income	83,681
D.	CORRECTED TAX	19,849
E.	Tax Shown on Return	15,180
F.	DEFICIENCY (Understatement)	4,669
G.	Interest on Deficiency	839
H.	PENALTY on Deficiency	933
I.	Interest on Penalty	168
J.	TOTAL ADDITIONAL AMOUNT DUE ▶	**6,609**
	SEE ATTACHED EXPLANATION OF ADJUSTMENTS AND PENALTY	
	IRC. Sec. 6662 (a)	

Fig. 4.3 - Abbreviated Audit Report With Sec. 6662 (a) Penalty

Regulations require that each examination change report be accompanied by an "explanation." As you'll see below, the explanation is computer generated and stereotyped. For the Figure 4.3 changes, the reason for the penalty was cited as follows:

Since you did not establish that the business expense shown on your tax return was paid or incurred during the taxable year and that the expense was ordinary and necessary to your business, we have disallowed the entire amount and have added the accuracy related penalty of IRC section 6662.

The reason for the disallowance was nonsense. The entire disallowed $15,096 in business expenses was adequately documented on appeal. The only flaw in the taxpayer's records was that he had only one repair invoice on his business auto for the year. The auditor demanded two such invoices: one near the beginning of the year, one near the end. This was to verify the total business mileage that he claimed. The true fact was that he had had the car in the shop only once during the year for repairs.

For this, the taxpayer got slapped with the 20% negligence penalty! Do you see what we mean? Auditors just don't use their heads. The purpose of a penalty is to encourage compliance with law: not to encourage contempt for the IRS.

Reasonable Cause Exception

The taxpayer in the example above was able to have his penalty removed entirely. He filed a written statement (protest) addressed to the auditor claiming reasonable cause and that he acted in good faith. He reminded the auditor that he had presented the records to her previously, and said that he would go over them again with her. He did so. Subsequently, the penalty was canceled and the deficiency (understatement) was reduced from $4,669 to $545. (The $545 deficiency was due to excess business entertainment expenses, which the auditor disallowed.)

An exception to the negligence and other accuracy-related penalties is set forth in Section **6664(c)(1)**. This subsection: (c) ***Reasonable Cause Exception***, (1) ***In General***, reads as follows:

No penalty shall be imposed under this part with respect to any portion of an underpayment if it is shown that there was a reasonable cause for such portion and that the taxpayer acted in good faith with respect to such portion.

The good faith aspects of the penalty exception are amplified in Regulation 1.6664-4: ***Reasonable cause and good faith exception to section 6662 penalties.*** Subregulation (b)(1) outlines the "facts and circumstances" that may be taken into account by the IRS for exception purposes.

Excerpts from this 400-word subregulation are—

> *The determination of whether a taxpayer acted with reasonable cause and in good faith is made on a* ***case-by-case basis****, taking into account all pertinent facts and circumstances. . . . Circumstances that may indicate reasonable cause and good faith include an honest misunderstanding of fact or law that is reasonable in light of the experience, knowledge, and education of the taxpayer. . . . An isolated computational or transcriptional error generally is not inconsistent with reasonable cause and good faith.* [Emphasis added.]

The "good faith" idea is that you do your best to prepare a correct return, and file it on time. But, if you wait until midnight on April 15th to prepare and file your return, and it contains understatement-of-tax errors, don't expect any reasonable cause exception to the Section 6662 penalties.

Example: Negligence Mitigated

Let us give you another example of how the Section 6664(c) penalty exception works. This also is a real-life case. The taxpayer, a small business contractor, was office audited and given an audit report showing a deficiency of $9,423. In the penalty portion of the report, the auditor entered—

> *6662(c): 20% of $9,423 = $1,885*

The taxpayer had no idea in the world what the "6662(c)" meant. After contacting his preparer, he learned that the "6662(c)" meant Internal Revenue Code Section 6662(c) which simply defines the term "negligence." The auditor provided no explanation whatever as to what portion of the $9,423 deficiency was due to negligence.

Upon analyzing the deficiency, the tax preparer determined that $6,472 was due to a transcriptional error from Schedule B; that $2,791 was due to a casualty-loss adjustment on Form 4684; and that $160 was due to a cost-of-sale error on Form 4797.

A written protest was addressed to the auditor. In edited and condensed form, the taxpayer pleaded that—

1. There was no understatement of income on Schedule B. There were 22 separate entries, all of which were verified.

2. The return was complex: a total of 118 entries was involved. In addition to Schedule B (22 entries), there was Schedule A (11 entries), Schedule C (9 entries), Schedule D (3 entries), Schedule E (22 entries), Form 4684 (16 entries), Form 4797 (6 entries), Form 2210 (9 entries), Form 4562 (3 entries), and Form 1040 (15 entries . . . plus 2 missing entries). Missing 2 entries out of a total 118 required does not warrant imposition of the negligence penalty.

3. The transcriptional oversight was self-discovered and promptly reported. This matter was called to your attention before you started the audit, and a check for $6,472 was handed to you at that time.

What was the auditor's response?

Answer: He abated the penalty on the $6,472 but asserted it on $2,791. His "explanation" was—

> *The 20% addition to tax is charged as per IRC Sec. 6662(c). It is asserted only on $2,791. This is the amount of deficiency due to your casualty loss adjustment. The penalty amount is 20% of $2,791 = $558.*

Although the $558 is a mitigation from the original $1,889 penalty, the taxpayer also had reasonable cause. He experienced a **7.1 earthquake** which caused the casualty loss. But the auditor would hear no more.

5

UNDERSTATEMENT PENALTY

The Difference Between What Income Tax You Show On Your Return, And What The IRS Imposes It To Be, Becomes An "Understatement." The 20% Accuracy Penalty Applies To Such Amount Unless You Can Show That All Or A Portion Of The Difference Is Due To SUBSTANTIAL AUTHORITY Or ADEQUATE DISCLOSURE. Either Showing Requires A Sensible Analysis Of Applicable Tax Law, Official Forms, And Relevant Court Decisions. You Must Show At Least A 50/50 Probability Of Prevailing. Even Then, The IRS Will Attack Any Grey Area Positions You May Take That Are Contrary To The IRS's Maximum Tax Goals.

In Chapter 4, we listed the five accuracy-related penalties that are identified in IRC Section 6662(b): ***Portion of Underpayment to Which*** [Imposition of Penalty] ***Applies***. In that chapter, we focused exclusively on penalty (1): negligence and disregard. In this chapter we focus exclusively on penalty (2): substantial understatement. We'll take up penalties (3), (4), and (5) in Chapter 6: Valuation Misstatements.

Penalty (2) relates to the amount of income tax shown on your return, when compared with the amount **required** to be shown thereon. It is the IRS, of course, which asserts the amount required to be shown. The difference between the amounts is your *understatement* of tax. The amount of understatement must be "substantial" before the 20% add-on applies. You may become disturbed when you learn how awkward the term "substantial" can be, justifying the IRS's imposition of the penalty. The correct full title of penalty (2) is: ***Substantial Understatement of Income Tax.***

The substantial understatement penalty brings forth two rather bizarre and difficult relief provisions. The two relief provisions are: (A) *substantial authority* for one's position, and (B) *adequate disclosure* on one's tax return. The IRS conveys a subliminal message to you in these provisions. If you do not accept the IRS's interpretation of a tax law, you have to convince it ahead of time that there is the greater than 50% likelihood of your position being upheld in court. Even if you can speculate sensibly a 65% likelihood, the IRS will challenge you if it decides to make a "test case" of your position. The idea is to dampen any creative interpretation on your part, that could lessen your burden of tax.

If you are a member of a tax shelter partnership or trust, or of a corporation engaged in tax motivated transactions, the relief-from-penalty provisions are stiffened even more.

In this chapter, therefore, we want to treat you to a special "twist of mind" that pervades the IRS bureaucracy. By our pointing out certain features to you about "substantial authority" and "adequate disclosure," you'll have a better sense of the realities to which you are tax law exposed. The substantial understatement penalty enables the IRS to bifurcate its accuracy penalty into a nonsubstantial part (where the reasonable cause exception may apply) and a substantial part (where relief from the penalty is extremely difficult).

How "Substantial" is Defined

The term "substantial" is defined in Section 6662(d)(1) as—

> *For the purposes of this section, there is a substantial* ***under-statement*** *of income tax for any taxable year if the amount of the understatement for the taxable year* ***exceeds the greater of***—
> *(i) 10 percent of the tax required to be shown on the return, OR*
> *(ii) $5,000* [$10,000 for corporations]. [Emphasis added.]

If the amount of tax required to be shown by the IRS is $10,586, for example, and that shown on the return is $5,386, the understatement of tax is $5,200. Because this exceeds $5,000 ["the greater of" vs. 10% of tax ($1,058)], the understatement is "substantial." Hence, the 20% penalty applies.

On the other hand, if the required tax were $76,586 and the amount actually shown on the return were $68,386, the understatement amount would be $7,800 (76,586 – 68,386). This is greater than 10% of $76,586 (7,658); thus, the 20% penalty applies. If the understatement were $5,800 (instead of $7,800), the penalty would not apply.

A 10%/$5,000 error tolerance is awkward and unrealistic. Most conscientious taxpayers prepare their individual returns in less than three weeks' time. The IRS has three years to examine it. This is a 50 to 1 time advantage in the IRS's favor. And adding to this, the IRS has all the benefits of hindsight. The consequence is that the substantial understatement penalty is another source of alternative revenue called: ***Additon to Tax***.

Particularly note that the statutory reference for applying the penalty is under**statement**. This differs from under*payment*. An understatement is that which is shown on a return when it is initially filed. This forecloses the opportunity on your part to correct the understatement by subsequent voluntary payments via an amended return. The IRS wants to hold your feet to the fire.

Understatement Defined

The term "understatement" is defined in subparagraph (A) of Section 6662(d)(2) as—

The excess of

(i) *the amount of tax required to be shown on the return for the taxable year, over*

(ii) *the amount of tax imposed which is shown on the return, reduced by any rebate.*

The "amount of tax required to be shown" is that which is imposed by the IRS when it examines your return. The "amount of tax imposed which is shown on the return" is that amount which you show. This is the amount that the IRS *freezes in place* for its penalty computation purposes. Remember, we are not dealing here with underpayment; we are dealing with under*statement*. The IRS wants to analyze your return and extract from it potential ideas for its adoption of new enforcement rules and regulations.

Once the IRS establishes an understatement amount, it goes through an elimination process to identify the specific item or issue to which the 20% penalty applies. This elimination process is prescribed by subparagraph (B) of Section 6662(d)(2): ***Reduction of Understatement Due to Position of Taxpayer or Disclosed Item***. This subparagraph reads—

> *The amount of understatement under subparagraph (A)* ***shall be reduced*** *by that portion of the understatement which is attributable to*
>
> > *(i) the tax treatment of any item by the taxpayer if there is or was* ***substantial authority*** *for such treatment, or*
> >
> > *(ii) any item if (I) the relevant facts affecting the item's tax treatment are* ***adequately disclosed*** *in the return or in a statement attached to the return, and (II) there is a* ***reasonable basis*** *for the tax treatment of such item by the taxpayer*. [Emphasis added.]

Other elimination rules apply if you are a shareholder in a multi-party corporate financial arrangement, or are a member of a tax shelter. If you are not such a shareholder or member, the sequence of elimination before the understatement penalty applies is depicted in Figure 5.1.

The whole idea of Figure 5.1 is to give you an opportunity to avoid the 20% penalty **before** it is imposed. This differs from relief from the penalty after it is imposed, such as is the case for the reasonable cause exception of Section 6664(c). Unfortunately, by stating your position and reasoning up front, you are bringing a matter to the IRS's attention, of which it might not otherwise become aware. Whether you pursue — or not pursue — the opportunity will depend on the extent of your research into

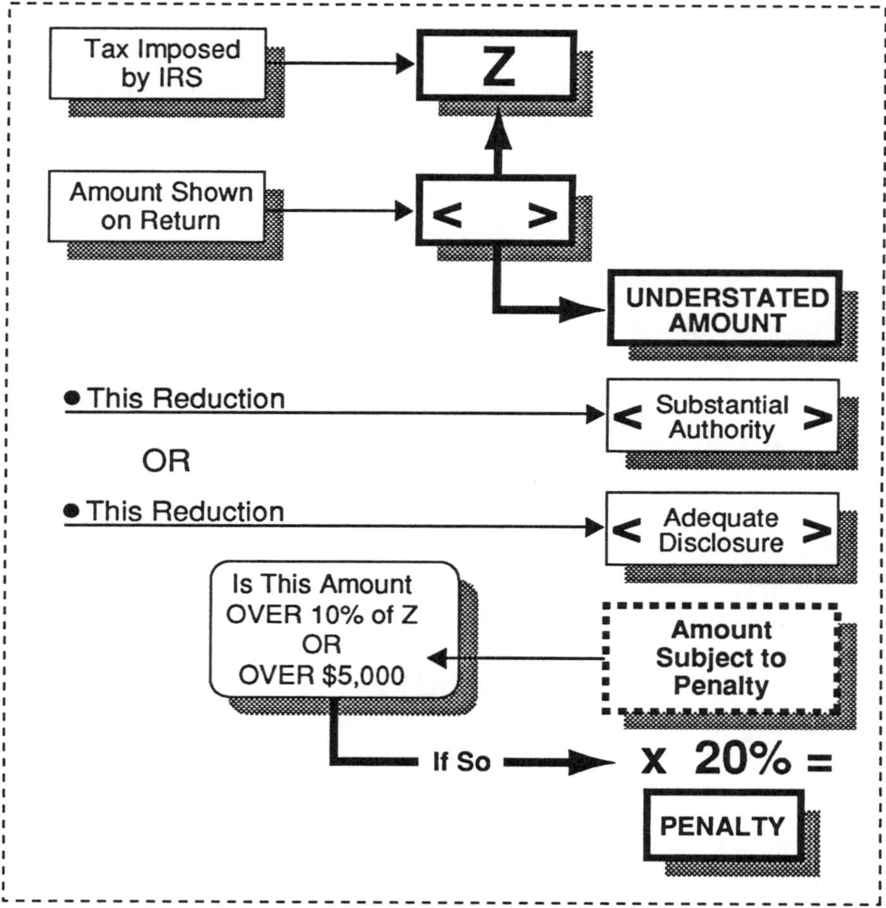

Fig. 5.1 - Reduction of the Understatement Penalty for Credible Showings

"substantial authority" and "adequate disclosure." Let us try to explain these matters more fully.

What is "Substantial Authority"?

Substantial authority: sounds impressive, doesn't it? It almost sounds like some quantitative measure that you can see and feel and hold up, to determine if you have it or don't have it. Actually, it is an elusive test whereby you try to prove, by citing relevant authorities, that you could probably win in court, if you are not frustrated before then.

Though cited in Section 6662(d)(2)(B)(i) as an accuracy penalty relief, the term "substantial authority" is not defined in the tax law itself. It is defined by the 1,680-word IRS Regulation ¶ 1.6662-4(d): ***Substantial authority***. The following is an outline of the contents of this regulation:

(1) Effect of having substantial authority.
(2) Substantial authority standard.
(3) Determination of whether substantial authority is present.
    (i) Evaluation of authorities.
    (ii) Nature of analysis.
    (iii) Type of authority.
    (iv) Written determination.
    (v) When determined.

Obviously, we can only present excerpts and digests which we believe are instructive. Otherwise, any attempt to cite the entire regulation would totally overwhelm you.

The effect of having substantial authority for the tax treatment of an item is that the item is treated as though it were shown properly on your return. As a result, the tax attributable to the item is not included in the understatement for that year. Each income taxable year stands on its own. This means that your substantial authority must be valid on the last day of the taxable year to which the return relates. Furthermore, the authority on which you rely must be supported by controlling precedent of a U.S. Court of Appeals to which you have the right of appeal with respect to the item. If your treatment of an item has no prior legal precedent, the IRS will give you a hard time. Count on it!

When there is no precedent for your treatment, you'll have to plod through a sophisticated analysis of the applicable tax law on which you rely. You have to address the: *substantial authority standard* (Reg. 1.6662-4(d)(2)). This is a mythical standard of probability which the IRS is supposed to respect . . . but rarely ever does. Each IRS agent interprets differently.

The IRS's own Regulation ¶ 1.6662-4(d)(2) says—

The substantial authority standard is less stringent than the "more likely than not" standard (the standard that is met when there is a greater than 50-percent likelihood of [your] *position being upheld* [in court]*), but more stringent than the reasonable basis standard (the standard which if satisfied, generally will prevent imposition of the penalty under section 6662(b)(1) for negligence). The possibility that* [your] *return will not be audited or, if audited, that an item will not be raised on audit, is not relevant in determining whether the substantial authority standard (or the reasonable basis standard) is satisfied.*

This regulatory citation is official IRS gospel. Can you understand it? Can you imagine any IRS auditor, revenue agent, department manager, district director, or regional counsel truly understanding it? No matter how valiantly you try to meet its 50/50 probability-of-winning-in-court standard, the IRS will disparage your efforts. It wants you to produce a "weighting analysis" of all of your selected authorities.

Weighting of Authorities

Regulation ¶ 1.6662-4(d)(3)(iii): ***Types of authority***, lists 12 different sources of tax authority. In order of their priority of weight, the top six sources are:

(1) the Internal Revenue Code,
(2) proposed, temporary, and final regulations,
(3) revenue rulings and revenue procedures,
(4) tax treaties and official explanations thereof,
(5) court cases, and
(6) congressional intent as reflected in committee reports . . . provided the intent is clear and unambiguous.

The regulation goes on to point out that—

Conclusions reached in treatises, legal periodicals, legal opinions, or opinions rendered by tax professionals are not authority. . . . Notwithstanding the preceding list, an authority does not continue to be an authority to the extent it is overruled or modified, implicitly or explicitly, by a body with the power to overrule or modify the earlier authority.

Selected excerpts from Regulation ¶ 1.6662-4(d)(3)(ii): ***Nature of analysis***, goes on to say—

The weight accorded an authority depends on its relevance and persuasiveness, and the type of document providing the authority. . . . An authority that merely states a conclusion ordinarily is less persuasive than one that reaches its conclusion by ***cogently relating the applicable law to pertinent facts****. . . . There may be substantial authority for the tax treatment of an item despite the absence of certain types of authority. Thus, a taxpayer may have substantial authority for a position that is supported only by* ***a well-reasoned construction*** *of the applicable law.* [Emphasis added.]

In the above regulatory pronouncements, there appears to be no clear definitive theme. Consequently, we ask, what is the essence of the above with respect to substantial authority?

It is that, if you are going to take a position that is contrary to what the IRS ordinarily ordains, you had better do some preemptive "case law" research. Line up your authorities and facts, pro and con, as we depict in Figure 5.2. Document your analysis in writing. Do so with the idea of deciding whether to persist with your contrary position. If you proceed, do **not** attach your weighting analysis to your tax return. It will be detached and thrown away at your IRS processing center. Instead, wait until you are audited — IF you are audited. Present it then to avoid the substantial understatement penalty. Your position would probably be disallowed, but at least no penalty would be applied.

Disclosure on Return

Another approach to avoiding the understatement penalty is to provide "adequate disclosure" on your return of the item or position that could be questioned. There are two approved disclosure

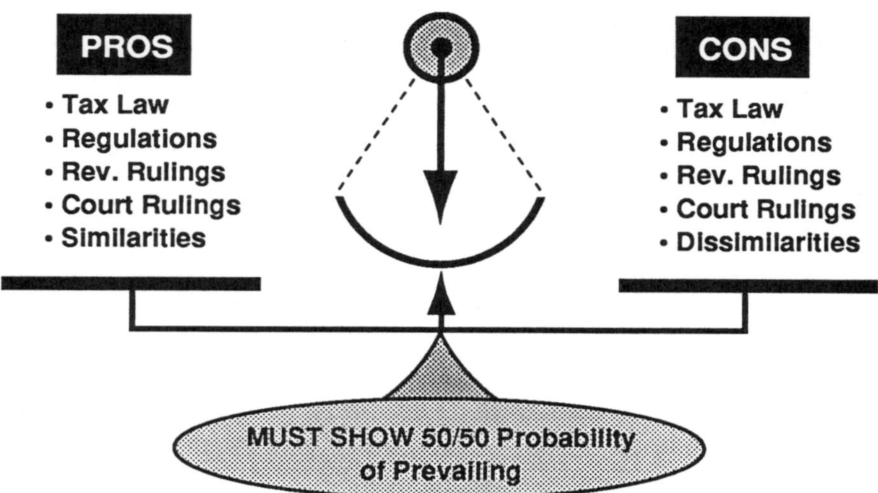

Fig. 5.2 - The Pros and Cons for "Substantial Authority" Relief

methods. One method is to complete the forms and schedules that comprise your return, by following precisely the official instructions thereto. The second method is to complete and attach a special form; namely: Form 8275 — Disclosure Statement. We'll address Form 8275 shortly below.

Regulation ¶ 1.6662-4(e)(1): ***Effect of adequate disclosure***, says that an item or position adequately disclosed will be treated . . .

> *as if such items were shown properly on the return for the taxable year. . . . Thus, for purposes of section 6662(d), the tax attributable to such items is not included in the understatement for that year.*

To be accepted as adequate, the disclosed item or position MUST—

(i) be based on a reasonable analysis which is neither frivolous nor "far out";

(ii) not be a pass-through item attributable to a tax shelter; and

(iii) be properly substantiated with adequate books and records with respect to the item or position.

Revenue Procedure 97-56 states the conditions on which various IRS forms and schedules, when properly filled out, constitute adequate disclosure. The essence of this 1,900-word procedure is that—

> ***Additional disclosure*** *of facts relevant to, or positions taken with respect to, issues involving any of the items set forth below* ***is unnecessary*** *for purposes of reducing any understatement of income tax under section 6662(d)* ***provided*** *that the forms and attachments are* ***completed in a clear manner*** *in accordance with their instructions. The money amounts entered on the forms must be verifiable. . . . A number is verifiable if, on audit, the taxpayer can demonstrate the origin of the number (even if that number is not ultimately accepted by the IRS) and the taxpayer can show good faith in entering that number on the applicable form.* [Emphasis added.]

The above revenue procedure goes on to list approximately 25 forms, schedules, and entry items that must be "completed in a clear manner." The procedure applies to your initial return as well as to a "qualified amended return."

Regulation ¶ 1.6662-4(f): ***Method of disclosure***, goes on to point out that—

> *(i) Disclosure with respect to a* ***recurring item*** *. . . must be made for each taxable year in which the item is taken into account.*
>
> *(ii) Disclosure . . . with respect to any loss, deduction, or credit that is carried to another year is adequate* ***only if*** *made in connection with the return . . . for the taxable year in which the carryback or carryover arises.*
>
> *(iii) If the revenue procedure* [97-56 or subsequent update] *does not include an item, disclosure is adequate with*

respect to that item ***only if*** *made on a properly completed Form 8275 or 8275-R, as appropriate, and* ***attached*** *to the return.* [Emphasis added.]

Disclosure Via Form 8275

From a tax point of view, a "questionable item" on a return is one which is neither all black nor all white. It is grey. It is in the grey area of ambiguity where, from the taxpayer's point of view (for fairness) it should be allowed, but from the taxtaker's point of view (maximum revenue) it should not be allowed. In other words, the grey item is a nonfrivolous, good faith situation which does not appear to be covered — nor precluded — by the nearest applicable law on point. In situations like this, it is often best to claim it on the return, then disclose it up front.

The upfront way of disclosing a grey item on your tax return is by means of Form 8275: ***Disclosure Statement***, or Form 8275-R: ***Regulation Disclosure Statement***. The two forms are almost identical. The "R" version, however, addresses a specific IRS/Treasury regulation to which you take a contrary position. Each form is one page; it is attached to your return like any other required schedule. Follow the Attachment Sequence number in the upper-right-hand corner of each form.

In Figure 5.3, we depict the general format of Form 8275. It is mostly an open-face form with a few numbered lines. Each numbered line represents a separate disclosure issue. In Part II, we suggest first a concise statement of each issue, followed by some analysis of the facts, circumstances, and law on which you base your rationale. The reverse side of the form is entirely blank, which permits continuing your analysis there.

The official instructions for using Form 8275 say, in part—

Specifically, the form is used for disclosures relating to the portions of the accuracy-related penalty due to disregard of rules or to a substantial understatement of income tax. . . . You cannot avoid the penalty by disclosure if you failed to keep proper books and records or failed to substantiate items properly. Disclosure will never avoid the penalty for a frivolous position.

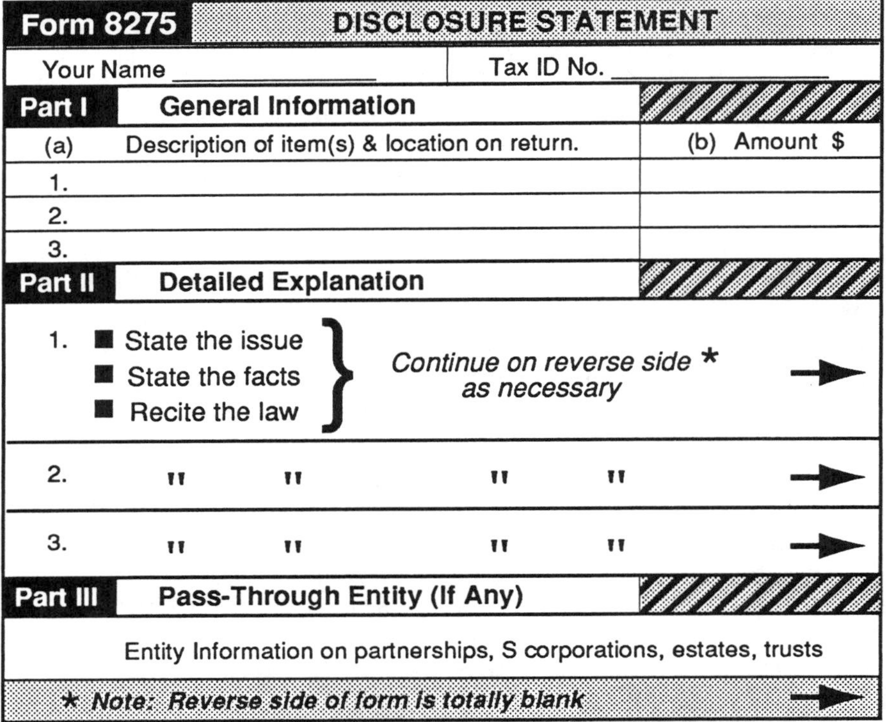

Form 8275	**DISCLOSURE STATEMENT**
Your Name ______________	Tax ID No. ______________
Part I General Information	
(a) Description of item(s) & location on return.	(b) Amount $
1.	
2.	
3.	
Part II Detailed Explanation	
1. ■ State the issue ■ State the facts ■ Recite the law	*Continue on reverse side * as necessary* →
2. " "	" " →
3. " "	" " →
Part III Pass-Through Entity (If Any)	
Entity Information on partnerships, S corporations, estates, trusts	
** Note: Reverse side of form is totally blank*	→

Fig. 5.3 - General Format of Disclosure Statement

The instructions to Part II of Form 8275 (Detailed Information) go on to say (in part)—

Enter either—
• A description of the relevant facts affecting the tax treatment of the item and the nature of the potential controversy concerning the tax treatment of the item; ***or***
• A concise description of the legal issues presented by such facts.

Disclosure will not be considered adequate unless the information you provide in Part II reasonably identifies the item, its amount, the location of the item(s) on your return, and the nature of the controversy to which the disclosure relates.

These instructions are concise and emphatic. If you don't provide in Part II the detail asked for, your disclosure will not reduce the 20% penalty. And if the penalty is not reduced, there is no chance that the grey item will be allowed.

Example: Part II Detail

You can play roulette on grey-area items on the chance that they will slip through the system. IRS processing staffs, DIF-scoring staffs, and audit examination staffs do miss things. So, if you are lucky, you might take a chance and not file Form 8275. But, on the assumption that your luck may have run out, or is about to, we present an example of the explanatory detail required on Form 8275.

The grey item of concern is a $31,640 expense entry on Schedule C (***Profit or Loss from Business***) identified as: *Other interest*. This amount derives from the portion of payment to the IRS of $52,541 for statutory interest on deficiencies asserted on Schedule A (***Itemized Deductions***) as well as deficiencies on Schedule C. The deficiency issues totaled $71,525 for Schedule A and $108,311 for Schedule C (grand total: $179,836). The deficiency issues were contested in Tax Court over a period of **10** years! It was this long period of contestation that drove the total deficiency interest ($52,541) so high.

The issue of concern for Form 8275 purposes was whether the interest paid on the tax deficiencies for Schedule C constitutes business interest or personal interest. The IRS treats all interest paid on tax deficiencies as nondeductible personal interest, regardless of the business form (except corporations).

To exemplify Part II of Form 8275, the Schedule C filer detailed as follows:

"(**a**) The Part I issue raised on line 16 of Schedule C: *Other interest*, is whether the $31,640 is personal interest or business interest, pursuant to IRC Sec. 163(h)(2)(A) and Treas. Reg. 1.163-9T(b)(1)(i). The total interest paid was $52,541.

"(**b**) IRC Sec. 163(h)(2)(A) exempts from personal interest that which is **properly allocable** to a trade or business. The properly allocable part in this situation is:

$$\frac{\text{Sch. C}}{\text{Sch. A + Sch. C}} = \frac{\$108{,}311}{\$179{,}836} = 0.6022$$

Hence, \$52,541 x 0.6022 = \$31,640.

"(**c**) Reg. 1.163-9T(b)(1)(i) exempts from the definition of personal interest that which is properly allocable **to the conduct** of a trade or business. The interest expense incurred was for a Tax Court determination of the 'character' of the audit-verified expenditures on Schedules C. The Court recharacterized the expenditures as Sec. 263A(h): qualified creative expenditures, amortizable over three years rather than currently deductible as Sec. 174(a) experimental expenditures. Said recharacterization constitutes determining 'the conduct' of a trade or business, and is therefore an ordinary and necessary expense for said business."

Ruling on Form 8275 Above

The use of Form 8275 in the above case went to trial in Tax Court in 1995. The primary issue was to gain acceptance of 60% of the deficiency interest as a business expense on Schedule C. Collaterally, the petitioner sought relief from the disregard-of-rules penalty. This case is unique in that the applicable rules were followed meticulously. The example case is—

H.F. Crouch, TC Memo 1995-289, Dec. 50,724(M).

The court ruled that the petitioner was liable for the disregard-of-rules penalty because—

> He failed to adequately disclose sufficient relevant facts on Form 8275 to justify a reduction in his tax understatement. An interest deduction which was based on a formula that allocated the interest between business and personal interest was disallowed, because the taxpayer

failed to produce sufficient evidence to prove that the amounts used in his formula were correct. The parties had stipulated to the authenticity of the taxpayer's Form 8275: not to the contents of the document. Standing alone, Form 8275 did not constitute proof that the taxpayer's computations were accurate.

This certainly appears to be an arbitrary ruling. And, it was! The petitioner had openly criticized the Tax Court and the IRS for disregarding the intent of Congress with respect to interest deductions "properly allocable to" a trade or business. The ruling was also a reprimand to the petitioner for taking up the court's time contesting a $94 penalty.

The $94 penalty was not the key issue. The important issue was the $31,640 interest expense that was sought to be allowed as a Schedule C business deduction. The court's main point was that Form 8275, in and of itself, is not proof of a claim. Even though the form cited ample substantial authority, and even though the IRS had already verified the evidence, the court was not persuaded.

Disclosure Presents Dilemma

As presented above, there are two components of "adequate disclosure" for avoiding the substantial understatement penalty. The disclosure may be on the return itself, or it may be on Form 8275 attached to your return. Based on various court rulings, the key ingredient of disclosure is that sufficient information be supplied to alert the IRS to the tax controversy that is likely to arise. Digests of two selected court rulings bear this point out.

☐ In *E.Fellouzis*, DC Fla., 95-1 USTC ¶ 50,287, substantial understatement penalties were not imposed against donors of art objects because they attached appraisals to their returns for the years in which the donations were made. They also attached Form 8283: ***Noncash Charitable Contributions***. Thus, the taxpayers provided sufficient information to enable the IRS to identify a potential controversy. The appraisals listed each art object and the amount the taxpayers deducted for each item. The taxpayers did not attempt to hide what they were doing.

☐ In *R.A. Adams*, TC Memo 1997-357, the taxpayer who excluded his disability severance pay from income was not liable for the substantial understatement penalty. He fully disclosed all relevant facts by attaching Form 8275 to his return, as well as a copy of the release he signed as a prerequisite to receipt of his severance pay. Further, there was reasonable basis for his position that the pay was excludable under Code Sec. 104 (compensation for injuries). Although the court ruled that the pay had to be included as taxable income, there was confusion in the law concerning disability severance pay.

As an individual, you always face a dilemma when trying to convey sufficient disclosures to the IRS regarding a questionable item on your return. There is temptation not to want to deliberately bring it to the IRS's attention. It is common knowledge that any item which is not all-black or all-white in tax law will be disallowed by the IRS. It is also common knowledge that, when you file Form 8275, you (most likely) will be audited. The IRS wants to make understatement matters as difficult for you as possible.

The IRS will argue — simultaneously —*four* ways against you. It will do so to force you to capitulate to its position, or to force you into court . . . as the above cases illustrate.

The IRS will argue, firstly, that you have no substantial authority for your position. If you cite a recent court case or revenue ruling that supports your fact situation, the IRS will assert that your citation does not apply. It will then argue that you did not provide adequate disclosure on your return. If you attempt to show that you did, it will switch its argument to your non-attachment of Form 8275. If you have attached Form 8275 to your return, the IRS will argue that the form doesn't prove anything. If you try to prove your point without going into court, the IRS will argue that you do not have a reasonable basis for your position. It all boils down to the reality of Tax Life USA. When it comes to ambiguities in tax law, the IRS CAN NOT BE TRUSTED to present a reasonable basis for its position against you.

6

VALUATION MISSTATEMENTS

The Correct Valuation Of Property Becomes A Disputive Issue When It Is OVERVALUED For Deduction Purposes, Or UNDERVALUED For Inclusion Purposes, On Your Tax Return. When An Underpayment Of Tax "Attributable To" A Valuation Misstatement Exceeds $5,000 ($1,000 For Overstated Pension Liabilities), The 20% Accuracy Penalty Applies. The Tolerance For Error Before The Penalty Is 200% Or More, Or 50% Or Less, Of The Correct Valuation. There Is Penalty Relief For Reasonable Cause And Good Faith. Engaging A Qualified Professional Appraiser To Make The Valuation Is Prima Facie Evidence Of Good Faith On Your Part.

We are not through with the accuracy-related penalty stack yet. There are still three more penalties — actually, four — that come under the umbrella of Section 6662: Imposition of Accuracy-Related Penalty. Penalty (1): negligence and disregard, was covered in Chapter 4, and penalty (2): substantial understatement, was covered in Chapter 5. The remaining accuracy penalties are:

(3) Substantial valuation misstatement [6662(e)],
(4) Substantial overstatement of pension liabilities [6662(f)],
(5) Substantial estate or gift tax valuation understatement [6662(g)], and
(6) Increase in penalty for gross valuation misstatements [6662(h)].

A valuation issue arises when there is a transfer of property or services, for which no or nil money changes hands. It is only for tax reasons — beneficial to the transferor — that a value is placed on the property or services. This occurs most often when trying to shift the tax burden between related taxpayers: family members, close friends, interlocking businesses, and self-owned businesses. Valuation distortions also occur in pension and estate plans.

When a transactional event is a deductible item to the transferor, the valuation of the property or services is often overstated. When the event becomes includible income, the valuation is often understated. Whether there is an overstatement (for deduction purposes) or understatement (for income purposes), there is a *misstatement* of the value of the property or services involved.

In this chapter, therefore, we want to review the valuation issue with you and explain why penalties may apply. Relief from the penalties is a little easier than is the case when a substantial understatement of income tax is involved. This is because, when valuing an item which is not actually sold in an arm's-length transaction, there is much comparative analysis involved. Unless the valuation misstatements are substantial or gross, a wider than normal tolerance for error applies. We want to explore with you the "tolerance bands" and explain why they are allowed to be so.

Why "Valuation" Important

When property changes hands between seller/transferor and buyer/transferee who are not related parties, and who are profit-motivated, the property is treated as conveyed for its *fair market value* (FMV). An "arm's-length" bargaining element has taken place which precludes any intentional overvaluing or undervaluing. As a result, the FMV is used by both sides of the transaction as the correct value for their subsequent tax accounting therewith. If the transaction goes through a commercially-recognized intermediary (broker), the IRS rarely ever questions the valuation amount.

But when there is no actual FMV sale or exchange, and property changes hands, the correct valuation of that property presents a problem. For example, if you were to contribute property to a charitable organization, you would want its value to be as high as possible. The higher the value of the property contribution, the greater the charitable deduction you get, and the lower the income tax you pay.

Similarly, for casualty losses, theft losses, abandonment losses, and inventory losses. The higher the value of the property involved, the greater the deductions . . . and the lower your tax.

In the case of tax shelters, property is intentionally acquired at inflated values. This is accomplished through nonrecourse loans, seller financing arrangements, and blue sky appraisals of what the property is worth. When allowances for depreciation or depletion are taken, a greater-than-correct tax benefit passes through to individual members of the arrangement.

When a person dies, all of his worldly assets are valued for inclusion in his gross estate. If his property is undervalued — intentionally or inadvertently — he pays less death tax than ordinarily. A similar situation occurs when property is transferred into an irrevocable trust. The lower the value of the property, the lower the transfer tax. The same undervaluation instinct applies to gratuitous gifts during life. A lower-than-correct value results in a lower gift tax than ordinarily.

When property does not change hands in an open-to-the-public offer, the valuation assigned is always tax suspect. This raises the question: What is the "correct value" of the property involved? Unavoidably, professional appraising techniques must be used to establish such value. Professional appraising is time consuming, costly, sometimes highly sophisticated, and often subject to controversy between appraisers representing opposite parties to the transaction.

IRS Valuation Coursebook

So important is the issue of valuation that the IRS has prepared its own valuation training manual. It is titled: ***IRS Valuation Training for Appeals Officers***, Coursebook No. 6126-002. It is a guideline for resolving valuation issues at the Appellate Division level of the IRS. Basic valuation concepts and their application to specific factual situations are presented therein.

The foreword to the IRS manual carries the notation that—

> *Although designed primarily to benefit IRS officials who negotiate income, estate, and gift tax cases in which the valuation of property is at issue, the Coursebook also provides taxpayers and their advisors with invaluable insight into the major valuation problem areas and the methods used by the IRS in resolving these issues. However, taxpayers and their advisors are cautioned that the material cannot be cited as authority.*

The manual goes on to address in 16 chapters the major valuation areas which we summarize in Figure 6.1.

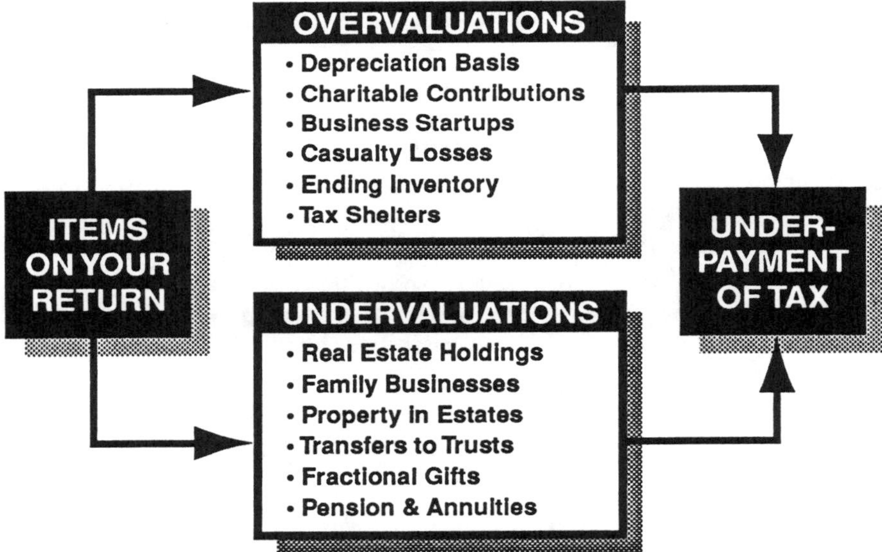

Fig. 6.1 - Types of Valuation Issues That Spark Penalty Disputes

The introductory chapter to the IRS valuation coursebook reveals two enlightening judicial rulings. We extract and pass the essence of these two rulings on to you:

- In *Messing*, 48 T.C. 502 (1967), the court stated that—

> Too often in valuation disputes the parties have convinced themselves of the unalterable correctness of their positions and have consequently failed successfully to conclude settlement negotiations. . . . The result is an overzealous effort, during the course of the ensuing litigation, to infuse a talismanic precision into an issue which should frankly be recognized as inherently imprecise and capable of resolution only by a Solomon-like pronouncement.

- In *Buffalo Tool & Die*, 74 T.C. 441 (1980), the court stated that—

> As the court repeatedly admonished counsel at trial, the issue is more properly suited for the give and take of the settlement process than adjudication. . . . The existing record reeks of stubbornness rather than flexibility on the part of both parties. . . . We are convinced that the valuation issue is capable of resolution by the parties themselves, thereby saving the expenditure of time, effort, and money by the parties and the Court — a process not likely to produce a better result.

The IRS was making a point to its own staff by citing the above two cases on page 2 in Chapter 1. The text goes on to say—

> *As appeals officers, we should always strive to settle cases. This is especially true with respect to valuation cases because of the* ***judicial distaste*** *for such issues.* [Emphasis added.]

We feel the same way. As you read the valuation penalty rules which follow, try to come within the official bands of error tolerance before contesting the IRS's assertion of the correct amount. Then, appeal *within* the IRS rather than stubbornly cornering yourself into court.

When is Misstatement "Substantial"?

Penalty (3) of the accuracy stack is identified as *any substantial valuation misstatement* of normal taxes and surtaxes of the IR Code. This penalty focus is on the misstatement of valuation: not on the amount or reason for underpayment of tax. Before penalty (3) is applied, supposedly, two tolerance thresholds must be exceeded. The two together define what is meant by the term "substantial."

Section 6662(e)(1)(A): ***In General***, defines the first tolerance threshold as—

> *The value of any property (or the adjusted basis of any property) claimed on any return* [which] *is **200 percent or more** of the amount determined to be the correct amount of such valuation or adjusted basis. . . .* [Emphasis added.]

The second tolerance threshold is prescribed by Section 6662(e)(2): ***Limitation***, as—

> *No penalty shall be imposed . . . unless the portion of the underpayment for the taxable year attributable to substantial valuation misstatements **exceeds $5,000** ($10,000* [in the case of most corporations]*). . . .* [Emphasis added.]

For further instructive emphasis, we depict these two tolerance thresholds in Figure 6.2. Suppose the valuation you assign to any property, or to the adjusted basis of any property, is 190, for example. If the IRS determines the correct value to be 100, there would be no valuation penalty imposed. The negligence penalty might be imposed, but not the valuation penalty.

If your valuation were 210, and the resulting underpayment of tax were exactly $5,000, again no valuation penalty would be imposed. BUT, if the underpayment of tax turned out to be $5,010, the valuation penalty would apply.

Keep in mind that we are talking about the *valuation* penalty. The negligence and disregard penalty could alternatively apply. The negligence or other penalty is not precluded when the valuation penalty is inapplicable. However, a showing of reasonable cause and good faith (IRC Sec. 6664(c)), if persuasively presented, may eliminate any collateral penalties.

Other Definitional Terms

Regulations ¶ 1-6662-5(e), (f), and (g) present other instructive definitions that apply to valuation misstatements. For example, the term "property" is defined in Reg. 1.6662-5(e)(3) as—

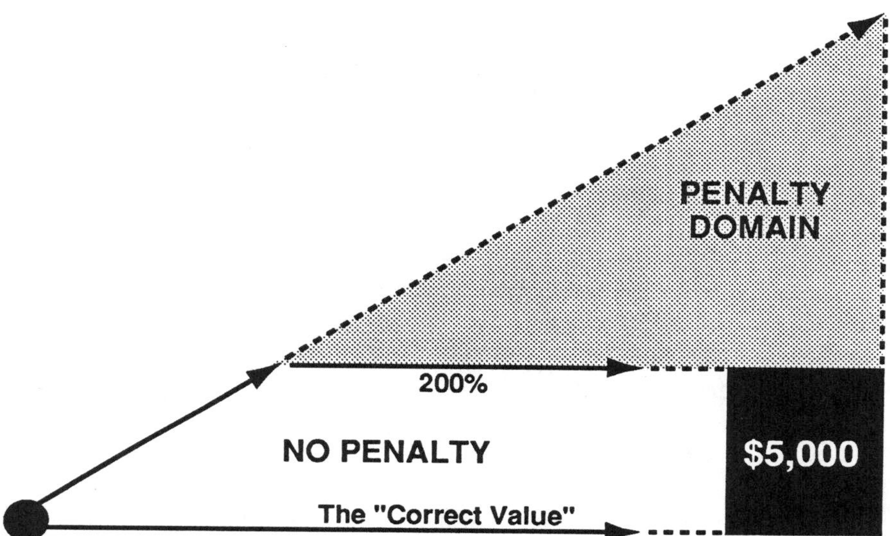

Fig. 6.2 - Error Threshold Before Substantial Misstatement Penalty

> [That which] *refers to both tangible and intangible property. Tangible property includes property such as land, buildings, fixtures, and inventory. Intangible property includes property such as goodwill, covenants not to compete, leaseholds, patents, contract rights, debts, and choses in action* [movable personal property items].

The corresponding statutory terms are "any property" or the "adjusted basis of any property." In other words, the valuation issue is wide open for tax administration purposes, when property changes hands. This is why Figure 6.1 is so extensive and why the IRS has found it necessary to develop its own valuation coursebook.

Regulation 1.6662-5(f)(1): ***Multiple valuation misstatements***, points out that—

> *The determination of where there is a valuation misstatement on a return is made on a* ***property-by-property*** *basis. Assume, for example, that property A has a value of 60 but a taxpayer claims a value of 110, and that property B has a value of 40 but the taxpayer claims a value of 100. Because the claimed and*

> *correct values are compared on a property-by-property basis, there is a substantial valuation misstatement with respect to property B* [250%: 100 ÷ 40], *but not with respect to property A* [185%: 110 ÷ 60], *even though the claimed values (210)* [110 + 100] *are 200 percent or more of the correct values (100)* [40 + 60] *when compared on an aggregate basis.*

With respect to the application of the $5,000 limitation for individuals, Regulation ¶ 1.6662-5(f)(2) says—

> *The determination of the portion of an underpayment that is attributable to a valuation misstatement is made by* ***aggregating all portions*** *of the underpayment attributable to the valuation misstatement.* [Emphasis added.]

In other words, if there are three properties on a return, each of which is valuation misstated, all three are dollar aggregated to ascertain exceeding the $5,000 tolerance threshold. If two out of the three properties are valuation misstated, only the two are aggregated for the $5,000 test.

Regulation ¶ 1.6662-5(g) addresses: ***Property with a value or adjusted basis of zero***. This regulation states—

> *The value or adjusted basis claimed on a return of any property with a correct value or adjusted basis of zero* ***is considered to be 400 percent or more*** *of the correct amount.* [Thus], *there is a gross valuation misstatement with respect to such property* . . . [for which] *the applicable penalty rate is 40 percent.* [Emphasis added.]

We'll have more to say about the 40% penalty rate, later. The point of this regulation is that there can be — and often are — transactional situations where the correct value (such as an unreported gift) or adjusted basis (such as depreciable property depreciated out) is truly zero. If property truly has a zero or negative basis, any attempt to assign a greater-than-zero basis to it — even a $1 valuation — is a gross misstatement. For this, a punitive penalty applies.

Section 482 Misstatements

We intentionally omitted from the valuation misstatement law above [Sec. 6662(e)(1) and (2)] any mention of Section 482 misstatements. Section 482 gets into "transfer pricing" rules between related manipulative entities. The term "section 482" is used three times in Section 6662(e)(1)(B). The focus of subparagraph (B) turns from the valuation of property to—

> *the* ***price*** *for any property or* ***services*** *(or for the* ***use*** *of property) . . .* [where] *the net section 482 transfer price adjustment . . . exceeds the lesser of $5,000,000* [5 million] *or 10 percent of the taxpayer's* ***gross receipts***. [Emphasis added.]

Whenever you see the term "gross receipts" in a tax law, the target is a *business entity*: not an individual filing his personal return. Whenever you see a penalty tolerance amount of $5,000,000 you know that substantial business activity is involved. Venturing into the pricing/valuation misstatements of related business activities is beyond the scope of this book. Nevertheless, we should at least say something about Section 482 misstatements.

Section 482 is titled: ***Allocation of Income and Deductions Among Taxpayers***. This section specifically addresses any—

> *two or more organizations, trades, or businesses (whether or not incorporated, whether or not organized in the U.S., and whether or not affiliated* [which are] *owned or controlled directly or indirectly by the* ***same interests****. . . .*

Such arrangements are multi-entity schemes where goods or services are regularly transferred among commonly owned or commonly controlled interests. These arrangements often lead to willful tax evasion: a subject for discussion in a later chapter.

Under Section 482, the IRS is authorized to *reallocate* income, deductions, credits, and other items to clearly reflect the results of an arm's length transaction between *unrelated* parties. The purpose of penalty Section 6662(e)(1)(B) is to encourage taxpayers engaged in related party transactions to prepare — and document — a factual and true economic analysis of their pricing structure for goods and services.

Significance of "Attributable to"

In the valuation misstatement penalty rule of Section 6662(e)(2): ***Limitation***, there is a key term over which there has been much court litigation. The litigation has centered around the significance of the term "attributable to," when the tax imposed on a return is based on a mixture of adjustments, not all of which are valuation related. The particular clause on point is—

> *No penalty shall be imposed . . . unless the* ***portion of the underpayment*** *. . .* ***attributable to*** *substantial valuation misstatements . . . exceeds $5,000* [for individuals]. [Emphasis added.]

A 20% penalty on a $5,000 underpayment is $1,000. This is no small piece of change to fork over to the U.S. Treasury just because of whim, confusion. or laziness of some IRS examiner. Therefore, it is important to distinguish clearly which underpayment amounts are valuation related, and which amounts are related to improper allowances, credits, or deductions claimed by the taxpayer. We try to depict this "distinction problem" for you in Figure 6.3. The misstatement penalty applies only to the valuation-related underpayment amount(s).

In several Courts of Appeal cases [*R.J. Todd*, CA-5, 89-1 USTC ¶ 9116; *J.B. Gainer*, CA-9, 90-1 USTC ¶ 50,024; *D.E. Heasley*, 92-2 USTC ¶ 50,412; and others], it was held that where the IRS disallows an entire deduction or credit which happens to include a valuation misstatement, the penalty does not apply. Such underpayment is attributable to an improper deduction or credit. In other words, to avoid or minimize the valuation misstatement penalty when there are other disallowed tax benefits on one's return, one must independently separate out those items of underpayment which are unrelated to valuation items.

The case of *B.V. Hartford*, TC Memo 1995-351 offers a good example of the separation of underpayments. The taxpayer

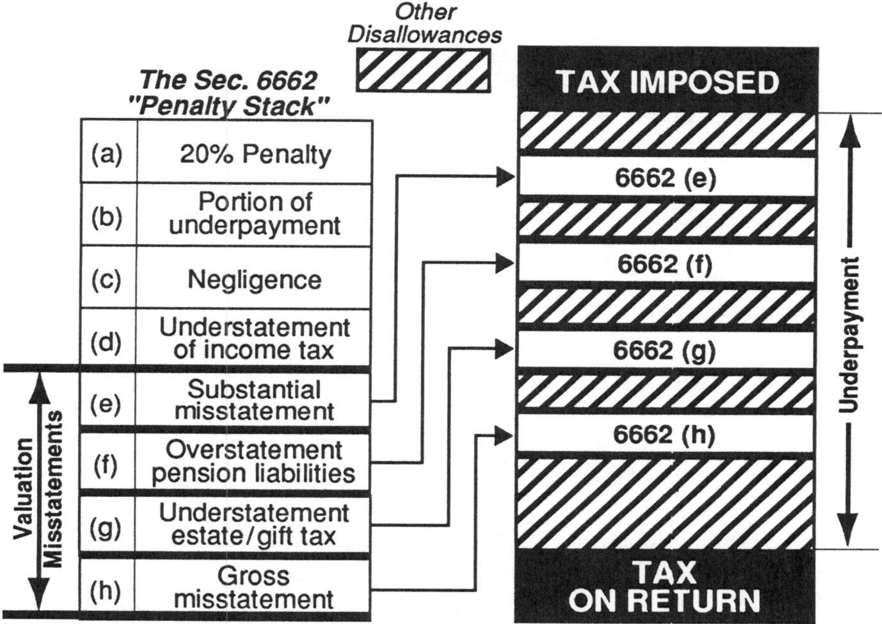

Fig. 6.3 - Matching Each Misstatement to its Portion of Underpayment

conducted a horse breeding operation where all expenses for board, care, and insurance were disallowed. They were disallowed because said expenses were related to an activity not engaged in for profit. No valuation penalty was assigned to the underpayment resulting from the disallowance of these expenses. However, the taxpayer was liable for penalty for disallowed depreciation deductions, because a valuation overstatement directly caused the inflated deductions.

Overstatement of Pension Liabilities

Corporate executives, high income professionals (doctors, attorneys), and self-employed persons are attracted to what are called: *defined benefit pension plans*. That is, one tries to define his annual pension benefits 20, 30, or 40 years before he actually retires. Actuarial estimates are made as to what one's working-year contributions are, in order to reach a targeted dollar benefit goal during one's retirement years. Whatever contributions to the plan are made during one's current earnings are deductible against total income. Consequently, the higher the contributions, the lower are one's current taxes. The temptation, therefore, is to overstate one's contributions in order to get more deductions on one's return.

Enter now, accuracy penalty (4): ***Substantial Overstatement of Pension Liabilities*** [Sec. 6662(f)]. The essence here is that—

> *If the actuarial determination of the liabilities taken into account for purposes of computing the deduction* [for contributions to pension trusts or annuities] *is 200 percent or more of the . . . correct amount of such liabilities, . . . there is a substantial overstatement* [thereof]. *No penalty is imposed . . . unless the portion of the underpayment attributable to . . .* [the] *overstatements exceeds $1,000.*

Note that the dollar threshold for underpayment is $1,000, instead of $5,000 as is the case for valuation misstatements.

The purpose of the lower underpayment threshold is to discourage the overvaluation of future liabilities of a defined benefit pension plan, with the corresponding excess deductions for current year contributions. The penalty provision is aimed at preventing unreasonable actuarial assumptions that can understate the expected earnings of the plan (for example, assumption of 5% yield where a reasonable assumption would be 9%). The provision is also intended to prevent overstatements of the amount needed to fund a future benefit (for example, assumption of an unreasonably high rate of inflation or an extended payout period for survivor's benefits) where the plan participant is presently unmarried.

Death Tax Valuation Understatements

When a person dies, his executor is required to prepare and file Form 706: ***U.S. Estate*** [Death] ***Tax Return***. This is a very formidable return. Excluding required attachments (such as death certificate, will, insurance statement, etc.), Form 706 consists of 44 preprinted entry pages and schedules. Of the 16 schedules, nine are asset schedules separated by property categories: real estate, stocks and bonds, jointly owned property, family-owned businesses, etc. Each asset schedule requires a verifiable inventory of property listings, with a valuation appraisal of each item. When completed, the nine asset schedules comprise the decedent's gross estate "wherever situated" (worldwide).

When a gross estate exceeds $600,000, the transfer tax rate *starts* at 37%. The rate increases to 50% for estates over $3,000,000. With such high graduated tax rates, the temptation is to provide valuations which are on the **understated** side of FMV. The particular temptation is to low appraise real estate, family businesses, and closely-held entities. With a gross estate FMV of $1,000,000 a 20% understatement of value can reduce the death tax by as much as $80,000. With a 50% undervaluation, for example, the reduction in death tax could be $180,000.

So powerful is the motivation to undervalue a decedent's gross estate, that another valuation misstatement penalty is imposed. This is Section 6662(g): ***Substantial Estate or Gift Tax Valuation Understatement.*** A substantial valuation understatement occurs when—

> *The value of any property claimed on any estate or gift tax return is **50 percent or less** of the amount determined to be the correct amount of such valuation. No penalty shall be imposed . . . unless the portion of the* [attributable] *underpayment . . . **exceeds $5,000**.* [Emphasis added.]

In the case of a death tax return (Form 706), the practice is to engage professional appraisers to determine the FMVs of all property items in the estate. Where comparable sales data on comparable property holdings are available, valuation disputes with IRS appraisers are generally minimal. But where there is a family business or a closely-held activity in the estate, valuation disputes are common. In the case of real estate, IRS values the property under the philosophy of: *highest and best use*. In the case of family businesses and closely-held enterprises, the IRS establishes its valuations on balance sheet analysis, valuation ratios, capitalization of earnings, minority interest discounts, and a complete liquidation analysis. For gross estates over $1,000,000, rarely does the IRS accept carte blanche the valuations stated on Form 706.

Section 6662(g) applies also to gift tax valuations on Form 709: ***U.S. Gift Tax Return***. In this domain, the valuation understatement temptation is not as severe as with Form 706. For one reason, gifts are made annually and are often in the form of money or readily marketable securities. For another reason, when gifts involve real estate or closely-held business, generally only fractional interests are conveyed. But if fractional interests in the same property are conveyed in a continuum of annual gifts, the IRS — "more likely than not" — will challenge the FMVs entered on Form 709.

Gross Valuation Misstatements

The focus above has been on *substantial* valuation misstatements. The term "substantial" applies when a valuation (property by property) is either 200% or more (for deduction type items) or 50% or less (for inclusion type items) when compared to what the IRS determines the correct value to be. In most good-faith valuation cases, this threshold-of-error tolerance seems within reason. Particularly so, when taking into account different generally accepted appraisal techniques.

Even so, there are instances of valuation misstatement aggressiveness. Aggressive taxpayers tend to be contemptuous of the FMV concept; they regard it as totally inappropriate to their situations. They value each property item with tax consequences in mind. They do so by assuming a large discount factor in their favor (for lack of instant marketability). Some consciously want to taunt the IRS as payback for their being badly mistreated by that agency.

To discourage valuation misstatement aggressiveness, Section 6662(h) applies. This section is titled: ***Increase in Penalty in Case of Gross Valuation Misstatements***. The penalty is increased from 20% for substantial misstatement to 40% for *gross* misstatements. The increase applies only to **valuation** misstatements. It does not apply to negligence, disregard of rules, nor to understatements of income tax. Section 6662(h) is not functionally a new penalty; it is an increased penalty for subsections (e), (f), and (g) above.

The term "gross" misstatement is the substitution of 400% for 200%, and 25% for 50%, in each place that it appears in subsections (e), (f), and (g). These subsections, recall, are property valuations used in the computation of income taxes, surtaxes, excise taxes, death taxes, gift taxes, and pension liabilities. Except for Section 482 (transfer pricing arrangements), the dollar thresholds for subsections (e) $5,000, (f) $1,000, and (g) $5,000 remain the same.

Engage a Qualified Appraiser

All of the valuation misstatement penalties are subject to reasonable cause relief, pursuant to Section 6664(c): ***Reasonable Cause Exception.*** The essence of this section is that—

> *No penalty shall be imposed . . . if it is shown . . . that the taxpayer acted in good faith with respect to . . . any portion of the underpayment.*

The above is paragraph (1) of Section 6664(c). There is also a paragraph (2): ***Special Rule for Certain Valuation Overstatements.*** This paragraph says, in pertinent part, that—

> *Paragraph (1) shall not apply . . . unless the claimed value of the property was based on a qualified appraisal made by a qualified appraiser . . .*

Although paragraph (2) is directed specifically at "charitable deduction property," the importance of engaging a qualified appraiser applies across the board to all types of property valuations where tax disputes can emerge.

Our experience has been that where a valuation issue has been raised by the IRS, it will seriously consider the statements, qualifications, and analysis made by the professional appraiser you have engaged. What the IRS wants to see is a "Certified Appraiser" in a designated specialty area (real estate, personal property, antiques, works of art, jewelry, collectibles, business equipment, etc.) or a "Certified General Appraiser." The term "certified" means some licensing designation under state law which requires a written test, continuing education, and a periodic fee to a state board. Being a member of a recognized professional appraisal society is also helpful. Your local telephone book or Internet provider is a good place to start your search for qualified persons. Our position is that, by engaging a qualified appraiser, you have established a prima facie case for "good faith."

IRS Regulations ¶ 1.170A-13(c)(3), (4), and (5) spell out what is meant by, and expected of, a qualified appraiser. In a nutshell, such person must—

1. hold himself out to the public as an appraiser who performs appraisals on a regular basis;
2. not be a party to the transaction or the return being examined;
3. understand that any intentionally false or fraudulent valuation misstatement is subject to penalty;
4. include a detailed description of the property, and where located on date of appraisal;
5. indicate the "accepted practice" method used for determining the property's fair market value;
6. indicate the property conditions and circumstances that could alter the valuation more than 60 days later; and
7. sign the appraisal and state the amount of fee he received for such.

No matter how well qualified your selected appraiser may be, be alert to the IRS's "testing" of him (or her) with *its* appraiser(s). If your valuation amounts and methods get pushed, shoved, and belittled too much, take a deep breath. Ask yourself: "Will my appraiser make a credible witness on my behalf in U.S. Tax Court?"

Seasoned appraisers who have been through the IRS grinder will display their qualifications as: ***Expert Witness in Court***! This should convince you that you are better off with an appraiser . . . than without one.

7

THE FRAUD PENALTY

The Most Bizarre Aspect Of Tax Life USA Is The 75% Penalty For Fraud. No Regulations Supplement Its Law And The IRS Publishes No "Indicia Of Fraud." The Term Itself Is Defined NOWHERE In The 3,600-Page Internal Revenue Code. Because Of a Secret Pact With Congress Going Back 60 Years, The IRS Does Not Have To Reveal Its Basis For The Penalty Until 10 SECONDS Before Court Trial. Though Often Derived From Weak Circumstantial Evidence, The IRS Allegation Is Tough To Withstand. YOU Must First Establish Its Implausibility, After Which The IRS Must Prove Its Case In A "Clear And Convincing" Manner.

We will tell it to you straight. The most malicious weapon the IRS has in its civil penalty arsenal is its fraud penalty. Fraud is too often asserted by the IRS strictly on whim. It is used to back a recalcitrant taxpayer into a corner, to force him into accepting the IRS's position on a disputive matter. The assertion of fraud is an attempt to blackmail and stigmatize a taxpayer.

When the fraud penalty is asserted, there is no statute of limitations. This means that the IRS can keep a tax dispute open for years, and dig into a taxpayer's past as far back as the IRS chooses. The whole idea of the fraud penalty is not to encourage compliance with tax law. Its purpose is to give a taxpayer a hard time, extract the maximum conceivable money, render him financially destitute, then — with the thrill and rush of victory — shove the IRS's will down his throat. Of course, the IRS will deny this.

The fraud penalty is 75% of the **entire amount** of underpayment of tax, whether the entire amount is fraud related or not. If, for example, there is a $10,000 underpayment of tax and only $100 is potentially fraud related, it is **not** the $100 that is 75% penalized. It is the entire $10,000 underpayment that is penalized! In other words, even if the $100 underpayment was admittedly a fraudulent act, the penalty would be $7,500 ($10,000 x 75%). You tell us where there is justice in this type of tax penalty.

Accordingly, in this chapter, we want to cover the imposition of the fraud penalty in a manner that you have never seen, read, or been told of before. We do this with the objective of informing you of, and of alerting you to, a deep, dark secret of tax administration. The secret has been kept from the general taxpaying public since 1913 when the income tax was first constitutionalized.

Fraud Not Code Defined

The 75% fraud penalty is prescribed by Section 6663 of the Internal Revenue Code. This section, titled: ***Imposition of Fraud Penalty***, consists of exactly 122 words. These words are arranged into three subsectional paragraphs, namely:

(a) Imposition of Penalty.
(b) Determination of Portion Attributable to Fraud.
(c) Special Rule for Joint Returns.

NOWHERE in these three paragraphs is the term "fraud" defined.

By contrast, the 20% accuracy-related penalty (Section 6662) consists of eight subsections totaling about 2,000 words. Subsection (c), for example, defines "negligence" in 18 words and defines "disregard" in 10 words. The respective key definitional clauses are: *any failure to make a reasonable attempt*, and *any careless, reckless, or intentional disregard.* Other definitional clauses and terms are used to describe the criteria for imposing each of the other accuracy penalties.

What goes on here? Why does Section 6663 not define and prescribe the criteria of conduct by taxpayers, before the 75% fraud penalty is imposed?

Perhaps Section 6664: ***Definitions and Special Rules***, may shed some light. It, too, has three subsections analogous to Section 6663. Subsection 6664(a) defines the term "understatement" in 48 words, and defines the term "rebate" in 38 words. Still, there is no defining of the term "fraud" in a section of the Tax Code where you would logically expect to find it. It's not there!

There is also a Section 6665: ***Applicable Rules***. It consists of two subsections, namely:

(a) Additions Treated as Tax — *penalties shall be assessed, collected, and paid in the same manner as taxes.*
(b) Procedures for Assessing Certain Additions to Tax.

Wouldn't "certain" additions to tax apply to fraud? No. The term "certain" applies to Sections 6651, 6654, and 6655 only.

In other words, there are no applicable rules and no applicable statutory procedures for asserting and assessing the 75% fraud penalty. Doesn't this strike you as being odd . . . and suspicious?

No Regulations Either

Predominantly, the tax laws are supplemented by a body of defining and procedural regulations prepared by the IRS. For example, if a tax law section is numerically designated as XYZ, its corresponding regulation would be: Reg. ¶ 1.XYZ-1. This could be followed by other regulations, such as 1.XYZ-2, 1.XYZ-3(a), or 1.XYZ-4(b)(2), all of which are directly applicable to tax law Section XYZ.

To exemplify more specifically, let's consider the 20% accuracy-related penalty: Section 6662. This section is supplemented with 18,000 words of IRS regulations (about 28 pages). These regulations start with Reg. ¶ 1.6662-1 and go through Reg. ¶ 1.6662-7(d)(2): *Definition of reasonable basis*. Let's be even more specific. Let's cite the subregulations of Reg. ¶ 1.6662-4: *Substantial understatement of income tax*. Under subregulation 4(b): ***Definition and computational rules***, there are—

4(b)(1) — Substantial defined

4(b)(2) — Understatement defined
4(b)(3) — Amount of tax required to be shown on return
4(b)(4) — Amount of tax imposed which is shown on return
4(b)(5) — Rebate defined
4(b)(6) — Examples of application

In incredible contrast, there is not one word — NOT ONE IOTA — of regulatory text supplementing Section 6663: the 75% fraud penalty. There is not one definitive word or procedural rule that applies to fraud.

"It can't be!" we can hear you saying to yourself. "The author must be wrong. Why would the IRS drum up 18,000 words of regulation on a 20% penalty, yet propose no regulations whatsoever on a 75% penalty. The author is surely wrong."

Think so? Check with your own tax advisor. Mention Section 6663: Imposition of Fraud Penalty, then request the citation of any regulation that is designated as ¶ 1.6663-1 . . . or whatever. We think you'll find that there is no such regulation.

The nearest regulation potentially applicable is Reg. ¶ 1.6664-1: ***Accuracy-related and fraud penalties; definitions and special rules***. The pertinent portion of this regulation reads—

> *Section 6664(a) defines the term "underpayment" for purposes of the accuracy-related penalty under section 6662 and* [for purposes of] *the fraud penalty under section 6663. . . . Ordering rules for computing the total amount of accuracy-related and fraud penalties imposed with respect to a return are set forth in ¶ 1.6664-3.*

Now, on to Regulation 1.6664-3(b): ***Ordering rules for determining . . . which adjustments are taken into account.*** Here, the substance is—

> *In computing the portions of an underpayment subject to the penalties imposed under sections 6662 and 6663, adjustments to a return are considered made in the following order:*
>
> *(1) Those with respect to which no penalties are made.*

(2) *Those with respect to which a penalty has been imposed at a 20% rate.*
(3) *Those with respect to which a penalty has been imposed at a 40% rate.*
(4) *Those with respect to which a penalty has been imposed at a 75% rate* [for fraud].

Still, no regulatory definition of fraud can be found. Nor are there any regulatory criteria as to what constitutes fraudulent behavior by a taxpayer. Nor are there any rules or tests that the IRS must use, for making its determination that the fraud penalty is justified.

Are you beginning to get a little suspicious? Could there by some secret pact that Congress and the IRS don't want you to know about? In our view, there is willful intent here to deceive taxpayers in some way.

What Does Congress Say?

The fraud penalty was upgraded from 50% to 75% in 1989. Congress did so via P.L. 101-239. This public law is dubbed the ***Omnibus Budget Reconciliation Act of 1989***. The term "omnibus" means a ragtag collection of unrelated revenue enhancement provisions called "budget reconciliations." Any omnibus legislation with tax increases presents the ideal opportunity for the IRS to put something over on Congress, and for Congress, in turn, to put something over on the public.

At any rate, what does P.L. 101-239 say about the fraud penalty? Based on excerpts from its Committee Reports, Congress said—

> *The fraud penalty, which is imposed at a rate of 75 percent, applies to the portion of any underpayment that is attributable to fraud. . . . If the IRS establishes that any portion of an underpayment is attributable to fraud,* ***the entire underpayment*** *is treated as attributable to fraud,* ***except*** *with respect to any item that the taxpayer establishes . . . by a preponderance of evidence . . . is not attributable to fraud. . . . The committee has*

> *not altered the present-law burden of proof imposed on the IRS in establishing fraud initially; the IRS must continue to meet its burden of proof by clear and convincing evidence. The committee believes that it is appropriate that the burden imposed on the IRS be higher than the burden imposed on a taxpayer in these circumstances.* [Emphasis added.]

In this statement by Congress, do you see any clues that might explain why there are no IRS regulations supplementing the fraud penalty? Did you miss the clause "burden of proof on the IRS for establishing fraud initially"? And, did you miss the clause about the IRS's burden being "clear and convincing"? Probably not. These clauses are probably signalling to you a false sense of security and belief, that the IRS has to be forthright by carrying some kind of burden. Don't **you** be naive . . . and be misled.

Supposedly, having the burden of proof that a fraudulent act has been committed, the IRS does not want to expose prematurely its position and procedures to taxpayers. The truth is, the IRS has no above-board position and procedures when it comes to alleging fraud. The matter is *purely discretionary* with *each individual* IRS person assigned to a case. There are NO INTERNAL STANDARDS OF JUDGMENT that apply! If there were, why aren't they codified into regulations?

Answer: The legal arm of the IRS is abusive, arrogant, and unethical. It does not initiate its burden of proof until *10 seconds* before a docketed Tax Court trial begins. Let us explain.

Burden of Proof in Fraud

When we look up the term: "Burden of Proof — Fraud" in the topical index to the Internal Revenue Code, what do we find? We find it listed as—

> ***Proceedings before Tax Court — Sec. 7454(a)***

So, now, let's look up Section 7454; its title is: ***Burden of Proof in Fraud.***

Its subsection (a): ***Fraud***, reads in full as—

> *In **any proceeding** involving the issue whether the **petitioner** has been guilty of fraud with intent to evade tax, the burden of proof in respect of such issue shall be upon the* [IRS]. [Emphasis added.]

A tiny printed footnote to this Code section reads:

> *Source: Sec. 1112, 1939 Code, substantially unchanged.*

In other words, on the issue of fraud, the IRS has kept its no-standards-of-judgment secret for over 60 years!

What does the term "any proceeding" mean? Its dictionary definition is: **the taking of legal action**. You know the IRS is not going to initiate any legal action on its own, to carry its burden of proof. Therefore, **you** as the taxpayer — the "petitioner" — must initiate legal action to require the IRS to disclose its judgment basis as to why the 75% fraud penalty was assessed.

Section 7454(a) appears in Chapter 76 of the Internal Revenue Code. Said chapter is titled: ***Judicial Proceedings*** (Sections 7401 through 7491). Section 7454(a) is further tucked away in Subchapter C of Chapter 76: ***The Tax Court***. Part II of Subchapter C is titled: ***Procedure***. Procedures in Tax Court extend from Section 7451: ***Fee for Filing Petition*** through Section 7465. This spread includes **Section 7454**: Burden of Proof in Fraud. We show in Figure 7.1 the Tax Code's organizational placement of Section 7454.

The essence of Figure 7.1 is that the IRS does NOT have to provide any information to a taxpayer when it asserts the 75% fraud penalty, until a Tax Court trial begins. Before actual trial begins, many other procedures have to be pursued. Court rules require that the parties exchange trial information between themselves within 30 days before trial begins. Trial starts to begin when the clerk of the court says: "All rise!" At this moment, the trial judge enters the courtroom, takes his/her seat at the podium, then says: "Be seated. This court is now in session."

The IRS's legal practice for exchanging trial information with the petitioner is to wait until the judge opens the door from chambers to the courtroom. The moment the door opens, the IRS attorney

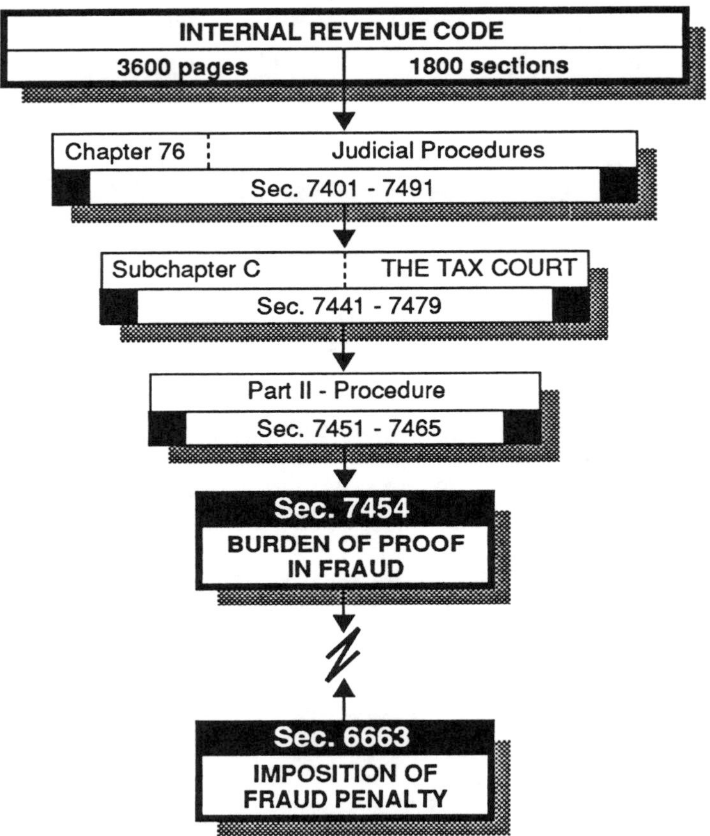

Fig. 7.1 - "Tucking Away" IRS's Burden of Proof on the Fraud Penalty

shoves all of his legal filings across the table to the petitioner's attorney. This action takes place literally *seconds* before trial begins. As the petitioner, you have no chance whatsoever to glean what specific fraudulent acts the IRS is alleging against you. Talk about "dirty tricks," this is it! Precisely speaking, 10 seconds before trial begins is "within 30 days before trial."

The Fraud Penalty Law

Now that we have given you the background on why no fraud penalty regulations exist, let us examine what the penalty law itself says. As mentioned previously, the applicable statute is IRC Section 6663: Imposition of Fraud Penalty. It consists of exactly 122 legal words. When counting legal words, any headings and subheadings are not counted as law. The headings/subheadings are for indexing purposes only. Accordingly, the full text of Section 6663 follows.

Subsec. (a): ***Imposition of Penalty.***

> *If any part of an underpayment of tax required to be shown on a return is due to fraud, there shall be added to the tax an amount equal to 75 percent of the portion of underpayment which is attributable to fraud.* [43 words]

Subsec. (b): ***Determination of Portion Attributable to Fraud.***

> *If the* [IRS] *establishes that any portion of an underpayment is attributable to fraud, the* ***entire underpayment*** *shall be treated as attributable to fraud, except with respect to any portion of the underpayment which the taxpayer establishes (by a preponderance of the evidence) is not attributable to fraud.* [Emphasis added.] [48 words]

Subsec. (c): ***Special Rule for Joint Returns.***

> *In the case of a joint return, the section shall not apply with respect to a spouse unless some part of the underpayment is due to the fraud of such spouse.* [31 words]

We show the word count [43 + 48 + 31 = 122] because we want you to see how devastating and destructive the few words can be. If a spouse knowingly signs a joint return on which the IRS asserts that some part is due to fraud, the assessable penalty jumps to 150%! It is standard practice that, before the IRS will assess the fraud penalty, it goes out of its way to maximize every conceivable underpayment issue that it can. By such tactics, when a formal Notice of Deficiency is legally served upon a taxpayer, he (and she) become traumatized, dazed, and incoherent. With its unlimited power to assert fraud based on its slightest whim, the IRS can strike terror in the heart, mind, and soul of any taxpayer . . . at any time.

Otherwise, since there are no regulations supplementing each of the 122 words of Section 6663, how else can one interpret its words and phrases?

Unlike the IRS, we will not let you down at this point. We will plow our way through various Tax Court cases, to apprise you of those rulings which are expressly applicable to Section 6663. Before we do so, however, we want to critique and point out a few things to you about those 122 words above.

Critique of Section 6663

There are features in the fraud penalty law that do not stand out when you read — and reread — its legal text. What may appear to be plain language and self-evident to you, is not so, when the IRS gets through twisting things around. It is upsetting to be the target of between-the-line interpretations, which the IRS will pull out of a hat . . . to beat you into submission. As one court ruling held: "The IRS's conduct made the petitioner's work more difficult due to the fact that the IRS was ***abusive, dishonest, and unethical***" [*W&S Distributing, Inc.*, DC Mich., 96-2 USTC ¶ 50,491].

In another case, *S.K. Regan*, TC Memo 1986-120, the IRS charged that the taxpayers were knowingly engaged in a falsehood. But the court ruled—

> There was no bad faith, intentional wrongdoing, sinister motive, or intent to mislead or deceive the IRS where taxpayers timely filed returns that set forth clearly their deductions . . . even though some of the deductions were questionable, and even though they were annoyed with government.

Section 6663(a) starts off with: *If any part of an underpayment . . . is due to fraud.* How small a part, relative to the entire underpayment does it have to be to warrant the 75% penalty? Because no regulations exist, and because the IRS can be dishonest and unethical, it can assert the fraud penalty without ever disclosing its identity of the part that it claims to be fraudulent.

For 75% penalty purposes, what really constitutes fraud? The plain language of the word requires some form of deception and willful intent (to understate one's tax). When it initially assigns the penalty, the IRS does not have to prove to itself or to the taxpayer that there has been deception or willful intent. It just blasts away.

What Section 6663(a) does not say is that, if the IRS cannot prove fraud in court, the IRS can alternatively assert the 20% or 40% accuracy-related penalty. Congress encouraged this penalty stacking when it increased the fraud penalty to 75% from 50%. In its Committee Reports on P.L. 101-239, it said:

> *Under the bill, the accuracy-related penalty is not to apply to any portion of an underpayment on which the fraud penalty is imposed. . . .* ***However,*** *the accuracy penalty may be applied to any portion of the underpayment that is not attributable to fraud.*

In other words, Congress rewarded the IRS with a bonus penalty of 20% (or 40% if gross valuation misstatement) if it fails in court to make a clear and convincing case of fraud. We doubt that this bonus penalty ever occurred to you when reading Section 6663(**a**) for the first, second . . . or third time.

Preponderance of Evidence?

Section 6663(**b**) provides a bizarre twist that you probably missed altogether. Its caption is: ***Determination of Portion Attributable to Fraud.*** Reading this caption alone, you could conclude that the IRS is required to be honest and upfront, and tell you what portion of your underpayment is attributable to fraud. We have already told you that headings and captions are not law. They are an index to each paragraph of law. Thus, the caption to Section 6663(b) is misleading.

As a taxpayer, you face two severe problems with Section 6663(b). Problem 1 is that the 75% penalty applies across the board to the entire amount of the underpayment that is IRS imposed. Problem 2 is that YOU have to prove the IRS wrong for each portion of the underpayment that is not attributable to fraud. You have to do this *by a preponderance of the evidence.*

Section 6663(b) starts off with: *If the IRS establishes that any portion . . . is attributable to fraud.* For whose ears and eyes does the IRS have to "establish" anything? Certainly not yours. The IRS only has to establish its position to a trial judge . . . and then only AFTER trial begins. So, right away, you know that the IRS is going to slam you with the maximum underpayment assertion that it can, in order to slam you with the 75% penalty across the board.

The only way out of your predicament is to pursue the exception clause in Section 6663(b). This clause, again, reads—

> *except with respect to any portion of the underpayment which the* ***taxpayer establishes*** *(by a* ***preponderance*** *of the* ***evidence****) is not attributable to fraud.* [Emphasis added.]

This is abominable tax legislation. The IRS is supposed to establish fraud by "clear and convincing evidence." Yet, you have to prove nonfraud by a "preponderance of evidence." How does one establish his preponderance of evidence without regulatory guidelines on point? Does the term mean some sort of preguarantee that the IRS will not prevail? Or, does it mean the presentation of "credible evidence," that puts the IRS to shame?

Fortunately, there is a new law (without regulations) that went into effect on July 22, 1998 [the IRS Restructuring and Reform Act]. The new law is Section 7491: ***Burden of Proof.*** The principal part which is pertinent here is its subsection (a): ***Burden Shifts Where Taxpayer Produces Credible Evidence.***

According to the Committee Reports on the IRS Reform Act (P.L. 105-206) the term "credible evidence" means—

> [That] *quality of evidence which, after critical analysis, the court would find sufficient upon which to base a decision on the issue if no contrary evidence were submitted.* [Such] *evidence must relate to a factual issue relevant to ascertaining the taxpayer's income tax liability.* [It is] *not credible for these purposes if the taxpayer merely makes implausible factual assertions, frivolous claims, or tax protester-type arguments.*

Being new law, Section 7491 has not yet been tested in court (as of this writing) with respect to fraud. It is quite ambiguous. For example, its paragraph (1) of subsection (a) starts out with—

> *If, in any court proceeding, a taxpayer introduces credible evidence with respect to any factual issue relevant to . . . liability for any tax, penalty, or additional amount . . . the* [IRS] *shall have the burden of proof with respect to such issue.*

But paragraph (1) is contradicted by paragraph (3) which says—

> *Paragraph (1) shall not apply . . . if any other* [section] *provides for a specific burden of proof with respect to such issue* [such as fraud?].

We are back to "square one," which is Section 6663(b). As cited above, the exception clause requires that the taxpayer, on each issue of fraud, prove that the IRS is wrong by a preponderance of evidence. From what we can gather from various critiques on new law Section 7491, the preponderance burden might be met by:

1. Raising a legitimate disputive issue with the IRS concerning its interpretation of fraud;
2. Identifying one's position with the plain language of a specific tax law or court ruling;
3. Substantiating one's position with books, records, and other documents relevant to each issue;
4. "Cooperating" with the IRS by supplying it with pertinent documents, information, and witnesses (WITHOUT agreeing to extend the statute of limitations); and
5. Appealing through the IRS's Appellate Division before petitioning to the U.S. Tax Court.

Badges of Fraud

Judicial minds often wrap themselves in emotional phrases that embody specific tests that are not privy to ordinary taxpayers. One such phrase is "badges of fraud."

What are the characteristics of fraud that make it so objectionable with respect to the filing of tax returns? After more than 60 years of administering the tax laws and aggressively asserting the fraud penalty, a reasonable person would expect that the IRS would have long ago set forth the type of conduct it views as constituting fraud. It is inexcusable why the IRS has not done so. A guideline listing of the "badges" or indicia of fraud would be as helpful to the IRS as it would be to taxpayers.

In as recent as a mid-1998 Tax Court case [*R.I. Ortiz*, T.C. Memo 1998-141, Dec. 52,660(M)], the fraud penalty was asserted . . . but it was **not** upheld. The court concluded that—

> Married taxpayers whose unreported self-employment income was reconstructed by the IRS were not liable for the fraud penalty. No evidence indicated that the wife had any intent to defraud. Although the husband had underreported the income and kept inadequate records, the indicia of fraud were too weak to constitute clear and compelling evidence.

The Ortiz case is a good illustration of how the IRS's arrogance can work against itself. Many of its fraud allegations are weak. Yet the IRS often gets away with its behavior for one simple reason. Most individual taxpayers do not have the time, money, or expert counsel to fight the IRS tooth and nail in court. Even if truly no fraudulent intent is involved, many taxpayers will give in to the IRS.

Once a fraud issue gets into Tax Court, seasoned trial judges follow certain precedents of the past. They start with the premise that fraud is **intentional wrongdoing** on the part of a taxpayer, who specifically intends *to evade a tax known to be owing*. The wrongdoing is evidenced by engaging in conduct intended to conceal, mislead, or otherwise prevent the collection of such taxes. Fraud should never be presumed. However, since direct proof of a taxpayer's fraudulent intent is not readily available, fraud may be proven through circumstantial evidence and reasonable inferences drawn therefrom [*O.C. Akland*, CA-9, 85-2 USTC ¶ 9593; *J.B. Kotmair*, 86 TC 1253; *J.E. Meier*, 91 TC 273].

The Ninth Circuit Court of Appeals (CA-9) has identified certain types of circumstantial evidence from which fraudulent intent may be inferred. Such "badges of fraud" include—

(1) **Understatements of income;**
(2) **Inadequate records;**
(3) **Failure to file returns;**
(4) **Implausible or inconsistent explanations of behavior;**
(5) **Failure to cooperate with the IRS.**

[*R.W. Bradford*, CA-9, 86-2 USTC ¶ 9602; *J. Edelson*, CA-9, 87-2 USTC ¶ 9547.]

The taxpayer's **entire course of conduct** is examined to establish the requisite intent. The courts commonly impose the penalty where they discern some "pattern" of behavior (such as consistently under-reporting income). Such prohibited behavior combined with overt acts designed to conceal such behavior (such as lying or being uncooperative during an audit) are generally required for imposition of the penalty [*C.P. Recklitis*, 91 TC 874].

The Examination Process

Rarely is the fraud penalty assessed without a thorough examination of at least three years of your tax returns. The reason for three years is to search for and identify some pattern of misconduct. Certain questionable items, if repeated three or more years in a row, are indicative of fraudulent intent. Examples of "certain questionable items" are flagrantly false deductions, ordinary income characterized as capital gain, extravagant business expenses, unusual/uncommon business expenses, gross valuation misstatements, reporting fictitious transactions, poor records of income . . . and so on.

Each IRS examination (audit) starts out with a routine selection notice. One specific year is identified, then the year before and the year after are included. The specific-year identity is considered the "target year": the reason for selection. The principal items to be examined for the target year are designated on the written notice. On such notice, there is no indication whatsoever that the likelihood of fraud is being investigated. You won't know until the audit is completed. When so, you will get a written report of proposed adjustments and the assessment of penalties.

In the meantime, you have to endure the audit. You have to do the best you can to answer the questions asked. You also have to do the best you can to substantiate every *significant* item of deduction, expense, or credit that you claim on your return. While every item that you substantiate with documents, records, or computational analysis will not be accepted by the auditor, at least you are demonstrating an effort to cooperate. Even if you have knowingly entered an item which is questionable or false, try to present a plausible explanation of your rationale for doing so. You want to give the impression that you are not hiding information. Adopt the attitude that you may have made erroneous entries, but you did so with good intent.

Every audit where fraud is suspected by the IRS starts with a reconstruction of your total income. Unreported income three years in a row is not, by itself, indicative of fraudulent intent. This is because not all items of income are tax accountable. Some items are exempt from tax, some are "return of capital," and some may be derived from gifts and inheritances. Taxable underreportings of 5% or less are treated as *de minimis*; they are not even considered from the perspective of fraudulent intent. It is not until your underreportings reach 25% or more of your reported income that the storm flag of fraud is raised.

Once the fraud flag is raised, you'll be in for a difficult time. Every "big ticket" item on your return will be examined, re-examined, and cross-examined. By "big ticket," we mean any basis, deduction, or expense of $10,000 or more per item, per year. This threshold does not eliminate lesser amounts as a source of fraud. It is just that those big items are where the IRS seeks to maximize your underpayment amount. Therefore, prepare yourself ahead of time to condition your conduct, responses, and reliance on researched tax-legal positions. As depicted in Figure 7.2, the general idea is to prepare for the worst, so as not to be caught off guard.

Cooperate Without Extending Time

During the course of an examination, you will never be told that you are under suspicion for fraud. You can sense this possibility on

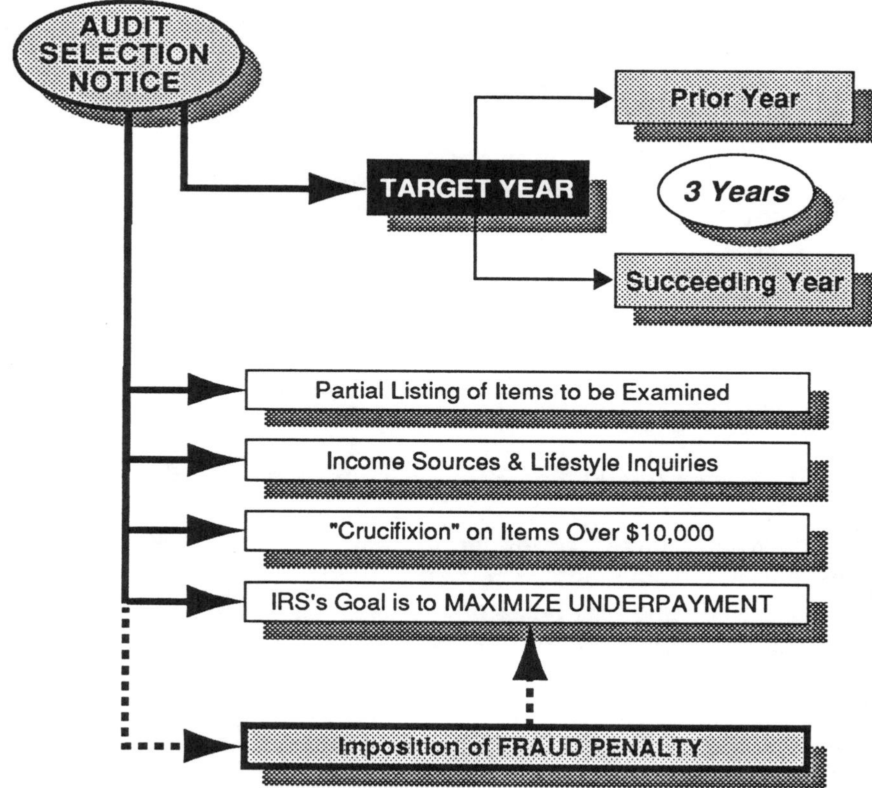

Fig. 7.2 - Preparation for IRS Examination of Returns When Fraud Suspected

your own by the line of questions asked — and reasked — and by the intrusion into your personal affairs and lifestyle which are not reflected on your return. Another telltale sign is when the audit drags on, seemingly endlessly. You will know that you are on the IRS's "fraud list" when the examiner asks you to sign a *consent form* extending the time to complete the audit.

The IRS will prepare two extension-of-time forms, with the expectation that you will sign at least one of the two. The two prepared-for-your-signature forms are:

Form 872: ***Consent to Extend Time to Assess Tax***, and
Form 872-A: ***Special Consent to Extend Time to Assess Tax***

You will be offered Form 872-A first. This is an *indefinite* extension of time to continue the audit. The only way to cut off the indefiniteness is for you to procure, prepare, and file Form 872-T: ***Notice of Termination of Special Consent to Extend Time to Assess Tax***. When offered Form 872-A, NEVER EVER sign it! The IRS is setting a disastrous 10-year financial trap for you. Even if you ultimately beat the fraud rap, 10 years of statutory interest plus alternate accuracy penalties will beat you down.

Next you will be offered Form 872. This is a limited extension of time: usually six to 12 months. If it extends *only* the one year that precedes the target year (the center of the three years), signing it may be as much for your convenience as for the IRS's. It gives you a little more time to disarm the profile "pattern" that the IRS may be building. However, if Form 872 extends the target year, decline to sign it. Hasten to add that you will likely sign it for the target year when the matter gets to the Appellate Division of the IRS. This will put the auditor on notice that you intend to appeal (within the IRS) whatever results the auditor comes up with.

By declining to sign Form 872, you'll be threatened and intimidated that you are being non-cooperative. If you are threatened, advise the IRS intimidator to review the Senate Finance Committee Report on P.L. 105-206: the IRS Reform Act of 1998. Point out that the definition of cooperation with the IRS is spelled out in the legislative intent behind Section 7491: ***Burden of Proof***. Or, *you* read the following excerpt to the IRS person harassing you about cooperation:

> *The taxpayer must cooperate with* ***reasonable requests*** *by the IRS for meetings, interviews, witnesses, information, and documents . . . within the control of the taxpayer. Cooperation also includes providing reasonable assistance to the IRS in obtaining access to an inspection of witnesses, information, or documents not within the control of the taxpayer including* [those] *located in foreign countries.* ***The taxpayer is not required to agree to extend the statute of limitations to be considered to have cooperated with the IRS.*** [Emphasis added.]

Examination Change Report

By not signing Form 872 for the target year, the auditor is under some pressure to issue promptly his or her Report of Examination Changes. If the examination is "incomplete" in the eyes of the auditor, all unexamined items of significance will be arbitrarily disallowed. Once under the cloud of fraud, all such items would be (most likely) disallowed anyhow. Thus, the idea is to get the change report as soon as possible, so as to start working on your contestation strategies.

The change report will definitely cover *three* years of your tax returns. For each year, the report will show: (1) Adjustments to Income, (2) Computation of Underpayment (Deficiency in Tax), and (3) Assignment of Penalties. Because of the 3-year "profiling," voluminous computer-generated data entries will be shown (for each year). An abridged arrangement of such report is presented in Figure 7.3. A fraud-alleged report will be more legalistic and obfuscated than that back in Figure 4.3 (on page 4-15). Depending on the complexity of your returns, and on the number of adjustments made and penalties assigned, the report can be anywhere from 20 to 35 pages in length. This includes its cover letter with instructions.

The report is lengthy because the IRS is required to give you an explanation of each adjustment and each penalty. The explanations are quite perfunctory . . . and computer generated, of course. An "explanation" consists of reference to the applicable tax code section, some alleged fact relating to your return, and a statement that you did not comply with the law. No convincing evidence, whatsoever, of the IRS's position is given. You are left entirely on your own to decipher each "explanation" spewed out by a computer key.

In the case of alleged fraud, the "explanation" goes like this:

IRC Sec. 6663(b) — Fraud Penalty

Since all or part of the underpayment of tax required to be shown on your return is due to fraud, a penalty of 75 percent of the underpayment is added to the tax. [33 words]

IRS	REPORT OF INDIVIDUAL INCOME TAX CHANGES		
Name of Auditee(s) / Soc.Sec. No.	Examiner's Name		Return Form #
	Year 1	Year 2	Year 3
Adjustments to Income ● ● ● ● ●			
Total Adjustments			
Tax Recomputation ☐ **Required to be shown** ☐ **Amount on return**			
Underpayment of Tax			
Penalties Assessed ● ● ●			
Total Adjustments			
Summary of Taxes ☐ **Balance Due** ☐ **Penalties** ☐ **Interest to** ____________			
Grand Total Due ▶			
Examiner's Signature	IRS District	Date of Report	

Fig. 7.3 - Abridged 3-Year Report Where Fraud May Be Alleged

This is the officially approved explanation of fraud. For a penalty that will always exceed $10,000, you get 33 words of computer disingenuousness. Such is the consequence of there being no IRS regulations supplementing Section 6663.

When the fraud penalty is asserted, you can count on other penalties being cited. This is because the IRS wants to cover its rear, in the event that you can show that all portions of the underpayment are "not attributable to fraud."

Response to Transmittal Letter

Every examination change report where fraud or other penalties are imposed is accompanied by a carefully worded transmittal letter. It is an official IRS letter with a head summary of: (1) underpayment of tax, (2) penalty assessments, and (3) statutory interest. Each of the three audited years is displayed. The letter provides information and instructions on what to do if you agree, and what to do if you do not agree with the report submitted.

The letter starts off with—

Dear Taxpayer:

We are enclosing a report proposing adjustments to your tax for the year(s) shown above. Please read the report, decide whether you agree or disagree, and respond within 30 days of the date of this letter.

IF YOU AGREE, you should sign and date the enclosed agreement form.

The agreement form is Form 870: ***Consent to Assessment and Collection***. By signing this form, you consent to the immediate payment of the increased tax, penalties, and interest. You also consent that—

By signing this waiver, I understand that I will not be able to contest these years in the U.S. Tax Court.

If fraud has been alleged and you sign Form 870, you should not be reading this book! You have wasted your time.

By agreeing to any amount of fraud penalty, you are opening yourself up to *more than* three years of return examinations. Ordinarily, the statute of limitations for examinations is three years. Section 6501(a): ***Limitations on Assessment and Collection***: ***General Rule*** says so.

But when you admit to fraud, Section 6501(c): ***Exceptions***, says—

> *In the case of a false or fraudulent return with the intent to evade tax, the tax may be assessed, or a proceeding in court for collection of such tax may be begun* ***without assessment, at any time****.* [Emphasis added.]

The term "any time" means just what it says: *any* time. In other words, by agreeing to any amount of fraud penalty, you are opening up the examination of three years *preceding* the years just examined, and three years *following* the years just examined. Obviously, we recommend strongly that you NOT agree to any fraud penalty.

The transmittal letter goes on to say—

> *IF YOU DO NOT AGREE and wish a conference with the Office of the Regional Director of Appeals, you MUST LET US KNOW within 30 days.*
>
> *An appeals officer, who has not examined your return previously, will review your case. The appeals office is independent of the district director. By going to the appeals office, you may avoid court costs, resolve the matter sooner, and prevent interest from compounding.*
>
> */s/ District Director*
> *Internal Revenue Service*

We urge that you promptly notify the district director of your disagreement. Don't even think twice about it. If fraud is one of the penalties assessed, call the "Person to Contact" in the upper right-hand corner of the transmittal letter. State your intention to disagree, then request the forms and instructions for doing so. Knuckle down, and get going on your appeal. We will discuss the appeals procedures quite fully in Chapter 12: Appealing Within IRS.

8

TRUST FUND FAILURES

If You Are, Have Been, Or Expect To Be An Owner In A Closely-Held Business (Proprietorship, Partnership, Or Corporation) Having Financial Difficulties, You Could Be In For A Shocker. If You Have Collected, Or Should Have Collected, Tax Withholdings From Workers, And Willfully Fail To Pay Over Such Withholdings, You Become Liable For The 100% TRUST FUND RECOVERY Penalty. This Is A Civil Liability Upon You As A "Responsible Person." It Is Separate And Apart From Your Business Entity. It Is NOT DISCHARGEABLE In Bankruptcy . . . Nor Is It Waiverable For Reasonable Cause. It Is "Government Money" Which Is Not That Of The Business.

Small business owners with one, two, or more employees are subject to a 100% penalty for failing to collect and pay over to the U.S. Treasury mandated withholdings from such employees. There are three types of required withholdings, namely: (1) employee income tax, (2) employee social security tax, and (3) employee medicare tax. Collectively, these three tax withholdings are called: *trust fund taxes*. The money withheld is **employee** tax money; it is NOT employer tax money.

The term "trust fund" is a legal doctrine for penalty administration purposes. In reality, no actual trust entity exists. The doctrine is based on the legal theory that a transitory trust takes effect, from the moment that withholding is first required, until all required withholdings are paid over. The actual trust entity is the U.S. Treasury itself.

The 100% trust fund penalty is distinct and apart from the failure-to-deposit penalty that we addressed in Chapter 3. The failure-to-deposit penalty (2% to 15%) addresses operating delinquencies in time, amount, and tax accounting forms. The intention is to deposit and pay over all payroll taxes, even though one is delinquent in doing so.

In contrast, the trust fund penalty is based on willful failures and avoidance attempts. The withholding money was either not collected, or, if collected, was not paid over . . . intentionally. The series of misconducts includes:

- ☐ Failure to *collect* the required withholdings.
- ☐ Failure to *account for* the required withholdings.
- ☐ Failure to *pay over* the required withholdings.
- ☐ Attempt to *defeat* the withholding requirement.
- ☐ Attempt to *evade* the payover requirement.

Whatever the operational cause of the failures and attempts, and whatever the form of the small business (proprietorship, partnership, or corporation), there is a *responsible person* for the collection, accounting, and paying over. The 100% penalty applies to that person only. It does not apply to any employee (who is not otherwise a responsible person) nor to the business entity itself. It is an individualized penalty for failures in carrying out one's withholding obligations. These obligations also extend to nonpayroll withholdings.

Accordingly, in this chapter we want to present and explain the tax law on point (namely: **Section 6672**). We also want to present the definitive ramifications of who is, in fact, the "responsible person." In doing so, we have to describe the procedural limitations that the IRS must go through before the 100% penalty can be assessed and collected.

Section 6672: General Rule

Section 6672 is officially titled: ***Failure to Collect and Pay Over, or Attempt to Evade or Defeat Tax***. Note that there are two distinct clauses in this title, namely: *Failure to* . . . and *Attempt to* . . . . The "failure to" pertains to small businesses whose workers are employees where the employer is cash short and having financial difficulties. The "attempt to" pertains to those businesses where the workers are independent contractors who are not subject to withholdings. The IRS comes along later, to ordain that the independent contractors are employees, and that, therefore, the employer has attempted to "evade or defeat" the withholding tax requirement.

Altogether, Section 6672 consists of about 1,100 words. Its first 100 words or so comprise its general rule (subsection (a)). The essence of this rule reads—

> ***Any person required to*** *collect, truthfully account for, and pay over any tax imposed by* [the Internal Revenue Code] *who willfully fails to collect such tax, or truthfully account for, and pay over such tax, or who willfully attempts in any manner to evade or defeat any such tax or the payment thereof, shall in addition to other penalties provided by law, be liable to a penalty* ***equal to*** *the total amount of the tax evaded, or not collected, or not accounted for, and not paid over.*

The term "any person" means any *responsible* person who is required to collect, account for, and pay over. We'll have more to say about such a person below. Expressly note, however, that the penalty target is a **person** — a human individual. The target is not the business entity itself.

In the full statutory wording above, we particularly want you to digest its seriousness and complexity. To do so, you have to read — and reread — Section 6672(a) several times. Then you have to break it down into distinct, stand-alone clauses. For this, the key focus clauses are:

- One who is *required to* collect, account for, **and** pay over—
- One who *willfully fails* to do so, knowing the relevant circumstances— OR
- One who *willfully attempts* to evade or defeat said tax—

SHALL BE LIABLE for a penalty *equal to* the amount not collected, accounted for, or paid over.

Can't you see the endless possibilities for interpretation disputes with the IRS? How do you define the person who is "required to" collect and pay over? When is such person considered to have "willfully failed" to do so? Or, when is such person considered to have "willfully attempted" to defeat such tax?

Suppose a small business owner genuinely believes that he can compete better in the market place with independent contractors than with employees. By not having employees, he is not required to collect, etc. the trust fund taxes. Is such an owner willfully attempting to evade or defeat said tax? In 99% of the cases, the IRS will assert "Yes" . . . and will impose the "equal to" trust fund penalty.

The "Rationale" Explained

As a penalty, what does the term "equal to" mean? Yes, we know it means 100% of the amount of tax which is not paid over. But does it mean that the penalty **is** the tax? Or, does it mean that the penalty is *in addition* to the tax not paid over? Most penalties are in addition to the underlying tax required to be paid. Said penalties are expressed as a percentage of the applicable delinquency. There is no statutory percentage expressed in Section 6672(a): just "equal to." What is the rationale here? The IRS is no help; it publishes no regulations on point.

The best explanation we can find is the case of *W.J. Ross*, 97-1 USTC ¶ 50,247; DC Ohio, 949 F Supp 536. The court did some background research into the Congressional intent of Section 6672. It explained the rationale this way:

> Under the system of withholding taxes prided by the Internal Revenue Code, employees are entitled to credit for the amounts of FICA [social security and medicare] and income taxes withheld from their wages, regardless of whether or not the employer turns the funds over to the government. Since, therefore, the government may actually be out-of-pocket by way of credit or refund of taxes never received, Congress has allowed the IRS more stringent protective devices to insure collection of payroll taxes, than in the case of many other taxes.

> The purpose of section 6672 is to protect the government against losses by providing it with **another source from which** to collect the withheld taxes . . . or those intended to be withheld.
>
> It is no excuse that, as a matter of business judgment, the [withheld] money was paid to suppliers and for wages, in order to keep the business operating as a going concern — the government cannot be made an unwilling partner in a floundering business.

Our take on Section 6672 is that it is treated as a penalty solely for purposes of IRS assessment and collection enforcement. As "another source" for the collection of not-paid-over withholdings, Section 6672 imposes a *civil liability* — not a punishment — upon some identifiable responsible person. As depicted in Figure 8.1, the trust fund doctrine gives the IRS a choice. It can collect the withheld tax (or that which was required to be withheld) either from the business entity itself, or from the responsible person in charge of the business entity.

Once the not-paid withholdings are collected by the IRS, *other penalties* and interest apply. The "applicable" penalties are those which relate to collection, accounting, and deposits of payroll taxes. Such is the meaning of the clause in Section 6672(a) which reads—

> *shall, in addition to other penalties provided by law, be liable to a penalty equal to . . .*

Withholding Requirements

The withholding of income taxes, social security taxes, and medicare taxes is a commonly known fact of life among employees and employers. Yet, despite this common knowledge, it is appropriate to review the high points on the requirements therewith.

The basic law on withholding is Section 3402: ***Income Tax Collected at Source***. Its subsection (a): ***Requirement of Withholding***, reads in principal part as—

> *Except as otherwise provided . . ., every employer making payment of wages* ***shall deduct and withhold*** *upon such wages a tax determined in accordance with tables or computational procedures prescribed by the* [IRS]. [Emphasis added.]

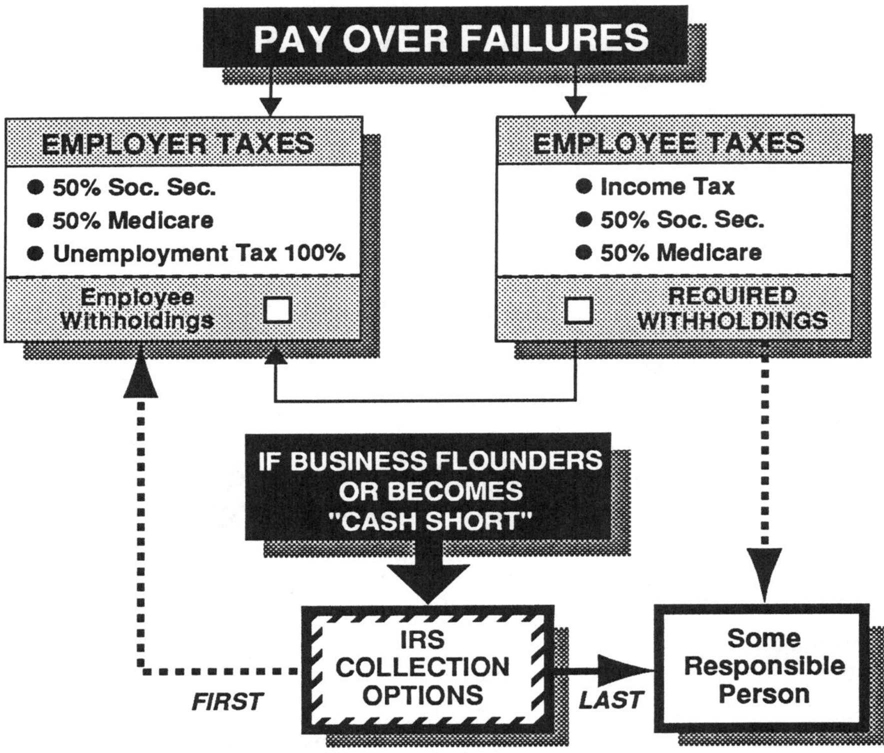

Fig. 8.1 - IRS's "Last Recourse" When a Business Flounders

The referenced "tables or procedures" are those prescribed in IRS Publication 15: ***Circular E, Employer's Tax Guide***. The "except as provided" relates to certain withholding exemptions outlined in subsection 3402(f). Otherwise, the withholding of income taxes "at the source" is a timeworn mandate.

Section 3402 is construed to also include FICA withholdings: Federal Insurance Contributions Act. The FICA is the combination of social security and medicare tax withholdings. The specific law on point is Section 3102(a): ***Requirement***. The first full sentence of this subsection reads—

> *The tax imposed by* [FICA] ***shall be collected*** *by the employer of the taxpayer,* ***by deducting*** *the amount of the tax* ***from the wages*** *as and when paid.* [Emphasis added.]

The FICA withholding law goes back to 1954. Ever since then, the employee pays one-half of the FICA tax; the employer pays the other half. Various new withholding requirements came on the scene in 1976 and subsequent years, classed as: *Nonpayroll withholdings.*

All forms of withholdings, whether payroll or nonpayroll, are subject to the provisions of Section 7501: ***Liability for Taxes Withheld or Collected.*** This provision reads in full—

> *Whenever any person is required to collect or withhold any internal revenue tax from any other person and pay over such tax to the United States, the amount of tax so collected or withheld* ***shall be held to be a special fund in trust*** *for the United States. The amount of such fund shall be assessed, collected, and paid in the same manner and subject to the same provisions and limitations (including penalties) as are applicable with respect to the taxes from which such funds arose.* [Emphasis added.]

This statutory wording defines the "trust fund doctrine" which we brought up earlier. As depicted in Figure 8.2, the withholdings are other people's tax money which belongs to the U.S. Treasury. It is NOT to be used as operating capital by the withholding entities involved. Herein lies the "responsible person" doctrine.

Responsible Person Defined

The trust fund recovery penalty (Section 6672(a)) can be assessed against the employer, but is most often levied on at least one "responsible person." Such person is usually that individual within the business entity who had sufficient authority to pay over the withheld taxes. This definition includes that individual who had direct responsibility for collecting, accounting for, and paying over the withheld taxes. Such individual is not easy to identify where businesses in closely-held corporate form "pass the buck" among officers, employees, directors, or shareholders.

When tax withholding matters go awry, many would-be responsible persons head for the exits. This behavior has led the

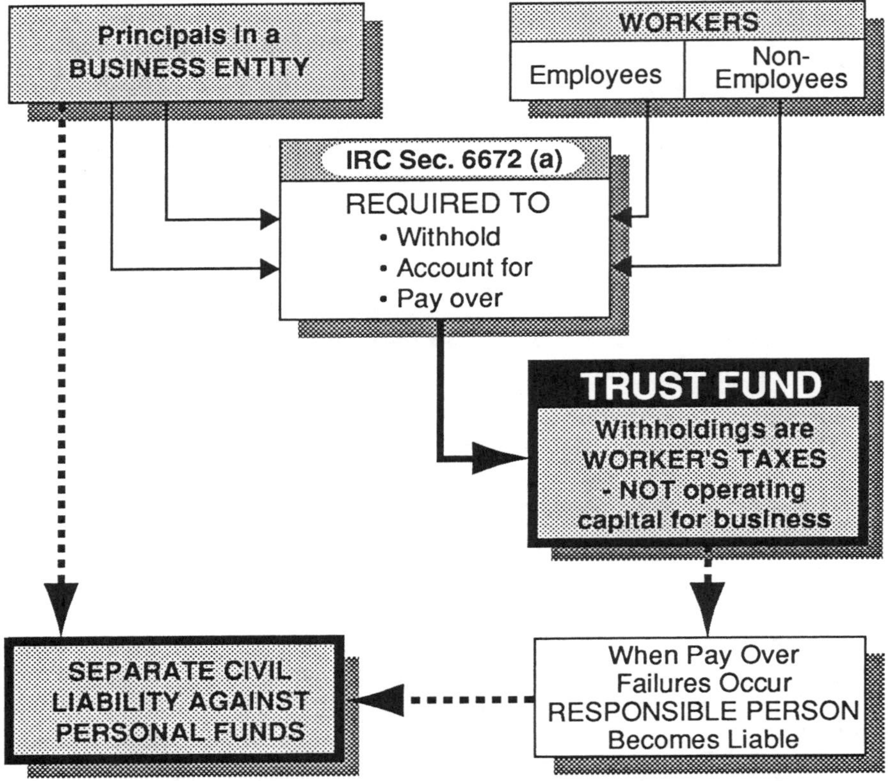

Fig. 8.2 - Civil Liability Feature of the "Trust Fund Doctrine"

courts to take a broad view when trying to pinpoint the one person ultimately responsible. This pinpointing includes determining who has—

(1) ultimate authority for the decision not to pay trust fund taxes;
(2) effective power to pay the taxes;
(3) authority over the expenditure of funds or the authority to direct payment of creditors;
(4) significant control or authority over the business entity's general finances or general decision-making; or
(5) power to control the decision-making process by which the employer allocates funds.

Thus, a person may be a responsible person for purposes of Section 6672(a), and not even know that withholding taxes have not been paid over. One does not cease to be a responsible person merely by delegating responsibility to someone else. Moreover, Section 6672(a) expressly applies to "any" responsible person: not the person "most" responsible for the tax payovers. There may be — indeed, there usually are — multiple responsible persons in any business entity engaging employees over a period of years. The IRS, however, can target any **one** of such multiple persons for its assessment and collection of penalty. In a separate civil action on his own, the targeted person—

> *shall be entitled to recover from other persons who are liable for such penalty an amount equal to . . . such* [other] *person's proportionate share of the penalty* [Sec. 6672(d)].

In the case of *R.D. Barnett*, CA-5, 93-1 USTC ¶ 50,269, the court summarized the circumstantial indicators of responsible person status. Among the factors considered are a person's—

(a) status as an officer or director of the business entity;
(b) substantial ownership interest in the entity;
(c) management of the day-to-day operations of the business;
(d) authority to hire and fire employees;
(e) making of decisions as to the disbursement of funds;
(f) making of decisions as to the payment of creditors; and
(g) authority to sign company checks.

No one single factor is determinative. The crucial inquiry is: Does the targeted person have "significant," as opposed to absolute, control over the financial affairs and decision-making processes of the business entity? That is: Does the targeted person have "sufficient" control to direct the disbursement of funds, whether or not he exercises that control directly? If he does, he is at least one responsible person. One responsible person is all that the IRS needs for implementing Section 6672(a). If more than one person is likely responsible, the IRS will assess each person separately. This way, at least one will be ultimately responsible.

Not Dischargeable in Bankruptcy

Predominantly, the Section 6672(a) penalty assessments deal with failing or failed small businesses. The principals of the business are scattering or have scattered. Through excuses and finessing, they assign some innocent employee to close out the books, if they are closed out at all. The close-out employee is given limited check-writing authority on dwindling entity funds, which have long since been raided by the principals. Either intentionally or unintentionally, they have designated the close-out employee to be the responsible person for IRS target purposes. This scenario is the very reason why the responsible person doctrine is the only recourse the IRS has for collecting the unpaid trust fund withholdings.

In typical situations, a struggling business that has fallen behind in its bills pays other creditors before the IRS. This is done to assure needed goods and services. Persons responsible for paying the bills hope that by the time the IRS catches up, the business will have turned around. Then it will have sufficient funds available to satisfy the trust fund taxes and other tax liabilities. Should the business not turn around, the hope is that by going bankrupt all tax liabilities will be discharged. In bankruptcy cases, not only do the business's tax liabilities gain a measure of priority, responsibility for paying over the trust fund taxes becomes a civil liability upon the IRS-determined responsible person. This personal liability is neither dischargeable in bankruptcy nor deductible as a business expense or bad debt.

There is no provision in law for bankruptcy discharge of the trust fund taxes. In fact, there is an express exception in Section 6658: ***Coordination With Chapter 11*** [Bankruptcy Code], to any such dischargeability. Subsection 6658(b): ***Exception for Collected Taxes***, says outright—

> *Subsection (a)* [dischargeability of "certain" tax liabilities] ***shall not apply*** *to any liability for an addition to the tax which arises from the failure to pay or deposit a tax withheld or collected from others and required to be paid to the United States.* [Emphasis added.]

Thus, Section 6658(b) makes it very clear that it is immaterial whether the responsible person himself/herself files separately for personal bankruptcy. The only relief for the "responsible person bankruptee" is to work out a protracted payment schedule either with the IRS or with the Bankruptcy Court.

Willfulness Defined

Imposition of the trust fund recovery penalty under Section 6672(a) requires that the responsible person's failure to pay over be "willful." The precise statutory wording on point is—

> *who willfully fails to collect such tax, or truthfully account for and pay over such tax, or* [who] *willfully attempts . . . to evade or defeat . . . the payment thereof.*

Consequently, before the IRS can assess the penalty against a targeted responsible person, it must show that the act of non-payment was voluntary, conscious, and intentional. It does not have to show a deceitful motive or evil intent on the part of the targeted person. In other words, the IRS need only show that the responsible party was aware of the trust fund taxes outstanding, and that he knowingly or intentionally used the funds to pay operating expenses and other debts of the business.

The issue of willfulness hinges on whether the responsible person has knowledge of the nonpayment of trust fund taxes. This aspect is best summarized in the case of *G.M. Lee*, BC-Md, 97-2 USTC ¶ 50,620. In its ruling, the court stated (among other things) that—

> Willful action under Section 6672(a) refers to voluntary, conscious, and intentional — as opposed to accidental — decisions to not remit funds. . . . The failure to pay trust fund taxes cannot be willful unless there is either knowledge of nonpayment or reckless disregard of whether the payments were being made. . . . The intentional preference of other creditors over the United States is sufficient to establish the element of willfulness. . . . A considered decision not to pay the taxes owed, evidenced by payments to other creditors with knowledge that withholding taxes are due, establishes willfulness.

The most succinct definition of willfulness is that of *A. Mardousian*, DC-Md, 98-2 USTC ¶ 50,754. Here, the court concluded that—

> ***His conscious and deliberate choice to prefer other creditors over the government constituted a willful failure to pay over the*** [trust fund] ***taxes. Reasonable cause did not negate his willfulness because his efforts to protect the trust funds were not frustrated by circumstances outside his control.***

When Notified of Assessment

Before the IRS can enforce collection of the trust fund taxes, it must notify the responsible person of the full amount it intends to assess. This is the tenor of Section 6672(b): ***Preliminary Notice Requirement***. The general rule reads (in part)—

> *No penalty shall be imposed under subsection (a) unless the* [IRS] *notifies the taxpayer in writing by mail . . . or in person that the taxpayer shall be subject to an assessment of such penalty.*

A preliminary notice must be delivered at least 60 days before any final Notice and Demand is issued. The purpose of the preliminary notice is to allow the responsible person to file a protest with the Appellate Division of the IRS. This affords opportunity to reconcile any factual differences between what the IRS says is owed, and what *you* — if you are the responsible person — say is owed. Said protest has to be filed within 30 days after receipt of the preliminary notice [Sec. 6672(b)(3)(B)].

If your appeal within the IRS turns out to be perfunctory and nonproductive, you have one other prescribed course. Pursuant to Section 6672(c), you can post a bond to stay the IRS collection process. You have to do so within 30 days of the IRS's Final Notice and Demand. Simultaneously file a refund-type lawsuit in the U.S. District Court or U.S. Court of Claims. You have to prepay the minimum amount required to commence a court proceeding on the penalty. This minimum is the amount of tax withheld or should have been withheld, on one employee for one calendar quarter.

The amount of bond required to stay IRS collection is prescribed under Section 6672(c): ***Extension of Period of Collection where Bond is Filed.*** The substance of its paragraphs (1) and (3) is that the amount of bond—

> *shall be 11/2 times the amount of excess of the penalty assessed over the payment . . . which is not less than the minimum amount required to commence a proceeding in court with respect to . . . such penalty.*

For example, suppose that the grand total of the trust fund penalty tax over several years, for several employees (or several workers who were reclassified by the IRS as employees) was $35,000. Suppose that you can show that the required withholdings from one worker for one calendar quarter came to $1,667. You prepay this amount, then file a refund claim with the IRS. When the IRS disapproves your refund, it keeps your $1,667 prepayment. You then commence court litigation against the IRS. At that time, you post a $50,000 bond [1.5 x (35,000 – 1,667)]. The combination of your posting of bond and commencement of litigation prevents the IRS from levying against your assets in the pursuit of its collection efforts.

Importance of "Accounting For"

If you are, have been, or expect to be a principal in a small business venture involving workers subject to withholdings, you should take heed. If you have *any* managerial, financial, or tax matters oversight responsibilities, you are on vulnerable ground. Especially so, if any trust fund failures occurred during "your watch" for one worker, for one calendar quarter. You are the very last recourse that the IRS has for recovering withheld tax money that was not your, nor your entity's, money to use. The fact that you may have left the company makes no difference. Once responsible, there is no escape. The sooner you face this reality, the sooner you can start resolving your plight.

Step One in the resolving process is to familiarize yourself with **Form 941** and, if applicable, **Form 945**. The titles and uses of these two forms are:

Form 941 — ***Employer's Quarterly Federal Tax Return*** — for *payroll* withholdings and accounting therewith: income, social security, and medicare taxes.

Form 945 — ***Annual Return of Withheld Federal Income Tax*** — for *nonpayroll* withholdings and accounting therewith.

Near the bottom of the front page of each form there is a recap block titled: ***Monthly Summary of Federal Tax Liability***. This summary is immediately above the signature block for the "responsible person." Whoever's name and title appear here, or were supposed to appear here, is the first target for the IRS's assessment when there are trust fund delinquencies.

The moment you learn of any trust fund failures in your company, get down to business. Meticulously review your job description and assignments. Do so in the light of the definitional tests of a responsible person who willfully fails "to account for." Try to truthfully establish (with documentation) those Forms 941 and 945 periods for which you are responsible . . . AND those periods for which you are NOT responsible. Your goal is to narrow down to only those periods for which you are truly responsible.

Suppose, for example, that the trust fund delinquencies extend over a period of 45 months (15 quarters). Also, suppose that you can show with convincing documentation, that you are responsible for only 12 of the 45 months (four quarters). If so, theoretically, you should be trust fund penalized for four quarters only: not all 15. But in order to help yourself, you have to help the IRS identify those persons who are responsible for those periods for which you are not responsible. So be prepared for what could be vicious finger-pointing by your business associates.

Stay mum. You want to be the first among your associates to establish the limitation(s) of your responsibilities.

Digest of What to Do

Face the inevitable. If you are truly trust fund responsible for only one month in a 45-month failure period, you will be assessed for the entire period! So, too, may other associates of your business be assessed. The IRS is spearing for the easiest responsible person it can find. Therefore, you owe it to yourself to prove the precise extent to which your liability accrues. Then prepare to "account for" and "pay over" those withholdings that were previously not paid over. Prepare to do this with your own personal funds. Ultimately, you will have to pay the trust fund penalty from your own funds, if your business entity is broke, bankrupt, insolvent, or in disarray.

Because trust fund failure circumstances differ from company to company, we summarize your what-to-do actions in Figure 8.3. There are three premises on which this figure is based. One premise is that you can establish with reasonable certainty that you are a responsible person for a limited period of time. The second premise is that you, yourself, did not prepare or sign the required Forms 941 and 945. These matters were handled either by an outside payroll service or by some worker under your control. The third premise is that you did not learn of the trust fund failures until several or more calendar quarters after the original failure occurred.

With these premises in mind, we urge that you study — and restudy — our Figure 8.3. It is a concise blueprint of what to do, that you won't find succinctly presented elsewhere. Start at Step 1 and plod your way down through Step 9. Seek tax professional assistance to help prepare and document your effort. By all means, familiarize yourself with Form 941-V and, if applicable, Form 945-V. The "V" is for ***Payment Voucher***, for each Form 941 and Form 945 that you "back prepare." Pay sufficient funds to cover at least one worker for each trust fund period. Stake your position promptly and affirmatively.

Also, attach to each Form 941-V or 945-V a filled-out Form 9465: ***Installment Agreement Request***. Read the instructions carefully, including the Caution that—

> *A Notice of Federal Tax Lien may be filed to protect the government's interest until you pay in full.*

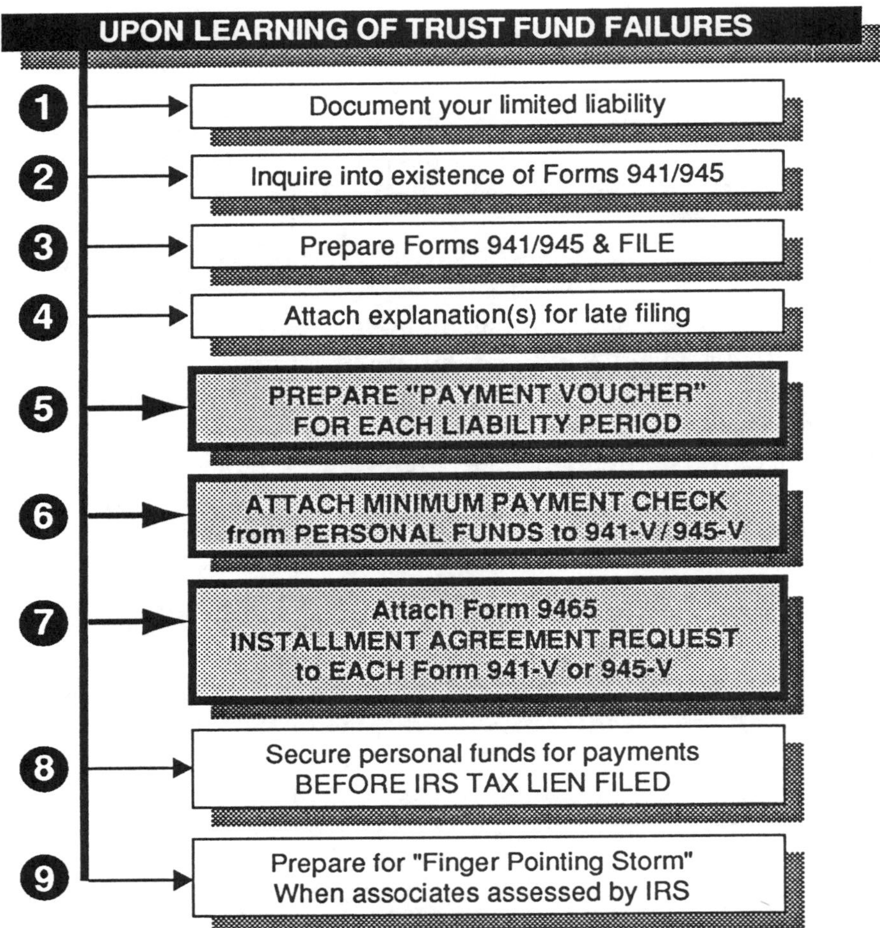

Fig. 8.3 - Facing the Inevitable by Arranging for Installment Payments

Before any trust fund tax lien is filed against your property and assets, secure the funding that you will need to make monthly payments on a regular basis. Unless you are forced to for other reasons, do not even think about filing for bankruptcy. As we tried to emphasize earlier, the trust fund recovery of withholdings is NOT dischargeable in bankruptcy.

9

WILLFUL TAX EVASION

The "Incentive" Behind Criminal Tax Penalties Is To Cause One To Pay His Taxes Voluntarily, And To File All Required Returns. Monetary Fines And Jail Time Can Be Imposed ONLY UPON CONVICTION In A U.S. District Court. The Department Of Justice (Not The IRS) Prepares And Serves The Legal Papers For Trial. After Service, A Request For PLEA AGREEMENT Can Be Entered. During Trial, A Good Faith Defense And Demeanor Are Essential. After Conviction And Sentencing, An OFFER IN COMPROMISE Can Be Made. Use IRS Form 656, Which Includes Many Pages Of Financial Data, For Computing The Offer Amount.

If you were seeking to evade tax willfully and intentionally, how would you go about it? One way would be to absolutely refuse to file a return, when required. Another way would be to file a false return with income knowingly underreported and deductions overly stated. Still another way would be to let the IRS assess a tax due (from third-party information), then you absolutely refuse to pay it. Or, you could make perjurious statements and pursue laundering acts to secrete your income and assets.

Nobody really likes to pay taxes. But overt acts of willful evasion up the penalty risks substantially. In all previous chapters, the penalties covered are classed as *civil* penalties. In the case of willful tax evasion, one crosses the threshold into *criminal* penalties. Criminal penalties are imposed **in addition** to civil penalties for the same tax delinquency. Criminal penalties invoke a fine or imprisonment . . . or both.

There are two grades of criminal penalties: misdemeanor and felony. For misdemeanors, the fine is not more than $25,000 (for individuals) or imprisonment for not more than one year . . . or both. For felonies, the fine jumps to not more than $100,000 (for individuals) or jail time not more than five years . . . or both. The message is that willful tax evasion is very serious business.

In this chapter, therefore, we want to focus on the distinctions between ordinary failure to pay, willful failure to pay, and willful tax evasion. To provide instructive guidance in this regard, we excerpt the highlights of landmark-type applicable court decisions. On tax evasion matters, the IRS provides little or no guidelines, other than to its own agents. The IRS's only concern is keeping its own agents out of jail for violating your constitutional rights. Otherwise, you — and your attorney — are on your own.

Basic Law: Section 7203

The basic law on willful tax evasion with which you should become quasi-familiar is Section 7203. Its official title is: ***Willful Failure to File Return, Supply Information, or Pay Tax.*** It consists of approximately 200 words. It identifies the key elements of what constitutes a misdemeanor. This is the "lesser penalty" than that which derives from criminal tax penalties. Yet, Section 7203 has tentacles to other tax crimes.

In our view, Section 7203 is one of those unique laws which are specifically directed at high tax-risk takers. The persons involved are knowingly taking a risk for which they hope they will not be detected. But, if detected, they acknowledge their error(s) and try not to repeat it/them. Instead, they go forward determined to "work the system" in every legal way they can. They are not hardened tax criminals; they are high-risk takers whose luck has run out.

The startoff wording in Section 7203 is: *Any person required to . . . .* This is what we call the "set-up phrase." It targets **any** individual, regardless of his or her organizational, fiduciary, or personal status, who is required to prepare a tax return of **any** kind. This "any person" doctrine applies to income tax returns, gift tax returns, death tax returns, trust tax returns, proprietorship tax returns, partnership tax returns. corporation tax returns, employer tax returns, excise tax returns, and any other type of tax return or tax information return addressed in the Internal Revenue Code. In short, there is no loophole escape from the all points inclusivity of the phrase: ***Any person required to*** . . . .

There are no IRS regulations expressly supplementing Section 7203. This means that the plain language of the law has to be used when contesting its application to a targeted person. The "plain language" technique is to focus on key phrases, then one by one apply them to the facts and circumstances at hand. This also means eliminating extraneous phrases which tend to cloud and confuse the basic requirements at issue.

Accordingly, the specifics of Section 7203 read:

> *Any person required . . . to pay any tax* [etc.] . . ., ***who willfully fails*** *to pay such tax, make such return, keep such records, or supply such information, at the time or times required . . ., shall, in addition to other penalties provided by law, be guilty of a misdemeanor and, upon conviction thereof, shall be fined not more than $25,000 ($100,000 in the case of a corporation), or imprisoned not more than 1 year, or both, together with the costs of prosecution.* [Emphasis added.]

There are four classes of willful failures to which Section 7203 applies. These are—

- failure to pay such tax, OR
- failure to make such return, OR
- failure to keep such records, OR
- failure to supply such information.

The term "such" refers to any applicable requirement in the Internal Revenue Code.

The phrase "in addition to other penalties" is self-explanatory. If civil penalties apply, they are neither negated nor superseded by Section 7203.

Meaning of "Willful Failure"

As listed above, there are four required acts preceded by the word "failure." In the text of Section 7203, the actual prefatory phrase is: *who willfully fails to*—(1) pay tax, (2) file return, (3) keep records, or (4) supply information. Thus, the whole premise of Section 7203 rests upon the interpretation of what constitutes willful failure . . . by *any person required.*

The short explanation is that willfulness is the **knowing omission** of a required act. In other words, the extent of one's *knowledge* as to the existence of any one of the four required acts is the first prerequisite to the willfulness issue. The second prerequisite is that having the foreknowledge, does the person *consciously omit* doing one or more of the required acts?

The landmark case on this willfulness issue is that of *J.L. Cheek*, 91-1 USTC ¶ 50,012. This was a 1991 Supreme Court case whose published findings and ruling approximated 6,000 words. Petitioner Cheek, an airline pilot, was charged with six counts of willfully failing to file a federal income tax return in violation of Section 7203. Although admitting that he had not filed his returns, Cheek testified that he did not act "willfully." He sincerely believed that his wages were not "income" and that he was not a "taxpayer," because the entire federal tax system was "unconstitutional."

Because this was a U.S. Supreme Court case, various erudite opinions were expressed. The more pertinent extracts for our purpose are as follows—

> Statutory willfulness, which protects the average citizen from prosecution for innocent mistakes made due to the complexity of the tax laws, is the **voluntary, intentional violation of a known legal duty**. . . .
>
> Claims that tax Code provisions are unconstitutional do not arise from innocent mistakes caused by the Code's complexity. Rather, they reveal full knowledge of the provisions at issue and a studied conclusion that those provisions are invalid and unenforceable. . . .
>
> Willfulness requires the Government to prove that the law imposed a duty on the defendant, that defendant knew of this duty, and that he voluntarily and intentionally violated that duty.

> We thus hold that in a case like this, a defendant's views about the validity of the tax statutes are irrelevant to the issue of willfulness. . . .

Meaning of "Willful Evasion"

There is a critical distinction between a willful *failure* to pay tax and the willful *evasion* of such tax. Whereas a "failure" involves the omission of a required act, "evasion" requires the commission of an affirmative act designed to conceal, or attempt to conceal, the required act. The distinction is a matter of punitive degree. Whereas willful failure is a misdemeanor, willful evasion is a felony. Willful tax evasion, *upon conviction thereof*, brings on a higher fine and increased jail time.

Whereas Section 7203 prescribes the punishment for a misdemeanor, Section 7201 prescribes the punishment for a felony. Section 7201 consists of approximately 70 words and is titled: ***Attempt to Evade or Defeat Tax***. This section reads essentially in full as—

> *Any person who willfully attempts in any manner to evade or defeat any tax imposed by* [the IR Code] *or the payment thereof, shall . . . be guilty of a felony and, upon conviction thereof, shall be fined not more than $100,000 ($500,000 in the case of a corporation), or imprisoned not more than 5 years, or both. . . .*

For better focus on the main distinction between a misdemeanor and a felony, we intentionally omitted from the felony citation above: *in addition to other penalties prescribed by law*, and, *together with costs of prosecution*. These two clauses are identical in Sections 7203 and 7201.

The key statutory clause—

> ***who willfully attempts in any manner to evade or defeat any tax imposed . . .***

is a clear indication that some affirmative act is required which seeks to "trick the system." In other words, an affirmative act is necessary to support a felony charge of willful tax evasion.

One of the clearest cases on point is that of *J.R. Williams*, 91-1 USTC ¶ 50,197. Here the defendant-appellant, Williams, filed a Form W-4: Employee's Withholding Allowance Certificate, claiming 50 exemptions. The W-4 was signed: ***Under penalties of perjury, I certify that—***. At the request of Williams, his W-4 form was kept on file by his employer for more than three years. Williams was a single person, entitled to only one exemption. Hence, claiming 50 exemptions was patently false. The only purpose for such a claim was "to evade or defeat" his correct tax.

The Court ruled that—

> Williams' offense is the willful failure to file a tax return [3 years in a row] **coupled with an affirmative act to conceal or mislead as to his tax liability.** Whereas the filing of the fraudulent W-4 was the affirmative act needed to enhance the crime to felony status, the failure to file a return was an essential part of his attempt to evade or defeat his tax liability. [Emphasis added.]

To summarize the distinguishing features of Sections 7203 and 7201, we present Figure 9.1. Keep foremost in mind that Figure 9.1 displays only the criminal tax penalties. Whatever civil penalties apply, apply *independently* of those in Figure 9.1.

Only "Upon Conviction Thereof"

Civil tax penalties can be proposed, assessed (finalized), and collected by the IRS without any court proceedings whatsoever. It has adequate authority within the Internal Revenue Code to do so.

It is a quite different story, when it comes to criminal tax penalties. Criminal penalties (fine, imprisonment, or both) are imposed by sentencing by a U.S. District Court, by a U.S. Appellate Court, or by the U.S. Supreme Court. The prosecutorial phase of the sentencing effort is under the jurisdiction of the Department of Justice (DOJ): **not** the IRS. However, the IRS conducts the investigations for formulating the Bill of Particulars (charges, allegations, counts), for transfer to the Tax Division of the DOJ. At the DOJ, the case is reformulated for trial. A lot of preparatory work is required before a criminal penalty matter can be submitted for trial. As per IRC Section 6531, the DOJ has **6 years** . . . *after*

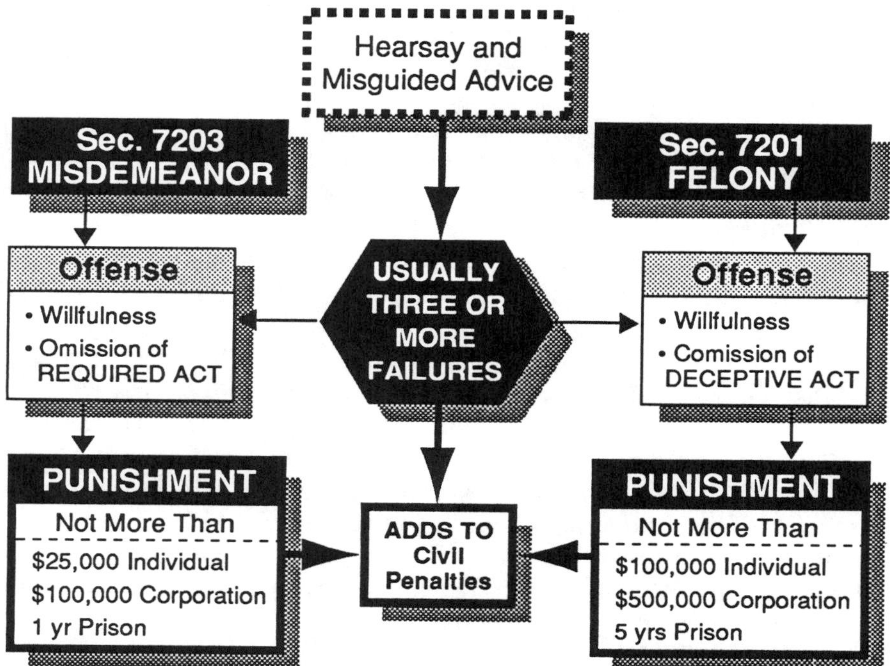

Fig. 9.1 - Differences Between Tax "Misdemeanor" and Tax "Felony"

the commission of the offense, within which to institute trial proceedings. The actual prosecutorial tasks at trial are conducted by U.S. Attorneys: **not** IRS attorneys.

As we have pointed out earlier, Section 7201 (felony) and 7203 (misdemeanor) both contain the identical phrase—

> . . . ***and, upon conviction thereof,*** *shall be* . . .

fined, or imprisoned, or both. Obtaining conviction is a rigorous process of its own. An example on point is the case of *R.W. Daniel*, 92-1 USTC ¶ 50,095; 956 F2d 540. He was charged with: ***Tax Evasion***; ***Failure to File*** (Sec. 7201).

Daniel operated a theater-seat installation business. He filed tax returns in the early years of his business, then stopped filing for three years in a row. Though notified by the IRS of his failures to file, he refused to file. He claimed that, based on his income and expenses, he was not required to file. After its investigation, the IRS determined that he owed $40,970 in taxes (*excluding* civil penalties and interest).

To convict someone under Section 7201, the government must show: (1) the existence of a tax deficiency, (2) willfulness, and (3) an affirmative act constituting an evasion or attempted evasion of the tax. The existence of a deficiency need only arise by "operation of law": not by any prerequisite that the IRS make an assessment and demand. In other words, the deficiency must arise from the taxpayer's own doing.

At trial, U.S. Attorneys introduced the following evidence against Daniel: [1] tax returns had been previously filed; [2] he stopped filing returns for a period of years; [3] business associates and accountants encouraged him to file; [4] he used other persons' credit cards for business and personal expenses; [5] he used cash extensively and converted checks to cash immediately; [6] he paid at least three employees in cash; [7] he changed the status of his employees to subcontractors; [8] he purchased investments under his second wife's name; [9] he titled several business-use vehicles in his son's name; [10] no checking or savings accounts were in his name; [11] more than $150,000 in large checks payable to his business were traced; and [12] for each of the three years at issue, he paid his insurance policies in cash.

A jury convicted Daniel on three counts (one count for each failure-to-file year) of income tax evasion. The court sentenced him to one year, four months incarceration; two years of supervised release; and ordered him to pay $154,343 in restitution to the U.S. On appeal, the amount of restitution was reduced to $40,970. This was the amount of tax deficiency, which is the amount of actual revenue loss to the U.S. Treasury. The difference of $113,373 (154,343 – 40,970) constituted civil penalties and interest. The $113,373 was collection enforceable by the IRS; the $40,970 was collection enforceable by the DOJ. The "costs of prosecution" (over $50,000) were also collection enforceable by the DOJ.

An oversimplified summary of the processing above is presented in Figure 9.2. The basic message there is that criminal penalties are established after conviction in U.S. District Court, whereas civil penalties are assessed by the IRS. Civil penalties,

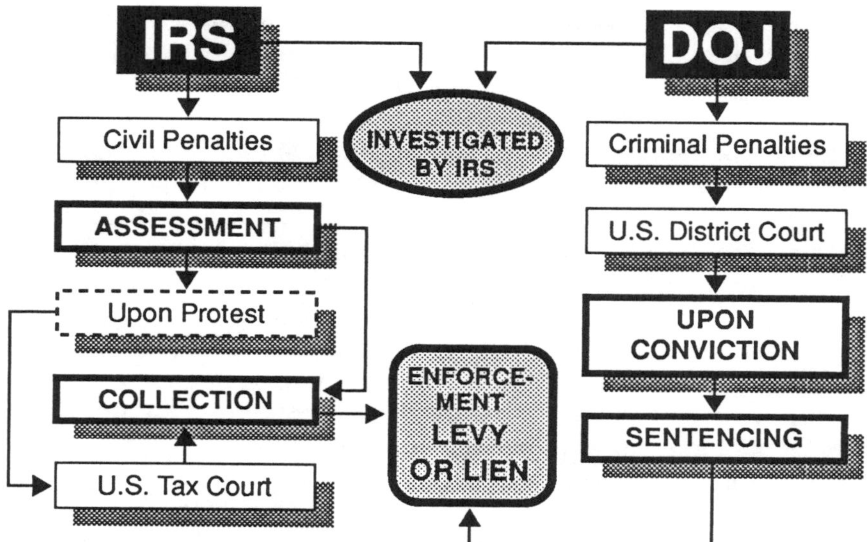

Fig. 9.2 - Process of Imposing Tax Penalties: Civil vs. Criminal

however, can be adjudicated in U.S. Tax Court, whereas criminal penalties cannot be heard in Tax Court.

Request a Plea Agreement

Prior to the *Daniel* case above, we had cited portions of the *J.R. Williams* case. We did not then tell you what that sentence was. Williams was convicted and sentenced to two concurrent 3-year periods of incarceration, and an additional suspended 3-year term, five years' probation, and a fine of $10,000. As a condition of his probation, Williams had to pay all outstanding tax deficiencies, civil penalties, and statutory interest.

There is one underlying message in the *Daniel* and *Williams* cases, and others similar. That message is, whatever the criminal sentence may be, the underlying tax, penalties, and interest are NOT WIPED AWAY! They continue to be due and owing to the IRS, irrespective of the amount of fine or jail time judicially imposed.

Realizing that all tax deficiencies and civil penalties have to be paid, suggests that an alternative to a full-blown criminal trial be sought. Indeed, such an alternative exists. It is called: *Plea*

Negotiation. The "negotiation" is conducted under the auspices of the Department of Justice. Before any consideration is given to a plea negotiation, legal papers have to be served upon the accused. The serving enables the accused person and his legal counsel to compare his factual evidence and knowledge of the circumstances with that which the DOJ alleges. The request for a plea agreement **must originate** through the attorney for the accused. IRS personnel are prohibited from suggesting or soliciting any such approach.

Before there is any serious consideration of your request for a plea agreement, the IRS must have sufficient evidence that the case is a "referable matter" to the DOJ for negotiation. For all practical purposes, this means that you prepare any required returns that have not been filed, and pay all taxes and interest due thereon. After sentencing, you'll have to pay the taxes and interest anyhow, so why not do so as part of the preparation for a plea agreement?

Contact a tax professional and get all required returns prepared. Do the best you can to reconstruct credible records of income, credible documentation of expenditures, and credible witnesses in your behalf. Once this information is assembled, arrange the financing to pay the tax and interest in full. Notify the DOJ and IRS agents in charge of your case, and request that they examine your returns. Disregard any IRS-imposed civil penalties for the time being. Include such penalties in your plea negotiation effort. Our Figure 9.3 presents a summary approach to the effort required.

If the DOJ agrees to consider your request for a plea agreement, your up-against-the-wall goal is to avoid any jail time. You could probably swallow a small fine, and any justifiable civil penalties. Do not expect too much from the DOJ and U.S. Attorneys. In criminal tax cases, government attorneys tend to be hostile, arrogant, sometimes malicious, and often unethical. If they sense blood, or get a narcotic rush from the kill, you will not get a plea agreement to your satisfaction. Even if not, your tax delinquencies and interest thereon are out of the way. This alone will save trial time and cost.

Pursue Good Faith Defense

If no plea agreement can be reached with which you are satisfied, your case will go to trial. The contestive issue will shift

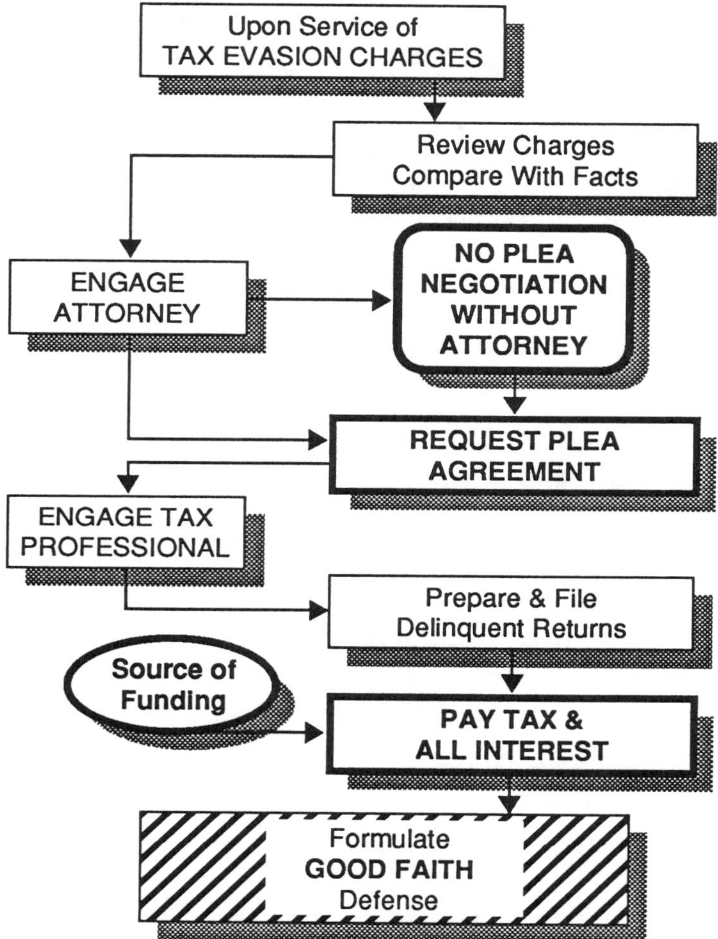

Fig. 9.3 - A Chance to Avoid Jail Time

from establishing your tax deficiency and failures, to why you did what you did. No matter what the real reason was, you — and your attorney — have got to come up with a plausible-sounding defense. You request a jury trial, plead not guilty, and try to present a good faith demeanor on the witness stand.

No matter how valid and verifiable your defense may be, the U.S. prosecutor will treat you belligerently. He will debase your character, belittle your plea, cast your defense into some evil motive, and portray you as a liar and tax cheat. Anticipate this and other despicable behavior from an adversary out to draw blood.

Whatever your defense, make it sound human and reasonable to a potentially sympathetic jury. Maybe you had some minor injury or disablement, some occupational setback, some family misfortune, son or daughter recently maimed, high blood pressure, prostrate (or breast) cancer, chronic lower back pain, tax laws too confusing and complex, too busy with other matters, hearing or eyesight difficulties, misguided advice from friends, . . . and so on. Surely you can come up with something that is not totally off the wall, that ties in with what you really did.

If you can't think of something reasonably plausible, take the position that you are a short-term tax protestor. Maybe you are, really. Assert that the tax laws are too cumbersome; that they favor wealthy persons and large corporations; that IRS agents are too threatening and abusive; and that your civil rights have been violated. (Discuss these items with your attorney.) Point out to the court and the jury that the only way to get your plight in the public record was to take the action that you did. It is a short-term protest to which you have a constitutional right. Your actions were not intended to be an ongoing pattern of willful tax evasion. Inform the court and jury that you have already paid the delinquent tax and interest. This fact alone should attest to the short-term nature of your protest.

Convictions have been averted or reversed by good faith positions genuinely held. Examples are:

- *W.P. Mann III*, CA-10, 89-2 USTC ¶ 9516; 884 F2d 532.
  - — good faith beliefs do not have to be rational, if irrational beliefs are truly held.
- *R.A. Pabisz*, CA-2, 91-2 USTC ¶ 50,316; 936 F2d 80.
  - — must consider whether beliefs are subjectively held in good faith, rather than being objectively reasonable.
- *R.G. Gaumer*, CA-6, 92-2 USTC ¶ 50,444; 972 F2d 723.

— cannot exclude evidence of an excerpt from the Congressional Record that would show a nexus between one's acts and his good faith belief.

A "Clever Scheme" Conviction

Ingenious schemes to "tweak" the tax system are exciting to speculate about. But, they seldom ever work. In a recent such case, *R. Huebner* [CA-9, 95-1 USTC ¶ 5008; 48 F3d 376], the accused was convicted on **12 counts** of willful tax evasion. It was not his own returns that he failed to file; he *aided and abetted* five tax protestors who, collectively, failed to file 12 tax returns.

Huebner's scheme was unique. He took advantage of the Bankruptcy Code to preempt the Internal Revenue Code. When a petition for bankruptcy is filed, the filing automatically requires that the IRS release any outstanding levies against a taxpayer/protestor. In the case at hand, all five protestors had IRS levies against their wages (Form 668-A: ***Notice of Levy***). When petition for bankruptcy is filed, the IRS must issue Form 668-E: ***Release of Levy***. This is a matter of jurisdictional precedence of long standing.

The Huebner scheme went like this. When a tax protestor received a Notice of Levy (against wages, bank accounts, etc.), Huebner — for a fee, presumably — would prepare and file a bankruptcy petition for such person. Simultaneously, he would prepare a promissory note of indebtedness to a fictitious creditor. The face amount of the note was set sufficiently large that, if actually paid, the protestor's income would be fully absorbed. There would be nothing left for the IRS to levy and collect on. Additionally, the note was backdated to precede the IRS's levy. This way, the levied amount would be mostly dischargeable in bankruptcy. The entire arrangement by Huebner was totally false and fraudulent.

At trial, the U.S. prosecutor conceded that: "There's nothing wrong with filing a bankruptcy petition to get a levy lifted." The prosecutor went on to point out that Huebner not only lied about the facts, he devoted special effort to fabricate documentary support. This constituted willful attempt ***in any manner*** to evade or defeat any tax . . . under Section 7201.

The Appeals Court (CA-9) concluded that—

> The case now before us does not involve concealment of assets, but does involve placing particular funds beyond the reach of the IRS levy. . . . The evidence is strong that the protestors do not intend voluntarily to pay their tax obligations. . . . Their actions are an attempt to evade willfully and defeat it by any means. . . . The convictions and sentences are AFFIRMED.

Altogether, there were eight defendant-appellants in the above case: Huebner, two associates, and five protestors. Huebner's sentence was the maximum: $100,000 fine and five years incarceration.

Form 656: Offer in Compromise

The *Huebner* case above raises a valid question about a taxpayer's ability to pay heavy fines, delinquencies, penalties, and interest. If one is incarcerated for five years, how is he going to pay a $100,000 fine? Even if one is not incarcerated, but is financially drained by contesting his delinquencies, penalties, etc., how does he pay? Does he file for bankruptcy? Or is there a better way?

Yes, there is a better way. It is called: ***Offer in Compromise***, Form 656.

An Offer in Compromise (OIC) is an authorized way to wipe your tax slate **nearly clean** of past wrongdoings. In addition to the 2-page **Form 656**, it requires the completion of a 6-page **Form 433-A**: Collection Information Statement for ***Individuals***, and, if applicable, a 6-page **Form 433-B**: Collection Information Statement for ***Businesses***. These must be accompanied by certifications: *Under penalties of perjury*, and the promise to be forthright and timely in your current and future tax obligations. The OIC procedure is a "light-at-the-end-of-the-tunnel" with certain strings. We depict the OIC procedural aspects in Figure 9.4. We do not intend to elaborate on these procedures; we just want you to be aware that they exist.

Offers in compromise are authorized under Section 7122 of the Internal Revenue Code. This approximately 1,000-word section is titled: ***Compromises***. Its subsection (a): ***Authorization***, reads in full as—

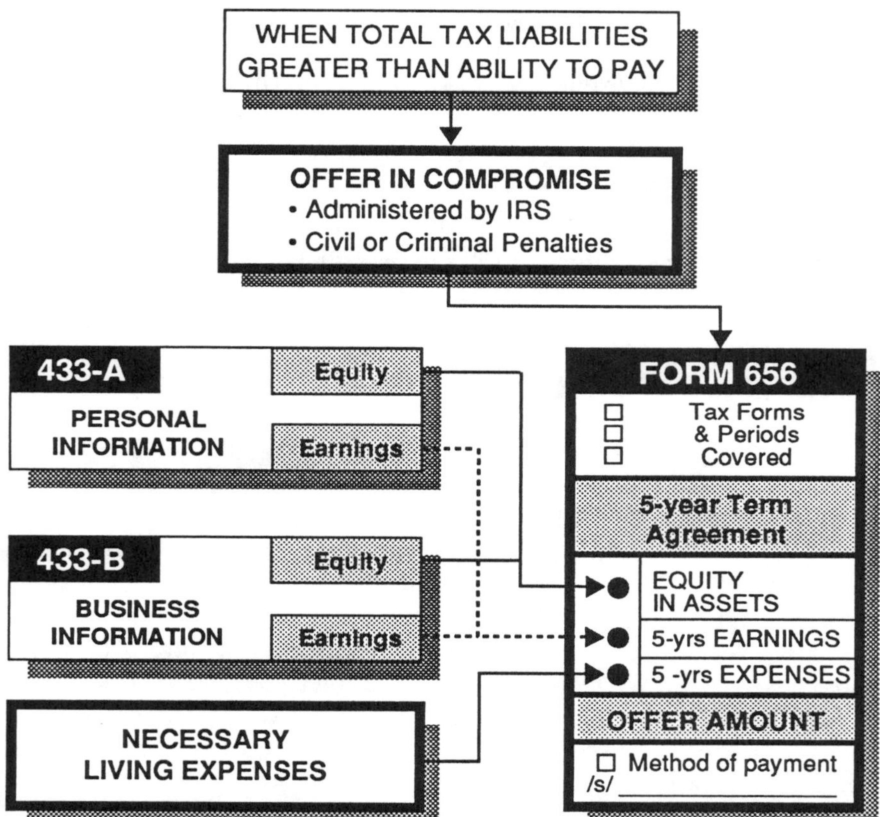

Fig. 9.4 - Relief Opportunity When Tax Debts Too Unbearable

> *The* [IRS] *may compromise* ***any civil or criminal case*** *arising under the internal revenue laws* ***prior*** *to reference to the* [DOJ] *for prosecution or defense;* ***and*** *the Attorney General or his delegate may compromise any such case* ***after*** *reference to the* [DOJ] *for prosecution or defense.* [Emphasis added.]

It is Congress's specific intent that the IRS — the Secretary of Treasury, actually — be given broad discretionary powers in its tax collection efforts. Congress wanted closure on long-pending tax delinquencies. In the Committee Hearings on P.L. 105-206 (the IRS Reform Act of '98), Congress said—

> *It is anticipated that the IRS will adopt a liberal acceptance policy for offers-in-compromise to provide an incentive for taxpayers to continue to file tax returns and continue to pay their taxes* [in a timely manner].

Before an offer can be seriously considered by the IRS, there must be in its possession a full and complete statement of the amount of tax assessed, all penalties and interest, verifiable financial statements, a "liquidity analysis" of the offerer, and a proffered cash sum of money on the line. If an offer is rejected, it can be amended and resubmitted. If it is rejected a second time, it can be appealed to the IRS Office of Appeals. Throughout the time that a good-faith offer is in process, no IRS levy will attach.

There is one final precautionary note: Section 7122 is not a tax giveaway. Each Form 656 contains a "must complete": ***Offer Amount Worksheet***. The worksheet requires separate totalization of [1] ***Equity in Assets***, and [2] ***Present and Future Income*** over a 5-year period. The whole idea behind Section 7122 is to provide reasonable relief from a lifetime of tax and penalty hardship.

For a quantitative perspective on such relief, here are recent statistics. In fiscal 1998, the IRS accepted 25,000 offers out of 105,000 Form 656 submissions. From these 25,000 offers, the IRS collected $290 million of the $1.9 billion outstanding [CCH Federal Standard Tax Reporter, '99 Vol. 16, ¶ 48,720A]. This is the collection of about 15^{+} cents on every dollar of tax, penalty, and interest owed. In the words of the IRS Commissioner—

> *It is better that we collect something rather than nothing, from taxpayers facing severe hardship.*

10

TRANSACTIONS IN CASH

If You Are In A Trade Or Business Selling "High Ticket" Items, There Will Come Offers To Pay In Full Green Cash. If The Amount Is Over $10,000 You Are Required To Prepare And File Form 8300 — A Currency INFORMATION Return. If The Customer Declines, Urge That He Exchange His Cash For A Bank Draft Or Cashier's Check From A Federally Regulated Financial Institution (Which Has To Prepare Form 4789). IN NO WAY Suggest How The Customer May Structure The Transaction To Avoid Forms 8300 Or 4789. If You Do, You Can Be Sentenced To Prison Time. Protect Yourself With A RELUCTANCE Towards Cash.

In the preceding chapter we introduced you to Section 7203. That section prescribed a misdemeanor penalty for willfully failing to file a return, supply information, or pay tax. We addressed all but the very last sentence in that 200-word section. Its last sentence reads—

> *In the case of a willful violation of any provision of section 6050I, the first sentence of this section shall be applied by substituting "5 years" for "1 year."*

Ordinarily, a tax misdemeanor involves one year or less jail time. But, here, we have an extension of that time. It is embodied in Section 6050I of the IR Code. What is Section 6050I, and what is so serious about it that warrants a five-year prison sentence?

The quick answer lies in subsection 6050I(a). Its title is: ***Cash Receipts of More Than $10,000.*** In other words, Section 6050I deals with large amounts of cash. It also includes smaller amounts as well. Section 6050I itself is titled: ***Returns Relating to Cash Received in Trade or Business, Etc.***

The implication is that all transactions in cash are illegal. This is **not** true! The further implication is that, if you transact more than $10,000 in cash, you are a criminal. There are a lot of legitimate reasons for handling cash. We present some examples below. Suspicion arises only because of the secretive manner in which cash is often handled.

In this chapter, therefore, we want to clear up some of the misconceptions re the criminality of dealing in cash, what the reporting requirements are, and the steps to take to avoid or minimize the penalties therewith. The cash transaction penalties cluster around the requirement to report or supply *correct information*. Both civil and criminal penalties apply. The distinguishing line between these two classes of penalties is $10,000. If the cash transaction amount is $10,000 or less, civil penalties **may** apply. If more than $10,000 criminal penalties **may** apply. The penalties apply only under specific circumstances.

Meaning of "Cash"

For purposes of Section 6050I, cash is not what you think it is. It is more than paper currency, U.S. or foreign. It is that which is defined by IRS Regulation ¶ 1.6050I-1(c)(1): ***Meaning of terms; Cash.***

This regulation defines "cash" as—

*(A) The **coin and currency** of the U.S. or of any other country, which circulate in and are customarily used and accepted as money in the country in which issued; and*

*(B) A **cashier's check** . . ., **bank draft, traveler's check**, or **money order** having a face amount of **not more** than $10,000—*

*(1) Received in a **designated reporting transaction** . . ., or*

> (2) *Received in any transaction in which the recipient knows that such instrument is being used in an attempt to avoid the reporting of the transaction . . . .*

A "designated reporting transaction" is a ***retail sale*** *(or the receipt of funds by a broker or other intermediary in connection with a retail sale) of—*
(A) A consumer durable,
(B) A collectible, or
(C) A travel or entertainment activity. [Emphasis added.]

The above regulatory detail is ostensibly focused on coin dealers, car dealers, jewelry dealers, pawn shops, boat dealers, loan and finance companies, real estate escrow accounts, attorney trust accounts, insurance companies, travel agencies, resort hotels, casino operators, sport shops, foreign exchangers, and a host of other retail activities where "cash is king." As this listing suggests, both property and services are covered.

Introduction to Section 6050I

Section 6050I (be sure to note the cap letter "I"; it is not a Roman numeral I) consists of approximately 800 words. It has seven subsections titled as follows:

Subsec. (a) Cash Receipts of more than $10,000

Subsec. (b) Form and Manner of Returns

Subsec. (c) Exceptions

Subsec. (d) Cash Includes Foreign Currency and Certain Monetary Instruments

Subsec. (e) Statements to be Furnished to Persons with respect to whom Information is Required

Subsec. (f) Structuring Transactions to Evade Reporting Requirement Prohibited

Subsec. (g) Cash Received by Criminal Court Clerks

Again, we want to state that the title to Section 6050I is: ***Returns Relating to Cash Received in Trade or Business, Etc.*** As the wording in this title suggests, the reporting emphasis is on **cash received**. Cash *expended* is not covered. The simple reason is that any cash expended is received by some other person, who has to do the reporting of cash received.

As is usual with all tax laws, subsection (a) covers the applicable general rule. Here, such rule reads—

> *Any person (1) who is engaged in a trade or business, and (2) who, in the course of such trade or business, receives more than $10,000 in cash in 1 transaction (or* ***2 or more related transactions****), shall make* ***the return described in subsection (b)*** *with respect to such transaction (or related transactions) at such time as the* [IRS] *may by regulations prescribe.* [Emphasis added.]

We'll tell you now that the IRS has prescribed approximately 10,000 words of regulations on the above. We'll cover the high points of Section 6050I and its regulations . . . but not everything.

For example, subsection (g) covers cash *bail* received by court clerks on behalf of persons charged with crimes of (A) drug trafficking, (B) racketeering, (C) money laundering, and (D) similar State offenses. These are clearly illegal activities. We are not going to cover these matters in any way whatsoever. We are only concerned with legal activities involving cash, and the proper reporting thereof.

The "Return Described"

Recall the second emphasized phrase in subsection (a) above: *the return described in subsection (b).* These words imply that there is a different type of return required, other than a tax return. Indeed, there is. It is an **information** return. No tax payments accompany it, though, separately, penalty payments may apply.

Subsection (b) reads straightforwardly as—

A return is described in this section if such return—

(1) is in such form as the [IRS] *may prescribe.*
(2) contains—
(A) the name, address, and TIN of the person from whom the cash was received,
(B) the amount of cash received,
(C) the date and nature of the transaction, and
(D) such other information as the [IRS] *may prescribe.*

The "TIN" is: **T**axpayer **I**dentification **N**umber. Ordinarily, this is one's Social Security Number (SSN) or Employer Identification Number (EIN). When dealing with cash transactions, attempts are made to avoid disclosing the transactor's SSN or EIN. In such case, the IRS can assign a TIN in order to facilitate its processing of an information return [IRC Sec. 6109]. If a TIN is requested of the transactor and there is no response, a notation to this effect on the "return described" will induce the IRS to probe further.

The particularly applicable IRS form number is identified in Regulation 1.6050I-1(c). It is **Form 8300**: ***Report of Cash Payments Over $10,000 Received in a Trade or Business***. This is a formidable form requiring up to about 60 information entries on its page 1 alone. Page 2 of the form requires about 15 additional entries for each separate person where more than one transactor person is involved. For familiarization purposes, we present the general arrangement of the form in Figure 10.1. Particularly note (in Part I) that some identifying document is required, such as a driver's license, passport, or other credential with a photo on it.

The 2,500-word instructions say that Form 8300 is to be filed—

> *By the 15th day* ***after the date the cash is received****. . . . If you receive more than one cash payment for a single transaction or* ***for related transactions****, you must report the multiple payments any time you receive a total amount that exceeds $10,000 within* ***any 12-month period****. Submit the report within 15 days of the date you receive the payment that causes the total amount to exceed $10,000.* [Emphasis added.]

Form 8300 | **Receipt of Cash Payments Over $10,000 Received in a Trade or Business**

Part I | **Identity of Individual From Whom Cash Received**

If more than 1 individual, check here, continue on page 2 ▶ ☐

Name, Address, Zip Code TIN: ____________

Date of Birth ____________ Occupation or business ____________

Document Used for Identity: ____________

Issued by ________ Date ________ Number ________

Part II | **Person on Whose Behalf Transaction Conducted**

If on behalf of more than 1, check here, continue on page 2 ▶ ☐

SAME AS PART I

- Also see instructions

Part III | **Description of Transaction & Method of Payment**

If cash received in more than 1 payment, check here ▶ ☐

SEE FIGURE 10.2

Part IV | **Business That Received Cash**

Name, Address, Zip Code EIN: ____________

Nature of business ____________ Phone No: ____________

● Under Penalties of Perjury . . .

____________ ____________ ____________
Signature Title Date

Fig. 10.1 - General Arrangement & Contents of Form 8300

In other words, for each person, group of persons, agent, or entity from whom you receive cash, you have to keep track of that cash for 12 months at a time. As long as the payments can be classed as "related transactions," they are all part of the same cash stream. This means that you have to keep a 12-month record of all *less than* $10,000 payments, until the total first exceeds $10,000. If and when it does, Form 8300 is mandated. Related cash payments received after the first report add to that report, until the 12-month period expires. You then have to file an *amended* combined report within 15 days of the end of the 12-month period. The descriptive details required are summarized in Figure 10.2. Figures 10.1 and 10.2 combined should convey the exhaustive amount of extracurricular activity required on your part.

Form 8300 Part III — **Description of Transaction & Method of Payment**

Date ________ Cash Received	Total ________ Cash Received	If More Than 1 Payment Received, Check ⟶ ☐

AMOUNT OF CASH RECEIVED (U.S.$ equivalent)

a. U.S. currency $________	c. Cashier's check(s) $________
(amount in $100 bills $________)	d. Money order(s) $________
b. Foreign currency $________	e. Bank draft(s) $________
(name of country ________)	f. Travelers check(s) $________

For items c, d, e, & f: Show issuers name(s) & serial number(s).

TYPE OF TRANSACTION

☐ Personal property purchased	☐ Debt obligations paid
☐ Real property purchased	☐ Exchange of cash
☐ Personal services provided	☐ Escrow or trust funds
☐ Business services provided	☐ Bail bond
☐ Intangible property purchased	☐ Other ________ *(specify)*

Describe, & give serial, registration, or docket number of each.

Fig. 10.2 - Descriptive Details of Cash Required on Form 8300

If you are in a trade or business in the U.S., you are mandated into being a "cash spy" for the IRS. You, of course, receive no compensation from the IRS for your extracurricular work. You get no thanks, either. Instead, you are treated as a conspirator in some illegal activity, such as money laundering, Mafia pursuits, or drug running. As such, you are subject to penalties for failure to file a correct and complete Form 8300 (where applicable).

Structuring to Avoid Reporting

Subsection (f) of Section 6050I is titled: ***Structuring Transactions to Evade Reporting Requirements Prohibited.*** The use of the word "evade" in this title is, we believe, stronger than necessary. It implies evil intent, where such may not be the case. For example, is a business that simply refuses to accept large cash sums trying to evade anything?

No; it is trying to avoid the thanklessness of Form 8300.

In some cash-attractive businesses, the practice is to refer the bearer of cash to a federally regulated financial institution (usually a bank or loan company). Said institution issues to the bearer an *exempt* cashier's check, money order, or bank draft. It does this **after** filing **Form 4789**: ***Currency Transaction Report*** (on the bearer of cash). The instructions to Form 8300 point out that a Form 4789 arrangement is not treated as a reportable transaction.

Nonreportable transactions are designated in Regulation ¶ 1.6050I-1(d): ***Exceptions to the reporting requirement.*** This regulation lists—

(1) Receipt of cash by certain financial institutions.
(2) Receipt of cash by casinos having gross annual gaming receipts in excess of $1,000,000.
(3) Receipt of cash not in the course of the recipient's ordinary trade or business.
(4) Receipt is made with respect to a foreign cash transaction.

Exception (3) exempts cash dealings over $10,000 which are outside of one's regular trade or business (a real estate agent selling a $12,000 motorboat, for example). Exception (4) exempts cash dealings of any amount (over $100,000 for example) which are formulated and consummated entirely outside the U.S. (such as delivering a small airplane to Mexico or to the Cayman Islands).

Other than the above exceptions, subsection (f): *structuring prohibited*, says—

> *No person shall for the purpose of evading the return requirements of* [Form 8300]—

(A) *cause or attempt to cause a trade or business to fail to file a return required,*

(B) *cause or attempt to cause a trade or business to file a return required that contains a material omission or misstatement of fact, or*

(C) *structure or assist in structuring, or attempt to structure or assist in structuring, any transaction with one or more trades or businesses.*

Although the term "structuring" is not defined by regulation, the focus of subsection (f) is quite clear. If a Form 8300 is otherwise required, any attempt to circumvent it is prohibited. This includes variant deviations to disguise the underlying transfer. Indeed, it is the element of disguise — the structuring part — that makes the prohibition criminal in nature, rather than civil. It is for this reason that subsection (f)(1)(C) is deemed the *money laundering* provision of Section 6050I.

Beware of Entrapment

Section 6050I(f) has become the most successful entrapment law in the entire Internal Revenue Code. The presumption is that the *origin* of cash amounts over $10,000 derives from some illegal source. Therefore, it is the source of the cash, not the recipient, that Form 8300 is primarily directed toward. It is, after all, an *information* return: not a tax return. But to get at the source, the IRS must entrap the recipient in order to enforce the preparation and completion of the form. For a recipient in a nonfinancial trade or business, Form 8300 is a BIG HASSLE. Verify this yourself, with an official copy of the form and its instructions.

An excellent instructive example of structuring entrapment by the IRS is the case of *P.C. McLamb*, CA-4, 93-1 USTC ¶ 50,143; 95 F2d 1284. McLamb was a licensed car dealer aware of Form 8300, but unaware of subsection (f)(1)(C): the structuring prohibition. One day, a female customer came into the showroom to buy a new van costing $13,930. She told the salesman that she had a poor credit rating, and had to pay in cash. When the legal papers were drawn up, she gave the salesman a stack of $100 bills (plus smaller ones) to cover the full amount. When the salesman showed the cash to McLamb, he instructed the salesman to write out a check from his personal account for $4,030 to the dealership, in return for handing the salesman $4,030 in cash. McLamb then deposited $9,900 cash plus the $4,030 check (totaling $13,930) into his dealership's business account. Subsequently, he accounted for and paid all tax on the $13,930 transaction. However, he did not prepare and file Form 8300.

Sometime later, the IRS became aware of the above transaction. It set out to entrap McLamb. A special IRS agent using a fictitious name and wearing a hidden tape recorder was assigned to the task. The undercover agent visited McLamb's dealership and expressed an interest in buying a $31,375 vehicle. For reasonable sounding reasons, the IRS agent offered to pay all cash. To which McLamb responded (to the effect that)—

> "I run a straight up business here. But handling that amount of cash can get us both into trouble. The better way to do it is to pay roughly $9,000 in cash and either finance the balance or purchase three separate cashier's checks in sub-$10,000 amounts to cover the balance. Otherwise, I have to report you to the IRS. I'll report the full $31,375 proceeds in my business, so that I am clean. I prefer not to lose you as a customer."

The next day, the undercover IRS agent came back with three sub-$10,000 cashier's checks. He left the cash balance in his car, not knowing exactly how much was needed. After all papers were drawn up, McLamb told the undercover agent that he would need $7,000 in cash to close the transaction.

Ostensibly, departing McLamb's office to go get the cash, the undercover agent signaled three other IRS agents outside. They entered McLamb's office and handed him a search warrant. They seized all of his car sales records, including the sham transaction that was in process of closing.

Subsequently, McLamb was criminally charged with multiple counts of violating Section 6050I(f). The jury returned guilty verdicts on two counts, namely: subsection (f)(1)(A) — failure to file Form 8300 on the $13,930 car sale, and subsection (f)(1)(C) — money laundering arising from the $31,375 sham transaction. Since there was no underreporting of McLamb's tax accountable income, and no discrepancies in his business tax returns could be found, there was no failure-to-pay tax. As a result, no monetary fines were imposed. Nevertheless, McLamb was sentenced to serve two concurrent prison terms of 60 months (5 years) each. The sentence was appealed . . . but was upheld.

The McLamb case illustrates quite vividly — and rather harshly, we think — the entrapment feature of Section 6050I. From a purely business point of view, McLamb reported all of his car sales income, including cash receipts. He filed all of his income tax returns and paid his tax when due. He was simply trying to avoid antagonizing his customers, and was trying to save himself the thankless task of preparing Forms 8300. For this, he gets five years' jail time. What a system!

Safest Course: Form 4789

It is not a very gratifying role being a cash snitch for the IRS. If you are too willing, it can give the impression that you are trying to curry favor with that agency. This can lead to the suspicion that you are trying to cover up your own wrongdoing. Consequently, protecting yourself against IRS suspicions is your first priority with respect to Form(s) 8300. This means that you pursue for your own trade or business a policy of *cautious reluctance* against any large transactions in cash.

If the nature and retail level of your business is such that you experience two or more over-$10,000 cash offers per year, you may want to think through how best to handle such affairs. We suggest you communicate with your own financial institutions which carry your business accounts. Inquire about their procedures for completing Form 4789: ***Currency Transaction Report.*** This form is very similar in format and content to Form 8300. The difference is that Form 4789 is prepared by a financial institution, whereas Form 8300 is prepared by any person in a trade or business.

For Form 4789 purposes, a "financial institution" is a bank, depository institution, broker/dealer in securities, money transmitter, currency exchanger, check casher, issuer/seller of money orders and traveler's checks, electronic transferor/transferee, or issuer/seller of bank drafts, cashier's checks, and negotiable instruments. Such an institution must file Form 4789 for each deposit, withdrawal, exchange of currency, or other payment or transfer **by, through, or to** the financial institution which involves a transaction in currency of more than $10,000.

Our position is that a commercial financial institution is more discreet than an ordinary business owner, when handling large amounts of cash. Your customer may feel more comfortable, and may feel that his identity and source of funds may be more confidential when dealing with a depository institution than with you. You, too, may feel more comfortable.

Consequently, we urge that you recommend to your large-cash customers that they obtain a cashier's check or other negotiable instrument from a depository institution of their choice. Insist that when (if) they return with the check, they also provide an authenticated statement from the institution that Form 4789 has been filed. As a preparatory guide towards this end, have a batch of Forms 4789 on hand. Give your potential customer a blank copy of Form 4789 so that he knows ahead of time what to expect.

As indicated earlier, a cashier's check drawn on a federally regulated financial institution, when received in your trade or business, is exempt from the return requirements of Form 8300. A list of regulatory authorities overseeing financial institutions is presented in Figure 10.3 Let the institutions use these authorities to protect you from any IRS suspicions of your activities.

Suspicious Transactions

What is a suspicious transaction?

Answer: It is a series of sub-$10,000 transactions, apparently related, by one or more persons with two or more recipient entities. The "suspicion" arises because of the extraordinary effort required to conceal the identity and source of the cash. The suspicion may also arise from circumstantial evidence that suggests attempts to evade the return requirements of Forms 8300 and 4789. Most suspicious transactions are reported by financial institutions to their federal regulator in Figure 10.3. Whether such suspicions are justified or not depends on what some U.S. District Court and jury may find. Instructive in this regard are the following excerpts from two actual court cases on point.

NAME	Acronym	Code
Comptroller of Currency	OCC	1
Federal Deposit Insurance Corporation	FDIC	2
Federal Reserve System	FRS	3
Office of Thrift Supervision	OTS	4
National Credit Union Administration	NCUA	5
Securities & Exchange Commission	SEC	6
Internal Revenue Service	IRS	7
U.S. Postal Service	USPS	8

FORM 4789	Part III
Financial Institution Where Transaction Takes Place	
REGULATOR CODE →[ ]	

Fig. 10.3 - Federal Regulators to Whom Financial Institutions Must Report

The case of *M.A. Simon*, CA-2; 96-2 USTC ¶ 50,358; 85 F3d 906, illustrates how the method of structuring can provide ample circumstantial inference of willfulness. Here, Simon was a licensed stockbroker in New York City. In a period of one week's time, he made 14 deposits of sub-$10,000 amounts in eight different branches of the same bank throughout the area. Specifically, the 14 separate deposits were for the amounts of: $9,730; $9,620; $9,000; $8,800; $9,900; $9,900; $9,920; $9,900; $9,900; $9,700; $9,600; $9,920; $9,920, and $5,400 (total: $131,210).

At trial, Simon conceded that he structured the deposits to ". . . avoid filling out that special $10,000 form." He denied that he knew such structuring was illegal, nor did he know that the bank was obligated to report all structuring deposits. Nevertheless, the court concluded that—

> The extensive effort Simon took in structuring his deposits amply supports a reasonable inference that he was attempting to hide his structuring activities because he knew his conduct was unlawful. His conviction and sentence are AFFIRMED.

In contrast to the above, the case of *C.J. Leak*, CA-4, 97-2 USTC ¶ 50,623 addresses subsub-$10,000 deposits that appeared suspicious, but had a valid reason. Leak was the owner of a nightclub in a high-crime area. In a period of about six months' time, he deposited 33 checks ranging in amounts of from $2,500 to $5,000 each, at various branches of three different banks. Subsequent to the deposits, he wrote a check on each of the three banks for approximately $50,000 each. He used the three checks to pay off the mortgage on his home and to buy a car. When the checks cleared, each bank reported what it thought was suspicious behavior to the same federal regulator. The regulator (not the IRS) had the U.S. Marshal seize the home and car.

At trial, Leak testified that he had "absolutely no knowledge whatsoever of any requirement of the bank to file a special form with the IRS" when the deposits exceeded $10,000 in cash. He further testified that his primary concern was his personal safety and security. His business was in a high-crime area where muggings and robbery were frequent. He denied that he was trying to conceal his deposits. His only desire was to foil would-be thugs who might trail him from his late-night business to his home, and the next day from home to his bank. The District Court held that Leak's claims were "too incredible to be believed," and ruled that his home and car were to be forfeited to the U.S. The forfeiture ruling was appealed.

The Appeals Court held that—

> The evidence proffered in this case . . . Leak's sworn denials and explanations . . . raises a genuine issue of material fact. Accordingly, this case is REVERSED AND REMANDED.

11

FRIVOLOUS & FALSE RETURNS

There Is Little Credible Justification For The Filing Of Frivolous Returns, Shelter Returns, Or False & Fraudulent Returns. A Frivolous Filer Does So To Express A Grievance By Delaying Or Impeding The Tax Process. A Shelter Filer Is More Motivated By The Expected Tax Benefits Than By Financial Gain. A False Filer Signs The Jurat Clause Knowing Full Well That His Return Is NOT "True, Correct, And Complete." Such A Filer And Those Who CONSPIRE With Him Are Subject To Fines Up To $100,000 And/Or 3 Years In Prison. Petitioning For Bankruptcy, Sending Money Offshore, Or Expatriating To A Foreign Country, Does No Good.

There is a lot of injustice in our tax system. Many individual and small-business taxpayers feel that too much tax money goes to corporate welfare, foreign aid (funneled through corrupt officials), and pork barrel projects within the U.S. sponsored by key members of Congress. Congress, it seems, doesn't use a clear head towards simplifying matters that could be simplified, nor clarifying ambiguities that could be clarified. Instead, Congress is perpetually adding complexity to the Internal Revenue Code which, to many, disguises the "loopholes" for the favored few. As a result, many taxpayers are frustrated to the point where they take some matters into their own hands. They use their tax returns improperly for political ends.

Trying to right a perceived wrong in the tax system involves one of three types of activities. These filing activities are:

- The filing of *frivolous* returns.
- The filing of *shelter* returns.
- The filing of *false* returns.

This listing order indicates the increasing frustration risk taken by such returns. The higher the risk, the more serious the penalties, and the more difficult it becomes to extricate one's self from the consequences thereof.

For each of the above filings, a specific basic penalty applies. Additionally, associated peripheral penalties may apply. The respective basic penalty sections are:

Sec. 6702 — Frivolous Income Tax Return
Sec. 6701 — Aiding & Abetting Understatement of Tax
Sec. 7206 — Fraud & False Statements

In this chapter, we want to review these penalties, indicate their deterrent purpose, and point out via selected court cases what your chances are of contesting them. When you get into the domain of a false return, whether intentional or not, there are a couple of legal defenses that might work in your favor. Whatever your frustration is with the system, do not stake your fortune on any easy penalty relief. Your best hope is that your proffered return be deemed a NONRETURN by the IRS. If you are so fortunate, take the opportunity to file an amended return to correct your errors and wrongdoings.

Frivolous Return Defined

A frivolous tax return is purported to be a return, but isn't. In most instances a Form 1040 or 1040A is filed on time and properly signed. In one sense, the return is mischievous, pure and simple. In another sense, it is a protest return, sincere and determined. In either case, the objective is to vent one's frustration by gumming up the tax works in a way that delays and impedes return processing by the IRS. Usually, the filer expects to pay the tax somewhere down the line. But he wants to make the IRS "work" for it.

Various tactics (some are clever) are used to disorient the IRS. They fit into well worn patterns of mischief over the years. Among these tactical patterns are the use of:

(1) irregularly shaped and physically altered official forms (parts cut off, bends, and tears).

(2) blank forms, other forms with every line showing "-0-" or "none," and other forms only partially complete, making it impossible to establish the correct tax.

(3) incorrect tax tables, exemption credits, filing status, and inconsistent treatment on one part of a return with that required on another part.

(4) computation made on "gold standard," "war tax" credits, wages not taxable because not paid in federal reserve notes, and that green paper dollars have no inherent worth beyond about one-half cent.

(5) spurious constitutional arguments based on involuntary servitude, self-incrimination, double jeopardy, taking without just compensation, right of privacy, freedom of expression, and so on.

The most common frivolity is altering, or striking out, portions of the jurat clause: *Under penalties of perjury . . . .* Many do so because they really do not understand what the clause means. It is **not** explained in the instructions accompanying Form 1040 or 1040A. The instructions simply say: *Form 1040 is not considered a valid return unless you sign it.* There is no explanation of what constitutes "perjury" for tax purposes (it's a criminal offense), and there is no explanation as to what degree of correctness you are swearing to. The signer is told: *If you have someone prepare your return, you are still responsible for the correctness of the return.*

Any "tampering" with the jurat clause, or any unsigned returns, are sent back by the IRS as unacceptable. An immediate frivolous penalty is assessed, plus failure-to-file, filing-late, or failing-to-pay penalties are imposed.

One District Court case on point is interesting: *L.P. McCormick*, 94-1 USTC ¶ 50,026. McCormick filed a true, correct, and complete return, and signed the jurat clause without change. Below his signature he added the words: "Under protest." In its knee-jerk, anti-protestor reaction, the IRS treated the return as a nullity. It charged McCormick penalties for frivolous filing and for a late return.

The court asked itself the question: "May a taxpayer protest when filing a federal tax return?" The answer is "Yes." "A taxpayer need not suffer in silent acquiescence to a perceived injustice," the court said. The court then had to educate the IRS on the meaning of the first amendment of the Constitution. If "Congress shall make no law" . . . prohibiting the right of petition and protest, the IRS could not do so either. The court concluded that McCormick's words "under protest" did not alter the meaning of the jurat clause. It ordered the IRS to reinstate the return as being timely filed and not frivolous.

Frivolous Return Penalty: $500

The penalty for filing what the IRS asserts to be a frivolous return is a flat $500. It is an *immediate* penalty: payable now! It is not based on tax liability; no advance notice by the IRS is given. The penalty cannot be appealed within the IRS. It must be paid, then judicial review sought only in a U.S. District Court or in the U.S. Court of Claims.

The tax law on point is Section 6702: ***Frivolous Income Tax Returns***. Its subsection (a): ***Civil Penalty***, reads in pertinent part—

> *If . . . any individual files what purports to be a return . . . which contains . . .* [insufficient information or incorrect information]*; and the conduct* [of such] *is due to—*
>
> *(A) a position which is frivolous, or*
>
> *(B) a desire . . . to delay or impede the administration of . . . tax laws, then such individual shall pay a penalty of $500.*

The subsection 6702(b): Penalty in Addition to Other Penalties, goes on to say—

The penalty imposed by subsection (a) shall be in addition to any other penalty provided by law.

When Congress enacted this penalty in 1982 [P.L. 97-248], it said—

The penalty of $500 would apply only on documents purporting to be returns that are patently improper and not in cases involving valid disputes with the IRS, or in cases involving purely inadvertent mathematical or clerical errors.

Thus, if you want to contest the penalty, you must do so on one of two justifiable causes, or both. Cause 1 is a valid tax dispute; Cause 2 is an inadvertent error, mathematical or clerical.

Statistically, for every 600 persons who seek recision of the penalty, only one prevails. In 599 of 600 cases, the IRS presents the court a copy of the "purported return" . . . and wins! It even wins when a corrected amended return is filed. An amended return cannot cancel the original frivolous return [*R.P. Lydon, Jr.*; DC, NH; 84-2 USTC ¶ 9670]. Filing a frivolous amended return results in TWO $500 penalties: one for the original, one for the amended [*R.B. Branch*, CA-8; 88-1 USTC ¶ 9317]. Filing a correct return unsigned is deemed frivolous because it impedes its processing [*E. Johns*, DC, HN; 84-2 USTC ¶ 9899].

The one (out of 600) winner was *J.H. Hoefker*, DC, KY; 86-1 USTC ¶ 9260. Although his return was correct and complete, he did not sign it. He testified that he simply did not understand the intent of the jurat clause. Hoefker interpreted the clause as being a sworn oath that everything on the return was positively accurate and complete. Because of the complexity of the tax laws, he did not feel that confident that everything was perfectly accurate. Besides, the IRS made no attempt to return the unsigned form, with an admonition that it must be signed in order to process it. The court held that the frivolous penalty was improperly imposed, and ordered that the $500 be refunded by the IRS.

Frivolous "Position" Penalty: $25,000

Emboldened by its 99% win on frivolous return cases, the IRS extends its assertions of frivolity and delay to many return filers who have valid tax disputes. As we all know, there are many ambiguities in tax law. If one's position — legal position, that is — for interpreting an ambiguity is based on flaky grounds, the IRS invokes the frivolous position penalty. Even so, the percentage of wins by the IRS on the penalty portion drops to 60% and below.

When a return is accepted for processing, it goes through, first, a mathematical check, then an out-of-norm check. This is where particular entries on your return appear to be unusual relative to the great majority of taxpayers in your similar income level. When an out-of-norm item is found, the return is flagged for examination and audit. After the audit, an "examination change" is prepared stating the amount of tax, penalties, and interest to be additionally paid. If you do not immediately acquiesce, you are sent a Notice of Deficiency. At this point, your only contestive option is to petition the U.S. Tax Court for a review of the deficiency findings.

The frivolous position penalty — up to $25,000 — is intended to deter meritless arguments and delays during Tax Court proceedings. The law on point is Section 6673: ***Sanctions and Costs Awarded by Courts.*** The meat of this section is in its subsection (a)(1): ***Tax Court Proceedings; Procedures Instituted Primarily for Delay, Etc.***

Subsection 6073(a)(1) reads—

Whenever it appears to the Tax Court that—

(A) proceedings before it have been instituted or maintained by the taxpayer primarily for delay,
(B) the taxpayer's position in such proceeding is frivolous or groundless, or
(C) the taxpayer unreasonably failed to pursue available administrative remedies,

the Tax Court, in its decision, may require the taxpayer to pay to the U.S. a penalty not in excess of $25,000.

Dilatory tactics, failure to cooperate with the IRS, failure to cite errors in the deficiency notice, failure to identify the law on which you rely, and failure to appear in court, are some of the indicators of a groundless legal position. These are cases where the IRS wins, hands down.

On the other hand, a half-way (at least) serious position based on a specific ambiguous provision in law is not cause for the penalty. As the case of *C.L. Troyer*, TC Memo 1989-218 illustrates, you do not have to win the tax issue to avoid the penalty. Troyer attempted to convert his for-profit business into a nontaxable entity by establishing his own private church. He lost the tax issue. The court did not assert the penalty because it felt that Troyer was testing the elements for establishing a legitimate nontaxable entity.

The frivolous position and frivolous delay penalty are a touchy matter with the IRS. At the slightest pretext, it will too often assert the $25,000 penalty . . . when it has no real basis for doing so. It is too bad that our tax system does not apply the penalty in reverse, when the IRS loses.

In Figure 11.1, we present a synopsis of the indicators of when the penalty would apply, and when it would not likely apply. Our point is that, if you are going to proceed into Tax Court, be sure you have a valid tax issue to dispute.

Shelter Return Defined

For our purposes, a "shelter" return is a bogus arrangement which follows the letter of the law, but not the spirit. The "arrangement" is a sham: no economic, arm's-length substance prevails. The arrangement is strictly tax motivated and self-serving. For a setup charge, some unrelated party promotes the arrangement and provides the documentation. It all looks legal and convincing.

For IRS processing purposes, a shelter return is not frivolous. It is only after the out-of-norm screening and subsequent audit that the shallowness of the arrangement comes to light. No bona fide business transaction actually took place. The IRS generically classifies all such artifices as: *abusive tax shelters*. In addition to imposing penalties on the return filer, the IRS has authority to penalize the promoter(s).

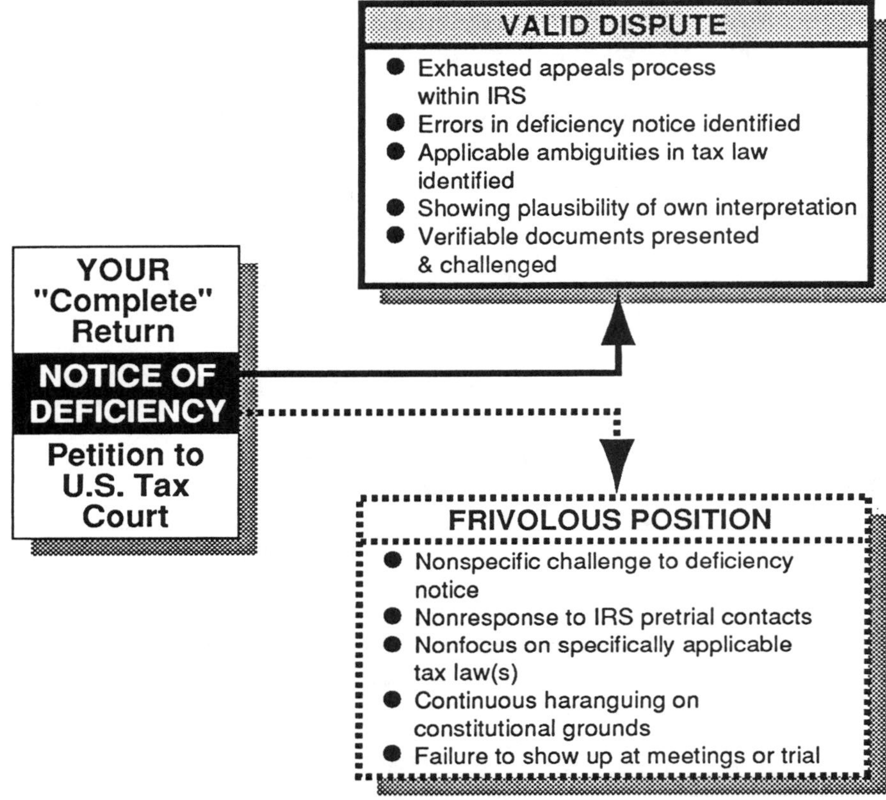

Fig. 11.1 - Valid Tax Dispute vs. Frivolous Position in Tax Court Proceeding

In a typical shelter return, the "hook" centers around one of six types of arrangements. Such arrangements are—

- Leveraged tax shelters
- Church oriented schemes
- Family estate trusts
- Pure business trusts
- Tax motivated shams
- Exotic sounding ventures

All have the same end goal of tax avoidance to the nth degree. They have some of the characteristics of a frivolous return, but they are far more sophisticated. They are well researched in that they follow the tax law to the letter. Their defect is that no real-world business activities take place. It's all on paper: nothing on substantive fact. Most boil down to a super-sales job of con artistry. International, as well as national, con artists do the "promoting." They base their operations in a "boiler room" beyond the reach of local law.

A recent noncourt case, of which the author herein has first-hand knowledge, will illustrate our point. The taxpayer — we'll call him ABB (his real initials) — purchased 1000 cubic yards of mineral aggregate in what was purported to be a California gold mining project, incorporated. ABB paid $5,000 and signed a promissory note for $20,000 which, purportedly, was money advanced to him to pay the full purchase price of $25,000 for the mineral aggregate. The mining agreement provided that the value of any gold and silver mined would first be used to pay off the note. The promoter instructed ABB on how to set up his own Schedule C (Form 1040): ***Profit or Loss from Business***, and on how to deduct the $25,000 as a mining development expense under IRC Sections 616 and 617: ***Mining Exploration and Development Expenditures***.

On paper, the arrangement was flawless. The only problem was: there was never any mine; never any mining lease; never any mineral aggregate; never any mining equipment; and, to top it all off, the alleged mining company had filed for bankruptcy. The whole arrangement was a total sham. In the meantime, ABB took a $25,000 Schedule C writeoff on his tax return.

Subsequently, ABB's return was IRS audited. It was the IRS who informed him that he was the victim of a sham. Consequently, his $25,000 writeoff was disallowed. He got no credit whatsoever for the $5,000 (documented with canceled check) he truly advanced. Altogether, ABB not only lost his $5,000, he had to pay $7,500 in deficiency tax (for the disallowed writeoff), plus a $2,500 accuracy-related penalty. His total loss came to approximately $15,000.

Tax shelter promoters are very clever. With professional help, they prepare an impressive prospectus. They induce (with high fees) some prestigious law firm or accounting firm (whose name is prominently displayed) to review the offering and make a statement thereon. It ends with the prospective investor being cautioned to contact his own tax advisor.

Shelter Promoter Penalties

There are two tax code sections that impose penalties on tax shelter promoters, and their aiding and abetting activities, for understating an investor participant's tax. The two sections are—

Sec. 6700 — Promoting Abusive Tax Shelters, Etc.
Sec. 6701 — Aiding & Abetting Understatement of Tax Liability.

In abbreviated text, the essence of Section 6700 is that—

Any person who organizes (or assists in the organization of) . . . [any] *entity, plan, or arrangement . . . and participates (directly or indirectly) in the sale of any interest* [therein], *and . . . causes another person . . . to* [claim] *a tax benefit by reason of holding an interest in the . . . entity, plan, or arrangement . . . shall pay . . . a penalty equal to $1,000 or . . . if lesser, 100% of the gross income derived from . . . each sale* [of an interest therein].

Similarly, in abbreviated text, the essence of Section 6701 is that—

Any person who—

(1) aids or assists in, procures, or advises with respect to, the preparation or presentation of any portion of a return . . . or other document,
(2) knows (or has reason to believe) that such portion will be used in connection with any material matter arising under the internal revenue laws, and
(3) knows that such portion (if so used) would result in an understatement of the liability for tax of another person,

shall pay a penalty with respect to each such document . . . $1,000 . . . or if the return or document relates to the tax liability of a corporation . . . $10,000.

The long and short of these two penalties is that they are NOT a severe deterrent to promoters (aiders and abetters) of sham tax shelters. By the time the IRS catches up with them — it takes three to five years to do so — the scam artists have filed for bankruptcy . . . and have gotten their money out of the U.S. The net result is that they may pay in penalties only about 10% of their gross take. The 11,000-word ruling of *Tax Refund Litigation* [TRL]; CA-2, 93-1 USTC ¶ 50,173; 989 F2d 1290, illustrates our point.

In *TRL*, there were seven general partners (principals) who formed, promoted, and sold investment interests in 95 interlocking limited partnerships. The scheme, ostensibly, was to lease to the investors special printing equipment for the republishing of rare and classical books. For $50,000, an investor would get a tax writeoff of from $62,500 to $75,000 over a 2-year period. There were 35 investors in each of the 95 limited partnerships: 3,325 investors overall. The gross take by the seven principals totaled $166,250,000 (3,325 x $50,000 per investor). No actual printing equipment was ever acquired or put in place. Upon discovery of this scam, the IRS assessed the seven principals a total of $29,668,000 in Section 6700 penalties.

After 10 years of litigative wrangling, the Appeals Court reduced the assessable penalties to $15,800,000. This netted the swindlers a cool $150,450,000 [166,250,000 – 15,800,000]. After attorney fees and court costs, our guess is that each of the principals netted nearly $20,000,000 (that is, 20 *million* dollars). Our further guess is that each principal had tucked away at least 10 million dollars in an offshore tax haven.

False Return Defined

A false return is one for which the underlying documents supporting the entries, or the entries themselves, are unequivocally false. On its surface, the return is true, correct, and complete. Below its surface, false statements and fraudulent intent can be uncovered. It is not a tax evasion issue like not filing or not paying; it is a falsification issue when filing and paying.

For example, if an item of one's true tax-accountable income is $10,762 and the return shows $2,762 — that is a falsity. Similarly, if a legitimate deductible item is $538 and the return shows $6,538 — this, too, is a falsity. Since anything and everything on a return is subject to verification, the factual extent of falseness is determinable. The relevant questions are: Was the falsity willfully done? Was it negligently done? Or, was it inadvertently done?

Statutorily, there are five characteristics of a false return. Any *one* of the five — **not** all five — is a required showing. The five targeted wrongdoings are:

1. Making a false declaration under penalty of perjury.
2. Aiding or assisting in the preparation of a return which is false as to any material matter.
3. Simulating or falsely executing any entry or document required by the IRS.
4. Removing or concealing property which has been levied upon (for tax collection enforcement).
5. Falsifying, destroying records, or making false statements in connection with an offer in compromise.

Each of the above is a separate offense of its own. Furthermore, each is a felony, punishable by fine or imprisonment, or both.

Each of the above offenses is formalized in a separate paragraph in Section 7206: ***Fraud and False Statements.*** The punch line of the 350-word tax code section is—

> *Any person who . . .* [does any of the above] *. . . shall be guilty of a felony and, upon conviction thereof, shall be fined not more than $100,000 ($500,000 in the case of a corporation) or imprisoned not more than three years, or both, together with the costs of prosecution.*

Jurat Clause & Perjury

If you have ever wondered what the jurat clause, *Under penalties of perjury . . .* on Form 1040 means, we now have the answer for you. For each individual who falsely signs the form, there is (potentially) a $100,000 fine and/or three years imprisonment. For a joint husband and wife return, there are **two** such penalties. Furthermore, the penalty applies to each year that a false return is filed. This is the substance of Section 7206(1): ***Declaration Under Penalties of Perjury.***

Paragraph (1) of Section 7206 reads in full as—

> *Any person who—*
>
> *Willfully makes and subscribes any return, statement, or other document, which contains or is verified by a written declaration that it is made under the penalties of perjury, and which he does not believe to be true and correct* ***as to every material matter***
>
> . . . *shall be guilty of a felony* [etc.]. [Emphasis added.]

We have selected two particularly interesting court rulings to exemplify the meaning of paragraph (1).

The first case is that of *R.K. Borman*; CA-7, 93-2 USTC ¶ 50,428; 992 F2d 124, a married taxpayer. The Bormans were charged with six counts of perjury: one count for each spouse, for each of three years. They filed a joint Form 1040A instead of joint Form 1040. Whereas Form 1040 consists of 15 different income disclosure lines, Form 1040A consists of only seven such lines. The Form 1040A does not ask for business income nor other supplemental income, which the Bormans had. The IRS charged that they should have used Form 1040, which they knowingly failed to do, thus subjecting them to the perjury penalty.

The court reasoned and concluded that—

> Although the taxpayers allegedly had a duty to file a different form, which called for a disclosure of their receipts from business, the IRS makes no claim that the answers on the Forms 1040A for the years at issue were untrue. . . . A charge that a taxpayer makes an implicit representation when filing the wrong form adds nothing beyond a charge of filing the wrong form. . . . Using the wrong form does not violate Section 7206(1). . . . Therefore, the taxpayers are not guilty of perjury since they answered the questions on the form filed fully and correctly.

The second case is that of *R.P. Mueller*; CA-11, 96-1 USTC ¶ 50,190; this case exemplifies two counts of (flagrant) perjury. Mueller filed his personal income tax return by reporting $160,000 in income, and business losses amounting to $156,000. As a result, he computed a zero tax, and signed the jurat clause accordingly. He also answered "No" to the foreign accounts question on Schedule B of Form 1040. This question asks:

> *At any time during* __(year)__, *did you have an interest in or a signature or other authority over a financial account in a foreign country?* ☐ *Yes,* ☐ *No. If "Yes," enter name of the foreign country.*

Upon extensive examination and investigation by the IRS, it discovered that Mueller was the president, majority shareholder, director, and trustee of five interlocking corporations. All entities were either in the process of being liquidated or being reorganized and renamed. It turned out that his gross personal income for the year at issue well exceeded $5,000,000 (5 million). Correspondingly, the IRS determined his correct tax to be $1,134,215. For this computation, the IRS found that Mueller showed a capital loss of $205,130 whereas in fact he had $911,975 in capital gain. This falsity, plus his zero tax falsity, sustained his perjury conviction on this item.

The IRS further discovered that Mueller had transferred $5,215,000 to three foreign bank accounts. All three foreign accounts were under Mueller's direct signature control. Thus, his answering "No" to the foreign accounts question was flat out false. His perjury conviction on this item was sustained.

Other False Statements

Paragraphs (2) and (3) of Section 7206 cover a wide range of false statements by others than the filers of false returns. These two paragraphs target anybody and everybody who, directly or indirectly, participates in the preparation and presentation of a tax deficient return. Paragraph (2) addresses the "aiding and abetting" concept of wrongdoing, whereas paragraph (3) addresses the "conspiracy" concept.

Paragraphs (2) and (3) start with the following wording:

Sec. 7206(2): ***Aid or Assistance*** — *Any person who . . .*

> *Willfully aids or assists in, or procures, counsels, or advises the preparation or presentation . . . of any matter arising under the internal revenue laws . . .*

Sec. 7206(3): ***Fraudulent Entries*** — *Any person who . . .*

> *Simulates or falsely or fraudulently executes or signs any bond, permit, entry, or other document required by . . . the internal revenue laws . . .* [or who] *connives at such execution thereof. . .*

With respect to paragraph (2): Aiding and Abetting, a published case on point is that of *M.G. Marshall*; CA-8, 96-2 USTC ¶ 50,678; 92 F3d 758. Marshall was a tax preparer charged with aiding in the filing of 60 false returns for others. The returns included fictitious dependents, incorrect filing status, and improper credits. All returns claimed refunds which were paid indirectly to Marshall who, in turn, paid the filers in cash. As such, the filers did not know that their refunds were larger than the sum they received. Numerous filers testified that they did not see their returns before filing; they signed blank tax forms and blank power of attorney forms. The loss in tax revenue asserted by the IRS was $2,004,961 (2+ million). Marshall was sentenced to 51 months' imprisonment under special sentencing guidelines based on the IRS's tax loss.

With respect to paragraph (3): Conspiracy, one published case on point is that of *R.W. Charroux*, CA-5, 93-2 USTC ¶ 50,628; 3 F3d 827. Charroux plus three other defendants-appellants (*James*, *Petr*, *McClain*) were in the real estate business in Dallas, Texas. At various meetings, they discussed a sophisticated "land flip" scheme for making big money without putting up any of their own. All of the money would come from local lending institutions. Charroux and James formed a land holding company (the "A" entity); Petr and McClain formed a land development company (the "B" entity). After the land flips were completed, a "C" entity was formed which took over the mortgage obligations of the "A" and "B" entities. The "C" entity would then file for bankruptcy, thereby defrauding the lending institutions. The nearest we can figure from the 8,500-word court ruling is the scheme depicted in Figure 11.2

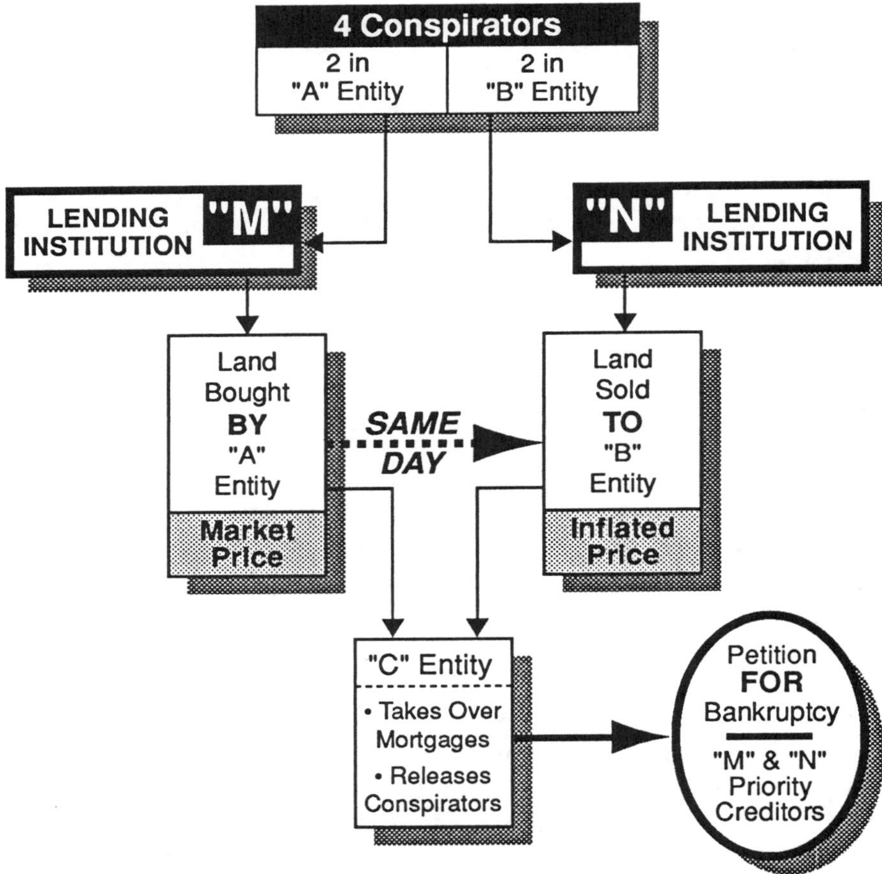

Fig. 11.2 - "Land Flip" Scheme for Defrauding Lending Institutions

The facts surrounding false or fraudulent entries on a return are difficult to trace. No one as careful as Charroux et al were is going to leave a clean paper trail for the IRS to follow. With multiple entities and multiple transactions taking place simultaneously, confusion is intentionally conjured up. Nevertheless, in the Figure 11-2 scheme, three land flips were conducted. In millions of dollars each, the flips were:

	Bought	Sold	Profit	Borrowed	Excess Proceeds
Flip 1	3.1	4.5	1.4	5.2	0.7
Flip 2	2.8	4.2	1.4	5.0	0.8
Flip 3	16.0	18.0	2.0	25.00	7.0
			4.8		8.5

Charroux, James, Petr, and McClain each made $1,200,000 in profit. They paid no tax. They doctored their papers and books so that their profit was disguised as the excess loan proceeds. The excess borrowings (in the "C" entity) were used to pay for the transactional costs, first few months of mortgage payments, and return of capital to the lenders, before filing bankruptcy. Each of the four conspirators was sentenced to 33 months in prison. Each was convicted also of tax evasion.

General Commentary

If caught red-handed in a false return situation, there is very little credible contestive recourse. In these situations, the more prevalent defensive positions are:

1. Blame it on one's tax preparer.
2. Haggle over the applicability of every word in the tax law which one is accused of violating.
3. Narrow down the year(s), period(s), or count(s) at issue.
4. Provide some rationale for the course taken, even if it is implausible.

In the *Charroux et al* case above, the defendants claimed that they had given all of the necessary information to their tax preparers. The lead tax preparer testified that the only records made available to him were the books of account for the "C" entity. The preparer explained that he had no settlement sheets on the three flip sale proceeds, and in fact was not notified that the sales had taken place.

His understanding was that the "C" entity was all that existed, and that the transactions were all loan proceeds in and out. Seasoned tax professionals are used to being blamed for the willful and wrongful acts of their clients. Consequently, they make copious notes in their own records to protect themselves against client attacks. A hoodwinked tax professional can be a formidable witness at trial.

Most (big time) false return filers wind up at some point filing for bankruptcy. This can be a stalling tactic while secreting one's ill-gotten gains. As per IRC Section 6871(a): ***Immediate Assessment in Receivership Proceedings***, the IRS can file its priority claim with the bankruptcy court. The claim includes all tax deficiencies, all accrued interest, all civil penalties, all additional amounts, and all assessable criminal penalties . . . *provided by law.* There may be other priority creditors, too. The process of reconstructing the debtors' assets can be painful and controversial. If assets are concealed and records destroyed, additional criminal penalties can apply.

The more sophisticated false filers transfer their monetary assets to a foreign trust of their own making. If they are smart about it, they file Form 3520 with the IRS Service Center, Philadelphia, PA 19255. Form 3520 is titled: ***Annual Return to Report Transactions with Foreign Trusts*** . . . etc. This is a legal and upfront way of avoiding criminal charges for secreting assets abroad. However, there is no guarantee that there will not be civil penalties.

For false filers who give up their U.S. citizenship and move abroad, there is a "shocker" in the Internal Revenue Code. Section 877: ***Expatriation to Avoid Tax***, extends the jurisdiction of the IRS to **10 years** after giving up citizenship. In addition, the U.S. has exchange-of-information Tax Treaties with 60 nations of the world where expatriate living is most preferred. In short, therefore, when a U.S. tax liability accrues, there is no legal escape from it!

12

APPEALING WITHIN IRS

The IRS Is Trying To Improve Its Image By Being Less Confrontational During Its Administrative Proceedings. One Area For Showcasing Its Effort Is The APPEALS PROCESS Within The IRS. After Any Examination Of Your Return(s) For Which Additional Tax Is Proposed And Civil Penalties Assessed, You Can Request A Conference With An INDEPENDENT Appeals Officer. This Is An INFORMAL Person-To-Person Meeting, Followed By Exchanges Of Information And Tax Law Positions On The Disputed Issue(s). Depending On The Credibility Of The Evidence Presented, You May Do Surprisingly Well.

The ***IRS Restructuring and Reform Act*** of 1998 (P.L. 105-206) was overwhelmingly passed by Congress by a 50-1 majority. It was signed into law by the President on July 22, 1998. As the "sense of Congress," the '98 Act directed that the IRS undertake a major overhaul of its mission and of its "rules of engagement" with taxpayers. In essence, the IRS is supposed to be more taxpayer friendly and less confrontational. **Don't you count on it!** We have already seen digests of the IRS's pronouncements that: *Although the '98 Act prohibits . . . the IRS still intends to* — continue business as usual.

There is one area, however, where the IRS has agreed to improve and liberalize its procedures. This area pertains to the appeals process within the IRS. Even prior to the '98 Act, the IRS had an Appeals Division which operated — we think — halfheartedly and perfunctorily. It acted as a modified rubber stamp on whatever the Examination Division and Collections Division did. The former Appeals Division also acted in a subservient role to the Technical Branch (tax law interpretation) and Legal Branch (chief counsel and prosecutor) of the IRS's National Office. Fortunately, lately, constructive changes are indeed underway.

The new direction for the appeals function in a "reorganized IRS" is an **independent forum** of its own. Towards this end, Section 1001(a)(4) of the Restructuring Act expressly states—

> *As part of ensuring an independent appeals function, the* [IRS's] *reorganization plan is to prohibit ex parte* [one-sided] *communications between appeals officers and other IRS employees to the extent such communications appear to compromise the independence of the appeals officers.*

Thus, in this our final chapter, we want to apprise you of the appeals function within the IRS, the prerequisites necessary before an appeal is made, and the realistic expectations of what your outcome might be. You cannot expect an Appeals Officer to wipe away all tax and penalties just because you have some personal beef with the tax system at large. No, you have to present some credible evidence and offer some credible rationale (based on tax law, court rulings, and good faith effort) as to why your penalty or penalties should be rescinded or reduced. Nor can you expect any penalty relief whatsoever until you have filed a "true, correct, and complete" return for the year or years at issue.

Jurisdiction & Authority

As envisioned by the '98 Act [IRS Restructuring and Reform] there are to be four primary operating units of the IRS. Unit A addresses the tax issues of individuals and investors; Unit B addresses small businesses and self-employeds; Unit C addresses mid-size and large corporations; and Unit D addresses exempt organizations and government entities. Within each of these operating units is an Appeals Office. This office has independent jurisdiction to settle most matters involving disputes over the amount of correct tax and the civil penalties relating thereto. The Appeals Office has no jurisdiction over criminal penalties for the simple reason that criminal penalties have to be adjudicated in a federal court other than the Tax Court. Consequently, our exclusive focus in this chapter is on civil penalties.

As is currently evolving, the appeals domain appears to be headed towards three levels of disputive issues. These levels are:

- Small case appeals — up to $ 50,000
- Large case appeals — up to $1,000,000
- Mediation case appeals — over $1,000,000

The dollar magnitude of the appeal includes the amount of tax deficiency **and** penalties *per year* or *per tax period.*

The net effect of these threshold amounts is that you do not appeal the penalties alone, without also appealing the underlying tax deficiency. This makes sense because most civil penalties are predicated upon the amount of tax deficiency in dispute. If the disputed tax is reduced in amount, the related penalty is automatically reduced. On the other hand, if you concede on the amount of tax, you can appeal the penalty as a separate issue.

The "small case" amount of $50,000 derives from IRC Section 7463: ***Disputes Involving $50,000 or Less***. Although this is a Tax Court provision, one of the procedures in Small Tax Court petitions is that the case is referred back to the IRS Appeals Office for possible settlement before trial begins. A petition to Tax Court is called a "docketed" case. If an appeals request is made before filing a petition in Tax Court, it is called a "non-docketed" case.

IRS Regulation ¶ 601.106: ***Appeals functions***, points out that the purpose of administrative appeals within the IRS is—

> *To resolve tax controversies without litigation, to the extent possible. Appeals is to approach those controversies in a fair and impartial manner to both the taxpayer and the government. Appeals authority on non-docketed cases has been delegated by the Commissioner* [of IRS], *while Appeals authority on docketed cases has been delegated by the Chief Counsel* [of the IRS].

Benefits of Appealing "Within"

The chief benefits of appealing within the IRS are the saving in time and cost, and the relative informality therewith. Generally, proceeding into U.S. Tax Court can take up to five years from time of dispute to time of resolution. If a disputive matter goes into a U.S. District Court or to a U.S. Court of Appeals, you are looking at up to 10 years of litigative time. Very rarely is a tax case accepted for adjudication by the U.S. Supreme Court. If, however, certiorari is granted, you are facing up to 15 years before the disputive issue can be resolved.

In contrast, if a dispute can be resolved during appeal within the IRS, your "limbo status" is approximately 18 months for small cases (under $50,000) and approximately 36 months (3 years) for larger cases. On both sides of a bona fide issue, time is money. You save money . . . and the IRS also saves money.

Another significant benefit is that the IRS Appeals Officer is a nonattorney. By training (and by their own inherent nature), attorneys — whether government or private — tend to be confrontational, unethical, and provocative of extreme positions via the "splitting of hairs." It is virtually impossible for an IRS attorney to be impartial towards a taxpayer. Our position is that, if the IRS sticks to its policy of assigning nonattorneys as Appeals Officers, it will have taken the right step in its new mission of addressing taxpayer needs.

Another benefit is that you, as the taxpayer, can represent yourself. This is called *pro se* (in proper person). Or, you can engage a nonattorney tax professional to represent you (or to accompany you). Nonattorney tax professionals are not eager to let a tax case go to trial. They cannot represent you in court: only attorneys can. Still, if a matter cannot be resolved at Appeals within the IRS, a nonattorney tax professional can be called as a witness in your behalf in court.

Whether an attorney or nonattorney represents you before an Appeals Officer, you will need to authorize the representation. You do so via IRS Form 2848: ***Power of Attorney and Declaration of Representative***. Even if you want to present your side of your story yourself, we think that executing Form 2848 is advisable. It enables the tax professional to make inquiries, do research, and cite pertinent tax law, regulations, and court cases in your behalf.

Still, another practical benefit is the relative informality of the IRS Appeals process. Except in rare cases, no sworn testimony is taken, and no acrimonious cross-examinations occur. Most personal statements are accepted on their face value and their merits weighed. However, if certain material and substantial evidence is required, it has to be submitted *under penalties of perjury.*

The underlying premise of the IRS Appeals function is that you take a position based on good faith, and on the recognition that bona fide differences between reasonable persons can indeed occur. Your reasons for disagreeing with the IRS must come within the scope of those tax laws cited in the Internal Revenue Code. You can NOT base your appeal solely on emotional, moral, religious, political, constitutional, conscientious, frivolous, or similar grounds. You have to cite the specific facts, the specific circumstances, the specific IRC section(s), and the specific case law (if any) on which you rely. Unless your positions are in the high-flying world of cyberspace, most Appeals Officers will take your case under advisement.

Disadvantages of IRS Appeals

Yes, there are certain disadvantages when requesting that your case be forwarded to Appeals for consideration. We abbreviate these disadvantages, alongside the advantages above, in Figure 12.1.

First off, Appeals will not accept "first impression" cases. These are disputive issues which derive from new law, new regulation, or new revenue ruling which have not been adversarially tested. Appeals decisions are not precedent setting. That is, the Appeals Office jurisdiction is limited to those tax issues which have been thrashed out judicially many times in the past. On old issues, a common theme of judicial wisdom exudes throughout. Unless your case is analogous to some common theme of the past, it will be rejected by Appeals.

A second disadvantage is that certain old issues (called: "prime issues") are used by the IRS — the Chief Counsel, particularly — to force you into court. Part of this forcing you into court is legal arrogance. It's the "thrill of the kill" that gives a power rush to IRS

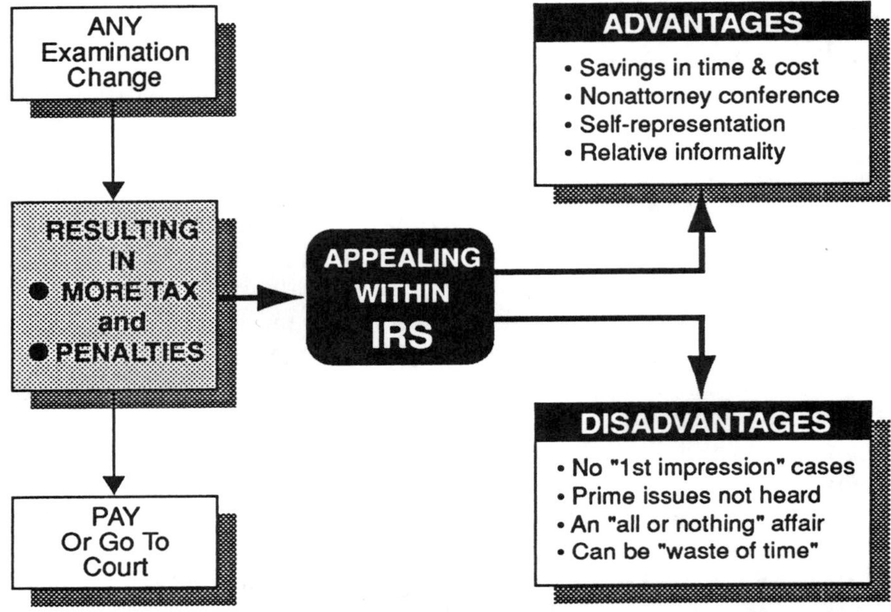

Fig. 12.1 - Advantages & Disadvantages of the IRS Appeals Process

attorneys. A "prime issue" is one on which the IRS had a mixture of wins and losses. It refuses to acknowledge its losses — called: *non-acquiescence.* The IRS then takes a hard-nosed and intimidating stance against you, on the chance that you will give up and let the IRS win by default.

The Appeals Officer does not have to disclose to you what the sacred prime issue is that you are encroaching upon. You disclose your position in good faith; you only get stonewalling in return. All of the arguments and evidence that you provide are used by the IRS against you in court. This is truly the most despicable side of the IRS Appeals function.

A third disadvantage of the Appeals process is that you cannot separate the various tax issues when going forward after your Appeal. It's an "all or nothing" affair. For example, for a given year, suppose you have a $11,000 tax deficiency (comprised of a $7,000 disputive issue and a $4,000 disputive issue) and a $2,000 penalty assessment. The Appeals Officer concedes on the $4,000 issue and rescinds the $2,000 penalty. He holds steadfast on the

$7,000 issue. Does the Appeals process allow you to accept the $4,000 and the $2,000 concessions, then permit you to go forward into Tax Court to judicially contest the remaining $7,000 issue? No; it does not. You either accept the $6,000 (4,000 + 2,000) Appeals concessions PLUS agreeing to pay the disputed issue of $7,000, or you go to court recontesting the entire $13,000 (7,000 + 6,000). This is a major inequity and disservice in the Appeals process which Congress has yet to address.

Another disadvantage is that the Appeals process can be a total waste of time. There is no guarantee that you will get any concessions at all. In some cases, a tidbit or two will be offered, after the case has been dragged on for awhile. The only forewarning you get of this is the perfunctory manner in which your case is being handled. It's a cut and dried matter. Either the Appeals Officer is not interested, or there is no professional challenge to him that will enhance his promotion within the IRS. A year or two later, you wind up where you started.

Initiating Your Appeal

Regulation ¶ 601.106(a)(1)(iii) says—

The taxpayer must request Appeals consideration.

(A) An ***oral request*** *is sufficient to obtain Appeals consideration . . . if the total amount of proposed additional tax including penalties . . . is $2,500 or less for any taxable period.*

(B) A ***brief written statement*** *of disputed issues is required . . . if the total amount . . . exceeds $2,500 but does not exceed $10,000 for any taxable period.*

(C) A ***written protest*** *is required . . . if the total amount . . . exceeds $10,000 for any taxable period.*

(D) ***Total amount defined.*** *The total amount includes the entire amount of additional tax and penalties proposed by*

> *the IRS, not just the portion . . . that the taxpayer disputes. Interest is not included in any of these amounts.* [Emphasis added.]

If you want to appeal any proposed additional tax and penalty, you must specifically request such. Usually, accompanying the IRS communication indicating the amount of additional tax and penalty, is information regarding your right to appeal. The window of opportunity for doing so is 30 days. Otherwise, it is presumed that you accept the additional tax and penalty, and will pay promptly.

An "oral request" consists of a phone call (if you can get through) followed up by a simple, signed request. As an example, after identifying the tax period, dollar amount, and tax form, you say—

> I disagree and wish a conference with an Appeals Officer.
>
> /s/ ______________________________
>
> signature date

A "brief statement" request is a written itemization of each disputed matter, and the reason for your disagreement. The disputed matter in character and amount must be cross-referenced to the latest communication you received from the IRS. This gives the Appeals Officer an indication of the particular portion of the tax and penalty that you dispute. The inference is that any portion which you do not dispute, you agree with and concede.

Keep in mind that you must identify each tax period separately. If you have three tax periods at issue and you want to appeal all three periods, you must make a separate Appeals request for each of the three periods. Otherwise, if you appeal only one period, it is presumed that you accept and concede on the other periods.

Preparing Your Protest

If the unagreed amount for any given tax year exceeds $25,000, a written protest is required. A protest requires a more structured format than a conference request based on a "brief statement." A protest must contain specific information so as to constitute an evidential document of its own. Because of their evidential role, the matters in the protest must be weighed and considered by the Appeals Officer. Serious protest matters cannot be waved aside or ignored, as so often happens with tax examiners and revenue agents.

Structured protests are usually initiated after one's return (or returns) has/have been audit examined and proposed adjustments made. An official report on the proposed adjustments is sent to you, with the instruction—

> *Please read the report, decide whether you agree or disagree, and* ***respond within 30 days*** *from the date of this letter.* [Emphasis added.]

If you intend to appeal via protest, notify the IRS office from which the proposed adjustments originated. Do so within 10 days. At the same time, if your case is complicated, ask for a reasonable extension of the 30-day response time.

A written protest is structured into four general parts, namely:

- I Reference-type information: for filing purposes, taxpayer identity, and tax year(s).
- II Main body: consisting of four specific paragraphs (described below).
- III Attachments and exhibits: documents which more or less speak for themselves.
- IV Perjury declaration(s): to assure that the main body statements are factual and pertinent.

There exists no official protest form. Consequently a suggested format is presented in Figure 12.2. The case reference information goes in the upper right-hand corner for taxpayer identification purposes. To make it clear that you are protesting unagreed matters resulting from the examination of your return(s), we think bold headliner words are appropriate: PROTEST: UNAGREED MATTERS.

The main body of your protest letter consists of four paragraphs as indicated in Figure 12.2. The first paragraph is a restatement of your request for an appeals conference. The second paragraph

Date: ____________
Phone No: ____________

District Director
Internal Revenue Service
____
____

Name: ____________
Address: ____________
TIN: ____________
Form(s): ____________
Year(s): ____________
Increase in Tax: ____________
Penalties: ____________
Reference: ____________

PROTEST:
UNAGREED MATTER(S)

1. Request is made for conference with the Appeals Office to discuss unagreed matters arising from examination of the income tax return(s) referenced above.

2. The unagreed matters for discussion are:
   (a) ____________
   (b) ____________
   (c) ____________

3. The facts pertinent to this protest are:
   (a) ____________
   (b) ____________
   (c) ____________

4. The applicable law and its relevance to this protest are:
   (a) ____________
   (b) ____________
   (c) ____________

● Attachments
(1)
(2)
(3)

/s/ ____________
Taxpayer(s)

■ Under penalties of perjury, I declare that -

/s/ ____________
Taxpayer(s)

■ Under penalties of perjury, I declare that -

/s/ ____________
Protest Preparer

Fig. 12.2 - Suggested Format for Protest and Appeal Letter

outlines the matter(s) on which you disagree with the auditor. If you can, make cross-references to the explanations on the examiner's change report. In the third paragraph, stress those facts important to your position which the examiner has sidetracked or ignored. The fourth paragraph is a "law and analysis" approach in which you try to rationalize within the context of the Internal Revenue Code. You do not have to be a tax expert on this, but you might want to do a little research, or have a tax professional do it for you. Try to cite at least one tax law, regulation, or court ruling for each issue raised in paragraph 2.

Each paragraph should be as succinct as possible, and not wander into emotional matters, criticism of the examiner, criticism of the IRS, or criticism of the tax system. Such criticism probably does more harm than good. Include as attachments those documents and portions of the tax return which you want the Appeals Officer to see first-hand.

Specific Protest Example

To give you an idea of the type of protest specificity desired, let us cite a real-life example. The taxpayer was a licensed general contractor doing business under the fictitious name of XYZ CONSTRUCTION. For nearly 20 years, XYZ engaged in the design, construction, remodeling, and repairs to residential and commercial buildings. He was getting older and getting tired, physically. He wanted to become more of a construction consultant and mortgage lender. Towards this end, he started two separate joint ventures: ABC and DEF. He advanced approximately $200,000 towards his new business directions, and claimed this amount as operating expenses on his Schedule C (Form 1040): ***Profit or Loss from Business***, for the principal year at issue. All of these items were summarily disallowed by the IRS examiner. The additional tax sought was $37,940; the penalty assessment was $7,588 (20% of 37,940).

Following the format depicted in Figure 12.2, XYZ's protest paragraphs read as follows:

2. The unagreed matters for discussion are:

(a) Whether the amount of $60,721 on Schedule C is a nonbusiness bad debt as recharacterized on Schedule 2A of the examination change report.
(b) Whether the amount of $56,760 on Schedule C is disallowable as advertising expense, as recharacterized on Schedule 2C of the examination change report.
(c) Whether the amount of $87,406 on Schedule C is disallowable as business expenses, as recharacterized on Schedule 2D of the examination change report.
(d) Whether the amount of $7,588 as a negligence penalty should apply, as asserted on page 4, Schedule 1B of the examination change report.

3. The facts pertinent to this protest are:
(a) The amount of $60,721 represents operating funds advanced to a joint venturer, ABC (and others), to open a business office under the dba name of "Preferred Loans." The money was used to pay office rent, purchase office equipment, install phone and faxes, and start an advertising campaign.
(b) The amount of $56,760 represents operating funds advanced to a joint venturer, DEF (and others) to open a business office under the intended name of "Infomercial Productions." The money was used to pay office rent, purchase office equipment, start art work, prepare advertising copy, produce 3 infomercials, and purchase and schedule TV airings.
(c) The amount of $87,406 was expended by the two joint venturers and the taxpayer to pursue and actively participate in the above business efforts. The expenditures were for car and truck expenses, rental of equipment, supplies, travel, legal and professional services, office expenses, utilities, production services, insurance, and other business expenses.
(d) None of the expenditures above were sham activities. They were properly classified by a professional tax preparer who allocated them in good faith to the categories designated on Schedule C (Form 1040).

4. The applicable laws and their relevance to this protest are:

(a) IRS Reg. 1.166-5(b)(1) defines a **business** bad debt as one . . . *which is created, or acquired, in the course of a trade or business of the taxpayer . . .* ***without regard*** *to the relationship of the debt.*
(b) IRS Reg. 1.162-1(a) expressly mentions . . . *advertising and other selling expenses* . . . as deductible business expenses.

(c) Code Sec. 162(a) states that a deduction shall be allowed for . . . *ALL ordinary and necessary expenses paid or incurred . . . in carrying on ANY trade or business.*
(d) Code Sec. 6664(c)(1) provides for a reasonable cause exception to the negligence penalty where the taxpayer has acted in good faith. Furthermore, IRS Reg. 1.6664-4(b) indicates that a reasonable cause is "most importantly" . . . *an honest effort to assess . . . the proper tax liability* . . . by taking a position reasonably relevant to existing law and regulation.

Under penalties of perjury . . . etc.

Refrain from trying to rationalize or argue your case at this point. Any discussion and rationalization of the facts and law is what the appeals conference is all about. Therefore, make your protest points as succinct as possible. Do not try to be persuasive. Just state the facts.

Acknowledgment by Appeals

Your written protest is addressed to the IRS District Director in your geographic area. The instructions tell you to mail it to the examiner who prepared your change report. Said examiner will prepare a supplemental report, countering your version of the facts with those of his own. Then, an *unagreed case file* is prepared (by the Examination Division) and forwarded to the Appeals Office.

Within six months thereafter, you will receive an official acknowledgment of your protest by an IRS Appeals Officer. You will be told that your case has been referred to him for consideration. He will provide his name and phone number, and will actually sign the acknowledgment himself. From this point on, contact is person-to-person rather than from you to a computer, and a computer to you.

Different acknowledgment forms are used, depending on the nature of each case, and on the IRS office where the conference will be held. The general thrust is in the opening paragraph which characteristically reads—

The income tax deficiencies proposed by the District Director's Examination Division have been referred to the Appeals Office *for our consideration. We would like to explore with you the possibilities of reaching a settlement without trial. I believe a **conference**, during which we could fully discuss the issues, would be mutually helpful. The conference will be informal.*

Do not get your hopes up too high. This acknowledgment wording is simply an approved formality, to say that you have one more chance before a more formal "deficiency notice" is issued to you. This is what is meant by: *the possibilities of . . . settlement without trial.*

The acknowledgment letter goes on to say that—

You may present facts, arguments, and legal authority to support your position. If you plan to introduce new evidence or information, please send it to me at least five days before the conference. Please call within 10 days [of the date above] *to arrange a mutually convenient appointment.*

Anticipate Form 872

If your appeals conference is scheduled to be heard anytime within six months of the statute of limitations for assessing additional tax against you, you'll be asked to sign Form 872. This form is titled: ***Consent to Extend Time to Assess Income Tax***. This is called a "waiver." That is, Form 872 waives your statutory rights and give the IRS Appeals Officer more time to consider your case.

Ordinarily, when you file your return on time, the IRS has just three years to determine whether additional tax is due from you. After three years, it's too late [Sec. 6501(a)].

Consequently, when you have protested an audit change, and you've requested an appeals conference, you are starting to bump up against the statute of limitations. If your conference is scheduled more than two and one-half years after the due date of your return, the IRS will press you to sign a waiver form. It does this by sending you filled-in Form 872.

Form 872 has a specific **expiration date** filled in on it. That is, it is a limited time waiver. The waiver of your right to limit the assessment of additional tax expires on the date indicated on the IRS-prepared form. When you are sent this form, be sure to look for its expiration date. If it is 12 months **or less** after the statutory assessment date, go ahead and sign it. If it is more than 12 months, DO NOT SIGN IT. Instead, phone the Appeals Officer and indicate that you'd like to limit the waiver to 12 months. Also indicate that you might further extend it for "good cause."

On average, it takes about nine months after your appeals conference to wrap up and settle the case, if it can be settled at all. Therefore, there is just no reason to allow the IRS more than 12 months to address your appeal.

Appearance at Conference

An appeals conference is **not** a bargaining session. It is a good-faith effort to resolve legitimate disputes where there are grey areas in fact or where there are ambiguities in law. It is not a matter of negotiation, compromise, "splitting the difference," etc.

The conferencing objective is to determine whether you come within the applicable law or regulation, as interpreted by the IRS. The IRS is a biased agency: biased towards maximum revenue. Nevertheless, the burden of proof is on you to establish that the IRS is wrong. After all, *you* are the "moving party." It was you who requested the appeal: not the IRS.

You have to do some preparatory homework. This means digging up the documents that you used, or should have used, when preparing your return. If it is a key document, you have to dissect it, line by line, word for word, dollar for dollar, to extract its true meaning in your favor. You may also have to do a little tax law research on point. You need to get the "flavor" of the legislative intent. You'll probably need some professional help in this regard. You want to be reasonably conversant with the applicable law on which you are relying.

To demonstrate your seriousness, it is a good idea to go to conference with a well prepared MEMORANDUM OF FACT, LAW, & CIRCUMSTANCES. Think of this memorandum as a legal brief, if you will. Describe your general background (education and experience), your occupation for the year(s) in which the tax issue(s) arises, your breakdown of each tax schedule and entry that was examined and disallowed, the documents that you intend to present, and a restatement of the tax law, regulations, and rulings on which you rely. In other words, go loaded for bear. You will be allowed only one conference meeting in person (by yourself, by your representative, or by both of you together).

After introductory courtesies, hand the Appeals Officer the *original* of your Memorandum. Then lay out all of your supporting documents on the desk or table across which you are conferencing. You want to impress him (or her) that you are ready for the nitty-gritty.

After one personal meeting, various follow-up matters can be handled by phone, fax, mail, E-mail, and through contacts with your representative. Matters will drag out for awhile, so don't get too apprehensive. Often, the outcome rests on a "judgment call" by the Appeals Officer, rather than on any proof-positive establishment of your position.

The Prospects of Relief

Civil penalties assessable by the IRS and appealable within the IRS are categorized as follows:

Class I — Reasonable Cause penalties
- those covered in Chapters 1 through 6

Class II — Willful Intent penalties
- those covered in Chapters 7, 9, and 11

Class III — Responsible Person penalties
- those covered in Chapters 8 and 10

The probability of relief from Class I (reasonable cause) penalties through Appeals is good to high. This is because the factual evidence presentable is more direct and less circumstantial. Facts, dates, amounts, and circumstances, if credibly presented, are the consequence of human error, negligence, oversight, "stretching," inadvertency, honest misunderstanding, etc. Willful intent is not an issue.

As to Class II penalties (willful intent), circumstantial evidence has to be probed and reprobed. The "indicia of fraud," for example, are not clear-cut criteria of whether fraud exists or does not exist. The Appeals Officer has to make a distinction between the *first* indications of fraud and the *firm* indications of fraud. A "first indication" is the mere suspicion of fraud. If an explanation of the discrepancies that form the basis for suspicion are reasonable and convincing, relief from the penalty is 50/50 possible. Contrarily, Appeals relief from firm indications of fraud (concealment and deception, for example) are highly unlikely. All the Appeals Officer has to do is to satisfy himself that the firm indicators are not "clearly erroneous."

Similarly for frivolous returns, false returns, and willful tax evasion. All of these penalties are based on some **overt act** by the return filer. The filer did something wrong, that he knowingly should not have done. Once the wrongful act has been committed, it is irreversible. Explaining the act away is extremely difficult . . . and unbelievable. Legitimate legal defenses can be raised, but their Appeals relief effect are virtually nil.

As to the Class III penalties (responsible person), Appeals relief is highly unlikely. In the IRS's eyes, SOMEBODY has to be the fall guy for trust fund failures (Chapter 8) and cash transactions in excess of $10,000 (Chapter 10). Unless you can pin the blame on some other taxpayer's back, it stays on your back. You either have to pay, or go to court to air your case in a more formal manner. The Appeals process, however is a good "practice run" on the IRS's position — and inquisition — facing you, should court trial become necessary.

In Figure 12.3, we summarize much of the above.

An Example That Worked

When appearing before an IRS Appeals Officer, use it as an opportunity for "testing the waters" with respect to your presenting *credible evidence*. In other words, go prepared to stand your ground with reasonable and verifiable evidence of your own. But also be prepared to cooperate with Appeals by furnishing additional information and documents that might be requested. Discuss each

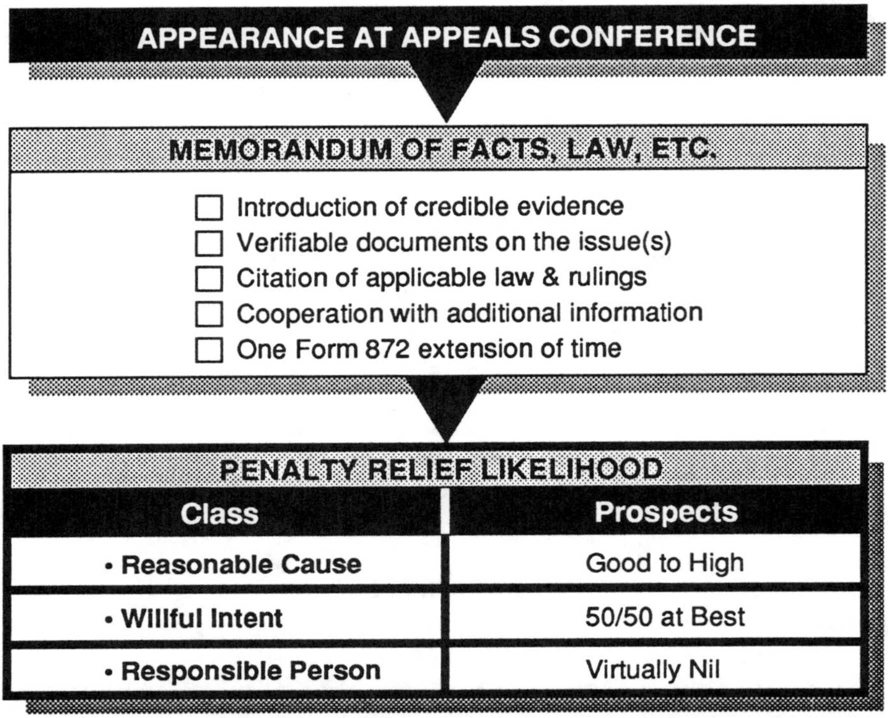

APPEARANCE AT APPEALS CONFERENCE

MEMORANDUM OF FACTS, LAW, ETC.

- ☐ Introduction of credible evidence
- ☐ Verifiable documents on the issue(s)
- ☐ Citation of applicable law & rulings
- ☐ Cooperation with additional information
- ☐ One Form 872 extension of time

PENALTY RELIEF LIKELIHOOD

Class	Prospects
• **Reasonable Cause**	Good to High
• **Willful Intent**	50/50 at Best
• **Responsible Person**	Virtually Nil

Fig. 12.3 - Weighing the Prospects of Success at Penalty Relief

issue openly and in a business-like manner.

For example, here are the results of the XYZ Construction case outlined earlier. Three consecutive tax years were at issue, though we presented previously only the mid-year. The tax and penalty for each year, before and after the appeal, turned out to be:

	Before Appeal		After Appeal	
Year	Tax	Penalty	Tax	Penalty
199X	$ 6,783	$1,357	$ 154	$-0-
199Y	37,940	7,588	1,864	-0-
199Z	4,834	967	-0-	-0-
	$49,557	$9,912	$2,018	-0-
	Total	$59,469	**Savings = $57,451**	

Thus, as the above case illustrates, the Appeals process can be well worthwhile. Initially, the XYZ owner was assessed a total of $59,469 in tax *and* penalties. He wound up paying only $2,018. In other words, his net payment was just 3% of the original IRS billing. We class this as "doing suprisingly well."

In many cases, however, appealing within the IRS is disappointing. You get your hopes up that maybe you'll win a major point or two. Then your hopes are dashed because you did not attain the satisfaction you sought. You conclude that appealing within the IRS is more of a PR (public relations) charade than substance. In such case, the only advantage is that it forces you to review your position thoroughly and decide whether you want to press on into Tax Court or other U.S. court. If you do go to Tax Court (or other), one of the prerequisites is that you have gone through the IRS Appeals Process.

Appeals Closing Procedures

For nontrial cases, the Appeals closing procedure is rather simple. **Form 870** (or its variants) is used. This form is titled: ***Waiver of Restrictions on Assessment and Collection of Deficiency in Tax and Acceptance of Overassessment.*** This title is quite a mouthful. The idea is that if you agree to the settlement terms — additional tax, reduced penalty, some overassessment (refund) — you have to allow the IRS adequate time to go through its billing, refunding process and its computation of statutory interest therewith. An edited and abridged arrangement of Form 870 is presented in Figure 12.4.

If you intend to close the case, do so by signing Form 870, as submitted to you by the Appeals Office. Of course, do so only after you are convinced that it is your best hope. The IRS needs at least 90 days to complete its processing of the case, before any Form 872 that you have signed expires. If your Form 872 expiration date is too tight for the IRS, expect to receive, by Certified Mail, a statutory NOTICE OF DEFICIENCY [Sec. 6212(a)]. This notice gives you 90 days to do one of the following—

1. Pay the tax and penalty, then file for a refund.

Form 870	CLOSING AGREEMENT & WAIVER (Edited Title)	Date received by IRS ______
IRS File No. ______	Your Name & Address	Soc. Sec. No. ______

INCREASE / DECREASE IN TAX AND PENALTIES

Year(s)	Item	Tax	Penalty 1	Penalty 2	Etc.	Refund
TOTALS						

Explanation(s)

Note: 1. "Increase / Decrease" is relative to that on the Examination Change Report.
2. "Decrease" is signified by < >.
3. "Refund" results from an overassessment in tax.

Consent to Assessment and Collection

See Text

▶ /s/ Taxpayer ______ (Date)
▶ /s/ Spouse ______ (Date)
▶ /s/ Representative ______ (Date)

Fig. 12.4 - Closing Agreement for Nontrial Appeals Case

2. Sign another Form 872, then request that the Notice of Deficiency by rescinded.
3. Petition the Tax Court; this automatically stays (suspends) any IRS assessment and collection action.

ABOUT THE AUTHOR

Holmes F. Crouch

Born on a small farm in southern Maryland, Holmes was graduated from the U.S. Coast Guard Academy with a Bachelor's Degree in Marine Engineering. While serving on active duty, he wrote many technical articles on maritime matters. After attaining the rank of Lieutenant Commander, he resigned to pursue a career as a nuclear engineer.

Continuing his education, he earned a Master's Degree in Nuclear Engineering from the University of California. He also authored two books on nuclear propulsion. As a result of the tax write-offs associated with writing these books, the IRS audited his returns. The IRS's handling of the audit procedure so annoyed Holmes that he undertook to become as knowledgeable as possible regarding tax procedures. He became a licensed private Tax Practitioner by passing an examination administered by the IRS. Having attained this credential, he started his own tax preparation and counseling business in 1972.

In the early years of his tax practice, he was a regular talk-show guest on San Francisco's KGO Radio responding to hundreds of phone-in tax questions from listeners. He was a much sought-after guest speaker at many business seminars and taxpayer meetings. He also provided counseling on special tax problems, such as divorce matters, property exchanges, timber harvesting, mining ventures, animal breeding, independent contractors, selling businesses, and offices-at-home. Over the past 25 years, he has prepared well over 10,000 tax returns for individuals, estates, trusts, and small businesses (in partnership and corporate form).

During the tax season of January through April, he prepares returns in a unique manner. During a single meeting, he completes the return . . . *on the spot!* The client leaves with his return signed, sealed, and in a stamped envelope. His unique approach to preparing returns and his personal interest in his clients' tax affairs have honed his professional proficiency. His expertise extends through itemized deductions, computer-matching of income sources, capital gains and losses, business expenses and cost of goods, residential rental expenses, limited and general partnership activities, closely-held corporations, to family farms and ranches.

He remembers spending 12 straight hours completing a doctor's complex return. The next year, the doctor, having moved away, utilized a large accounting firm to prepare his return. Their accountant was so impressed by the manner in which the prior return was prepared that he recommended the doctor travel the 500 miles each year to have Holmes continue doing it.

He recalls preparing a return for an unemployed welder, for which he charged no fee. Two years later the welder came back and had his return prepared. He paid the regular fee . . . and then added a $300 tip.

During the off season, he represents clients at IRS audits and appeals. In one case a shoe salesman's audit was scheduled to last three hours. However, after examining Holmes' documentation it was concluded in 15 minutes with "no change" to his return. In another instance he went to an audit of a custom jeweler that the IRS dragged out for more than six hours. But, supported by Holmes' documentation, the client's return was accepted by the IRS with "no change."

Then there was the audit of a language translator that lasted two full days. The auditor scrutinized more than $1.25 million in gross receipts, all direct costs, and operating expenses. Even though all expensed items were documented and verified, the auditor decided that more than $23,000 of expenses ought to be listed as capital items for depreciation instead. If this had been enforced it would have resulted in a significant additional amount of tax. Holmes strongly disagreed and after many hours of explanation got the amount reduced by more than 60% on behalf of his client.

He has dealt extensively with gift, death and trust tax returns. These preparations have involved him in the tax aspects of wills, estate planning, trustee duties, probate, marital and charitable bequests, gift and death exemptions, and property titling.

Although not an attorney, he prepares Petitions to the U.S. Tax Court for clients. He details the IRS errors and taxpayer facts by citing pertinent sections of tax law and regulations. In a recent case involving an attorney's ex-spouse, the IRS asserted a tax deficiency of $155,000. On behalf of his client, he petitioned the Tax Court and within six months the IRS conceded the case.

Over the years, Holmes has observed that the IRS is not the industrious, impartial, and competent federal agency that its official public imaging would have us believe.

He found that, at times, under the slightest pretext, the IRS has interpreted against a taxpayer in order to assess maximum penalties, and may even delay pending matters so as to increase interest due on additional taxes. He has confronted the IRS in his own behalf on five separate occasions, going before the U.S. Claims Court, U.S. District Court, and U.S. Tax Court. These were court actions that tested specific sections of the Internal Revenue Code which he found ambiguous, inequitable, and abusively interpreted by the IRS.

Disturbed by the conduct of the IRS and by the general lack of tax knowledge by most individuals, he began an innovative series of taxpayer-oriented Federal tax guides. To fulfill this need, he undertook the writing of a series of guidebooks that provide in-depth knowledge on one tax subject at a time. He focuses on subjects that plague taxpayers all throughout the year. Hence, his formulation of the "Allyear" Tax Guide series.

The author is indebted to his wife, Irma Jean, and daughter, Barbara MacRae, for the word processing and computer graphics that turn his experiences into the reality of these publications. Holmes welcomes comments, questions, and suggestions from his readers. He can be contacted in California at (408) 867-2628, or by writing to the publisher's address.

ALLYEAR Tax Guides

by Holmes F. Crouch

Series 100 - INDIVIDUALS AND FAMILIES

Series 200 - INVESTORS AND BUSINESSES

Series 300 - RETIREES AND ESTATES

Series 400 - OWNERS AND SELLERS

Series 500 - AUDITS AND APPEALS